Raids on Australia

Raids on Australia

1942 and Japan's Plans for Australia

Pam Oliver

Australian Scholarly Publishing

© Pam Oliver 2010

First published 2010
Australian Scholarly Publishing Pty Ltd
7 Lt Lothian St Nth, North Melbourne, Vic 3051
TEL: 03 9329 6963 FAX: 03 9329 5452
EMAIL: aspic@ozemail.com.au
WEB: scholarly.info

ISBN 987 1 921509 60 5

Copyediting by Ally Cheah
Design and typesetting by Sarah Anderson
Printing and binding by BPA Print Group
Front cover photograph of Japanese Training Squadron in Sydney Harbour, HIJMS *Asano*.
    Photograph by Ichiro Kagiyama of Sydney, c1935. Courtesy of Kenji Hirodo.
Back cover photograph; members of 2/7th Australian infantry Battalion, 17th Australian
    Infantry Brigade, who have returned from New Guinea, enjoy a meal of good food, not
    dehydrated food. Left to right: WX13342 Sergeant C.E Hubble (1); NX31900 Sergeant A.
    E. Griffiths (2); Private (PTE) G. Bailey (3); WX1503 PTE P.A Woodman (4); WX13231
    PTE H.J. Broome (5) Black and White photograph. Wondecla, QLD. 1943–10–07.
    Australian War Memorial (057863).

To my mother, Patricia Malloch,
who did not live quite long enough to see the book in print,

and to two supportive souls,
Mason Oliver and Erik Toller

Contents

When I was a small girl living in Melbourne's leafy Blackburn, my mother told me horror stories of the war that had ended before my birth. She had a very strong sense of history. On her side of the family, a Scottish immigrant family from the tenements of Glasgow, all the men had been to war, either World War One or World War Two. Remarkably they had all survived. On my father's side of the family, which was very large, many of the men, including my father, were enlisted in the Reservists because they were working in essential services and remained so for the duration of the war. But some cousins enlisted in the AIF and RAAF and served in the Pacific on Bouganville, Morotai, at Milne Bay, and in the Middle East. One saw service on the high seas on the 2/2 Hospital Ship *MV Wanganella* for the duration of the war travelling from Suez in the Middle East to Borneo in the Pacific where they picked up released Australian prisoners of war. These relatives saw action and survived it. There is no name recorded on the Honour Roll at the Australian War Memorial in Canberra where I can place a poppy in memory of a loved one.

Our neighbours in Blackburn were Methodist missionaries and worked in South Korea to help orphaned children in the early 1950s. I well remember even as a preschooler the shocking stories of what the Korean people were living and dying through. My closest encounter with the horrors of conflict is life in London during the IRA bombings near my home. So I do not know what it is to experience war or lose someone in a war but have heard enough of the horrors and sacrifices to have a great respect for those who go through such experiences in the field and on the home front.

War at home in World War Two was "tough but everyone did their bit", my mother would say. Stories of trenches in the yard, blackout curtains, rumours of raids, fear of telegrams, bartering for local produce, making do, eating home-grown cabbages and silver beet day after day, working incredibly long hours in essential services were part and parcel of my mother's stories. She was also terribly angry at "the Japs" and had an inherent fear of invasion. "They almost succeeded, you know, in 1942. But for our boys in New Guinea … and of course the Yanks. Goodness knows what life would be like today." Such was the impression those times had made on her, she still told these stories when she was 90 just before her death in 2006. Perhaps the bombing of Darwin five days before she was married explains the persistence of memory. Growing up, I often wondered what life would have been like under the Japanese but had no chance to even meet and talk to a Japanese person until 1991.

I am an historian and as such try, like my colleagues, to achieve impartiality, work thoroughly on all the evidence available and examine the questions carefully and seriously. This book asks some questions which are new. I am also a person with a particular life history and experience, and recognise that, as with all of us who write history, this needs acknowledging and keeping in perspective. So let me say here, that I am of no particular political persuasion. I am not "taking sides" in any recent debate between the "there was no planned invasion therefore our troops could not have saved us from one" perspective – nor – the "Battle for Australia" perspective that Japan did plan to invade and our troops stopped this. The evidence is and has been for the last 40 years that a few elements in the Japanese naval command only briefly considered some sort of invasion of part of mainland

Australia in 1942 when the war was going very well for that country as one of four options for the next stage of the war. The invasion option was not taken up but abandoned in favour of another on the table. This does not mean that Australia was never under any real threat. Neither does it mean that "our boys" as my mother called them died in vain. Clearly the events of 1942 and 1943 testify to Japan's need to harass, scare and raid Australia. Rather, I am taking the questions of the debate, with a couple of key ones that *both* sides leave out, to examine the evidence for what Japan planned for Australia in the event of achieving territorial and commercial gain in the war. In effect I am seeking to answer a life-long question that my mother never satisfactorily answered, and neither has any book that I have read since: "What did 'our boys' save us from?" It was clearly not a mainland invasion but had Japan succeeded in New Guinea, life in Australia would not have been pleasant.

How I am in a position to research and answer these questions is fortuitous. But for a request in 1996 at Monash University to undertake a biography of a Japanese man who had emigrated in 1897 and become a very successful merchant in Sydney, I would not have encountered the material needed to write this book. The story of merchants and large Japanese companies doing business in Australia during the White Australia years to 1941 was a missing piece of our history, which has never been considered in relation to Japan and the wars. White Australia did not keep Japanese people out, it merely controlled who could enter and for what purposes. The discovery among the records of the National Archives of Australia of 3,114 boxes containing those of the pre-World War Two Japanese trading companies or *zaibatsu* provided a very detailed picture of what Japan was doing in Australia before 1941 and why. They give us the best key to answers about the war.

Many people and organisations enabled the research. Monash University provided research grants and many colleagues in the School of Historical Studies encouraged me. Colleagues in Australia–Japan relations, such as Professor Peter Drysdale and Professor Bill Purcell have provided invaluable insights into economics and trade and were the only ones to have seen the value of the Japanese company records. I would also make particular mention of D.C.S. Sissons whose interest, professionalism and depth of scholarship was inspirational throughout the project. Unfortunately he did not live to see it in print. Many Japanese people who have been prepared to provide family records, photos and documents have made the book more personal. I am grateful to them for sharing their amazing stories. They are acknowledged in the chapters as their stories unfold.

The National Archives of Australia provided material assistance. Their reference officers have also provided constant support through what was a very heavy workload for many people in all states and territories. I would mention especially Kerry Jeffrey in Canberra, Paul Wood and Edmund Rutlidge in Sydney and Brian Pitcher, Anne Piggott and Mark Brennan in Melbourne, who between them organised the processing of thousands of boxes of records through Access Examination and the inevitable photocopying and digitisation that resulted from reading those boxes. Regional officers in South Australia, Darwin, Western Australia and Queensland assisted me, and my small team of research assistants, over the years. A special mention goes to Ross Gibbs, the Director General of the National Archives who has been generally supportive and introduced me to valuable contacts in New Caledonia.

The staff of the Australian War Memorial Research Centre and Australia–Japan Project provided invaluable help. The staff of the National Library in Canberra, particularly in Manuscripts, Newspapers and Petherick provided expertise at critical points of the work. Linda West and staff of the Mitchell Library in Sydney hunted out little used rare books. The Battye Library staff in Western Australia assisted my research assistant Varrunika Darmapala. The staff of the Northern Territory Archives Service and National Archives in Darwin assisted my research assistant in that city, Dr Steven Farram. Liliane Tauru worked hard to uncover information in New Caledonia through the staff of the National Archives in Noumea. Finally I would thank the good people of Australian Scholarly Publishing for their work on the project.

Pam Oliver
Adjunct Research Associate
Monash University
May 2010

Australians' worst fears of a Japanese invasion seemed realised in Darwin at 10 am on 19 February 1942. Claude Leonard, a Post Master General linesman at the Post Office, heard the wail of the sirens, an awful sound, but he did not grasp the significance of it. Halfway through the second blast, "I hear Boom Boom. There was no time for thought then, I just acted. I skipped through the door, ... and into the trench." Two waves of nine bombers passed. Claude hugged the earth as the bombs fell with ear-splitting noise. When all went quiet:

> We poked our heads curiously over the sandbags. What a sight – The old
> P/O was wrecked and we got a better view of it than we should have done
> ... The P/Ms house had been hit, fences were down everywhere.[1]

A further wave of bombers attacked Darwin again at 12.10 pm destroying much of the aerodrome and the aircraft on the ground.

During the weeks after 7–8 December 1941, when Japan bombed Pearl Harbor and Malaya, Australians followed the daily newspaper reports of the Japanese armed forces' continuing southward advance as they drew ever closer to Australia. Everyone expected something to happen. The fall of Singapore on 15 February 1942 was particularly alarming because Australia had relied on this last bastion of British defence in the East to assist in the event of an attack. The raids on 19 February were just the beginning for Darwin. Sergeant Albert Fletcher No. 13 Squadron RAAF tells how, on 30 March 1942, they dashed into the open wearing their tin hats.

> And, hell! The sky was packed with formation after formation. All Jap planes and all with a belly-full of hate and sudden death .... The familiar crackle, fascinating and deadly of the Zero sent us crouching in our trench. From where we were, about three hundred yards from the hangars, we saw the bombers screaming down to within a hundred feet of the same hangars, releasing a single black bomb and then twisting away.[2]

This pattern of attack, often with little damage, continued for a further 62 raids in the Darwin area alone. Between February 1942 and November 1943, dozens of raids, most of them just nuisance value like the single bomb raid of 30 March, occurred along the north from Broome in the west to as far as Sydney in the southeast, but no invasion ever came.

Australians were warned early in 1942 to prepare for an invasion. The continuation of raids into 1943 suggested to many people that this was indeed still likely. The panic and sheer terror at times that Australians felt throughout 1942 accompanied preparations for attacks all over the country. People built trenches in their backyards and in local parks. Public buildings reinforced windows and packed valuable archives for safe storage. One 1942 image of the consequences of an invasion, with the caption 'A united "fighting mad" Australia can never be enslaved' was used by the Department of Aircraft Production. It depicts an Australian worker pulling a wealthy Japanese business magnate in a rickshaw past Flinders Street Station in Melbourne. Would the white race finally be reduced to slavery to the Asiatics of the north? In NSW, Les Sullivan returned home for holidays on the train south to Kempsey. Passing the beaches at Coffs Harbour, he saw that they were covered with barbed wire entanglements and that military personnel manned foxholes in the dunes. As he watched from the train, a Lockheed Hudson bomber took off on submarine patrol because several ships had been torpedoed off the coast. At his home, the emergency meeting of farmers was told that if a Japanese landing took place, they should burn all crops, smash their boats and drive stock inland. Les wondered if there would be a farm to return home to next holidays. As the air attacks continued into March 1942, Stan Tutt, serving in a militia unit in northern Queensland outside Townsville, wrote: "I expect a Japanese attempt on Australia within the next six weeks, ... An American says this place may be raided tomorrow. We'll see." The three Japanese raids on Townsville did not take place until July 1942.[3] Further news of raids on Broome and of the sinking of dozens of ships along the east coast kept Australians edgy.

The frequent raids, but the absence of an invasion, have led historians to ask many questions about Japanese activities and intentions. One of the most enduring questions is whether Japan really intended to invade Australia. We know now that Japan did not have that intention except early in 1942 when Japan considered the option of invading part of Australia alongside three other military options but rejected it as impracticable. However, if Japan did not intend to invade why did it raid Australia? Military historians provide one reason: that isolating Australia was important in Japan's attempt to keep the USA out of the areas that Japan wished to acquire in order to build a Greater East Asian Co-prosperity Sphere that included much of South East Asia (SEA), the Netherlands East Indies (NEI, modern-day Indonesia), the islands of Micronesia, Rabaul, the Solomon Islands and New Caledonia. Japan needed good harbours and the rich mineral, oil, marine and agricultural products that these areas offered. Australia was a convenient base from which the American armed forces could thwart this advance. But Bob Wurth, a journalist, argues that the raids were an "unimportant sideshow" and nothing to do with the serious debate in Japan in the early part of

1942 about the course of the war in Australia's region or the possibility of invading Australia.[4]

Despite the fact that Japan did not invade, the belief persists strongly in a planned Japanese invasion that failed. Why? There are three main reasons. Some historians argue that Australians had so feared Japan for decades before the war that when the raids came in 1942 they believed that this was the beginning of a long-planned invasion. In support of this view, these historians maintain that the popular invasion novels and stories of the 1910s and 1920s reflect a real fear of Japan deep in the Australian psyche.[5] But what evidence is there that Australian people believed these fictional ideas and were actually terrified of Japanese people and Japan for 50 years before World War Two, and, as a result, still continue to believe in a failed invasion long after the war? The historians do not give us any other information to resolve this question.

The second reason that historians offer, which is found in popular belief, is that Japanese people in Australia prepared for the raids. This would explain the knowledge that the bombers possessed and used to select and attack their targets with such accuracy. These historians point to the official report of the bombing of Darwin, which squarely placed the blame for the raids on the Japanese who were living in Darwin before the war. Further information on alleged Japanese spying in Australia is used to strengthen the case for a long preparation for the raids in other areas along the north. The argument is that because Japanese people spied, they must have intended to invade.[6] This argument makes sense only if Japan intended to invade and if Japanese people in Australia gathered information overwhelmingly for military purposes. It does not answer the following questions. If Japan did not intend to invade, why did it raid? Why did it gather all the information it did? What was its interest in Australia? What part would Australia play in relation to Japan's planned Greater East Asian Co-prosperity Sphere to the north if Japan was not interested in conquering part of Australia?

The third popular reason, and perhaps the most powerful, is the remembered experience of 1942. Many people can recount personal experiences of the war or have, like myself, had relatives tell them stories about the raids. Many still remember the preparations to repel an invasion, the reports of Japanese activities in the press and Prime Minister Curtin's speeches on the radio that contained dire warnings against complacency. Few historians even briefly compare what the public was told and what the government actually knew about the possibility of invasion or of Japanese activities within the country at the time.[7]

Neither the popular experience nor historians' arguments answer the following questions. What happened before Japan bombed us? What activities were the Japanese people, who visited and lived in Australia, engaged in within the country before 1942 and for how long? Were these activities harmless or military in purpose? What connection did any of these activities have to the events of 1942? No historians have investigated the records, recently released by the National Archives of Australia, of the extensive Japanese networks, particularly the large trading companies or *zaibatsu* and their international operations that fuelled Japan's war preparation in the 1930s and were broken up in 1945. Importantly, the same *zaibatsu* firms operated in Australia from the 1880s to 1942. These records give us a true picture of what the Japanese were doing in Australia before the raids.[8]

It is my purpose in this book to show the full extent of Japanese settlement and activities in Australia before World War Two in order to fill the gap in our history and enable us to see what part the Japanese people in Australia played in preparing for war. This completed story of what happened before the Japanese raided shows an Australia confident in the operation of its immigration laws, feeling safe behind the 'great white walls' provided by the White Australia policy after 1901 and not particularly worried about invasion by the hordes from the north except in moments of international crisis. It shows the workings of an

Australia efficient in intelligence and security and aware of its defence needs. It reveals an even more remarkable narrative of a resident Japanese population spread all over the country, well integrated into every aspect of Australian life and able to travel freely back and forth to Japan, the Pacific and SEA. This older, pre-war story that has been buried by the war narrates the constant activities of Japanese networks in Australia at diplomatic, international, business, social, local and family levels from the 1860s–1940s. The records left by Japanese companies, Australian security services and individuals show us the complex relationships and distinctions between genuinely co-operative activities of a peaceful nature and the clandestine world of intelligence gathering.[9] We can ask where the fictional stories stand and how these influenced people's feelings of the Japanese at the time. What was the social and commercial reality? We can ask particularly: if Australians were scared stiff of a possible Japanese invasion and strongly suspected Japanese people were spying and planning for that, why did Australia let them through the great white walls at all between 1901 and 1941?

In 1942 and since, Australians have also seen the raids as one offensive by Japan. We know now that the attacks on the north were not one front but three.[10] This military assessment must be taken into account when we look at any preparations for the raids and consider the possible part played by the Japanese people whom Australian authorities allowed to visit and live in Australia in the decades before the war. This book aims to leave us with a better understanding of our experiences and memories of World War Two and of the raids by Japan. It is a more remarkable story than the current one. To examine the pre-war story we will first look at 1942 and what Australians knew about Japanese intentions and plans at the time of the attacks. Different assessments of what happened in 1942 have led to five different beliefs about the nature of Japanese activities in Australia and their relationship to what happened in the war. If we examine these beliefs, especially the mistaken assessments of the nature of pre-war Japanese settlements and their status under immigration law, it is possible to see other reasons, apart from military ones, why Japan did not seriously contemplate an invasion of Australia, and what part Japanese immigrants played in preparation for the raids.

1942 and the invasion belief

During the twelve months after World War Two began, it became increasingly clear that Japan, a formal ally of Britain and thus Australia between 1894 and 1922, and a member of the League of Nations until 1933, would enter the war on the side of the Axis powers, Germany and Italy. Since 1937, Japan had been engaged in full-scale war with China. Japanese troops entered Nanking on 13 December 1937. For six weeks following the fall of the city, they engaged in rape, murder, theft and arson on an extraordinary scale. The news leaked out from the few westerners who managed to film some of their experiences and report to newspapers. What became known as 'The Rape of Nanking' horrified Australians and sparked fear of Japanese brutality. Australians were further shocked to read of the surrender of France to Germany in June 1940. In September 1940, Japan signed the Tripartite Pact with the Axis nations, an act that many Australians saw as a betrayal of a longstanding friendship. Japanese residents like Mr Iida, a manager of Okura Trading in Australia for 20 years, was shocked to be spat on in the street and called a traitor on the day Japan signed the treaty.[11] As an ally of Germany, Japan was able to occupy French Indo-China (modern-day Vietnam) in September. In response to these actions, the Australian government gradually began to prepare for a possible war with Japan.

Internally, in late 1937, the Australian government took the first security measures to prepare for a war with Japan. This involved documenting the names and addresses of all men, women and children resident or born in Australia who were of Japanese descent, whether they were naturalised or not. Hirokichi Nakamura, a resident of Sydney since

1897, was married to an Australian, had three daughters and owned his house in Mosman. He had run his own very profitable import business since 1907. His NSW security service dossier begins:

> Urgent. A confidential inquiry is required as to status and general character of a Japanese Hirokichi Nakamura residing at Countess St Mosman, and in business in the City .... See me. 2.11.37

This was one of thousands started from this time onwards when state security services regularly followed Japanese people and reported on their daily activities. Agent '63' had the job of shadowing Mr Nakamura, and, in May 1941, reported Nakamura's conversations on the golf course with another Japanese man, Ken Shimada, manager of Nosawa & Co., who had been in Australia 20 years and was also married to an Australian and living in Mosman. Warrant Officer G.H. Hawkes of the Intelligence Corps in Sydney followed Mrs Nakamura and reported on 19 October 1941, just weeks before war broke out with Japan, that she was engaged in war work as an instructor in the Volunteer Aid Division.[12]

From 1940 onwards the Australian War Cabinet took very seriously the possibility of some form of attack on Australia if Japan entered the war but it only expected raids on Australia's coast, not invasion. When Japan occupied French Indo-China, the army prepared arrest warrants for the internment of all Japanese nationals and Australian-born Japanese regardless of age or gender. Further, the War Cabinet followed the USA and Britain and froze Japan's Sterling assets on 1 July 1941.[13] This made Japan's overseas trade almost impossible. Dozens of Japanese trading companies in Australia had goods on the way to Australia and exports on their way to Japan. They advised most of their Japanese staff and families to return to Japan but to keep a skeleton staff at their offices around the country to handle the goods in transit. Many firms were still open in December 1941. Most of the millions of pounds worth of imports of fabrics and household goods were intended for Australian department stores and corner shops. The equally large amounts of exports of wool, minerals, wheat and other produce were destined for Japan, SEA or Manchuria. J.F. Guthrie of Geelong wrote to Ken Shimada of Nosawa & Co. in Sydney on 17 November 1941 worried about the fate of 142 of his Corriedale sheep in transit for Hokkaido in northern Japan that were caught in the pre-war asset freeze and suspension of trade. Both regretted the unfortunate "international complications" that were interrupting the trade.[14]

Japanese-Australians who worked for the trading companies found it difficult to respond to the situation. Many of the men had families in Australia where they had lived for decades. Many wives and children left to live with relatives in Japan. Other wives and children refused to go to a Japan they no longer knew or had never known. The last direct ship to Japan left in August 1941. Hirokichi Nakamura stayed with his Australian family and friends. He closed down his business, the Austral Nippon Indent Co., in September 1941. Ken Shimada, his friend and colleague, was booked to sail on 2 December, but the sailing was postponed to 9 December and Ken was arrested and interned.[15]

By the time Japan attacked Malaya, the Philippines and Pearl Harbor in December 1941, Australian authorities were in a position to arrest and intern all Japanese people in the country. Hirokichi Nakamura and his family were holidaying at their beach house at Woy Woy, near Gosford, north of Sydney, when they heard the report of the bombing of Pearl Harbor on the radio. Nakamura decided to return to Mosman because he felt that Japanese nationals might be questioned. He was correct. At 1.30 am on 9 December, Constables Walsh and Hughes from the North Sydney Police Station arrived to arrest Nakamura. Constable Walsh, who had known Nakamura for 20 years, was embarrassed at the situation and apologised. Nakamura told his distressed family that they should not worry because he had not committed any offence. He was sure that he would only need to answer some questions and would return later. He left with the police, taking nothing with him. They did not see him again for almost three years.[16]

Over the next two days, police very quickly entered all Japanese trading houses and businesses Australia-wide. They closed down the small businesses and took steps to place the large firms under administration. They entered the offices of Mitsui & Co., Kanematsu Australia, Mitsubishi Shoji Kaisha and over 50 more firms. They took the names of the staff and began to interview them and check their friends, families and associates. The officers emptied all the contents of the desks and filing cabinet draws into cardboard boxes. The Christmas cards for 1941, ornaments, personal effects and photos along with files of invoices, correspondence on commercial matters and account books remain like a time capsule in the National Archives of Australia today.[17]

The War Cabinet put military precautions in place to protect Australia and its territories. Early in February, a battalion of the 8th Division went to reinforce Rabaul, parts of New Guinea and northern Australia. Once the raids began on Australia's north, the War Cabinet placed the area north of Alice Springs, from the Kimberleys to Mount Isa, under the military control of Major General Sir Edmond Herring. The Chiefs of Staff decided that Broome and Wyndham in Western Australia were indefensible. In effect the townspeople had left and 40 army engineers were prepared to blow up Broome if the Japanese landed. It was felt that "less effort would finish the others". Cabinet discussed the protection of the outlying islands such as New Caledonia and of Australia's sea-lanes, which were crucial to supply. In December 1941, Australia sent the 2/3rd Independent Company to garrison New Caledonia as a temporary measure until a much larger American division could relieve them. They were not withdrawn until August 1942.[18]

During 1942–43, Japan attacked many places along Australia's north coast including the pearling town of Broome in WA and as far east as Thursday Island and Townsville, a stretch of coastline where Australian master pearlers had employed Japanese men, many of them long term residents, for over 50 years. But the raids on Australia were three separate Japanese operations, not one concerted attack. Japanese air commanders in NEI fought an air war over northern Australia as part of the occupation of Timor and NEI and so Darwin was bombed. Japan's bombing of Broome in March 1942 attacked flying boats and ships carrying evacuees from NEI. Japanese naval commanders in Rabaul and Truk embarked on submarine campaigns to support operations in the southwest and central Pacific and targeted shipping along the east coast of Australia. In May 1942, Sydney and Newcastle experienced raids. These cities had been prime sites of the Australia–Japan trade, where the *zaibatsu* had opened their Australian head offices, and had provided facilities to Japanese merchant and passenger ships since 1896. Land operations in Papua and New Guinea were unrelated to either of these operations.[19]

During the early part of 1942, war preparations were in full swing all over Australia. Coastal areas considered the threat of attack to be very real. Many localities including Sydney's famous Bondi beach prepared barbed wire defences to hinder any Japanese landing. Air raid trenches were dug and gun emplacements set up at key points on harbour frontages. Even in Port Phillip Bay in Victoria civil defence forces held exercises at Frankston to repel a Japanese invasion. The Kalumburu Benedictine Mission at Drysdale River, in north WA recorded that on 3 January, "An order came from Darwin to make trestles to place on the [air] strip to prevent enemy planes landing there."

The preparations were not always welcomed or thought necessary. On the outskirts of Adelaide, at Tonsley, the Ragless family's mixed farm was six kilometres from the coast. Alice Ragless noticed two army men in a car "Spying our property" in preparation for possible enemy invasion. Later on 6 January Alice records that:

> seven military men arrived. They had come to make a place for putting a gun in, in case the Japs come. Very near the cow bail, we are very cross about it.

This was one of an ongoing series of visits from the military.[20]

The preparation was justified throughout most of 1942. Out to sea German mines sank ships along the east coast and Japanese submarines attacked merchant vessels, including the steamer *Barwon,* off Gabo Island in Victoria on 4 June. On 8 June 1942, Japanese mini submarine I-24 entered and fired 10 rounds in Sydney Harbour sinking the *Kuttabul.* One shell exploded at Bellevue Hill. At Newcastle on 8 June at 2 am, submarine I-21 commanded by Captain Matsumura fired 34 shells nine kilometres off Fort Scratchley at the mouth of the Hunter River. In an attack lasting 20 minutes, shells landed near the customs house and power station. But the community was divided on the reality of the threat of invasion in 1942 despite the dire reports surrounding the bombing of Darwin. A survey conducted by the *Daily Telegraph* on 26 February 1942, just five days after the raids began, reported that 54 per cent believed Japan would invade but 46 per cent did not believe it or did not know.[21]

To counter this reluctance and awaken the people to concentrate on the war effort in case the worst happened, Prime Minister Curtin and his ministers did nothing to allay the fear. From mid-1942 and part of 1943, what the government knew about Japan's intentions from intelligence intercepts and what it could tell and did tell the public differed. Japan not only terrified many Australians through the raids in late February but threatened specific areas of the country through propaganda broadcasts from Tokyo. One broadcast to the south Queensland coast in the week after the bombing of Darwin announced that Japan would bomb the entire coast from Darwin to Port Kembla and kill every woman and child. The report noted:

> At Coolangatta and Southport last week the A.R.P. Wardens went around from house to house asking them if they wanted to be evacuated and the people got such a scare they all packed up and left.[22]

Such experiences left very deep impressions.

Although an invasion felt imminent, the reality was quite different. The government knew by mid April 1942 that an invasion would not happen but could not share this information with the Australian public because this would have revealed that the Allies could read enemy codes. The initial assessment of Australia's situation at the beginning of the Pacific war brought Prime Minister Curtin and Sir Frederick Shedden, the Secretary of the War Cabinet, to canvass this as a 'new war', not just an escalation of or incident in the existing war. The War Cabinet called for a detailed appreciation by the Chiefs of Staff of the armed forces about what Japan might do. They concluded that Japan might occupy Rabaul, Port Moresby or New Caledonia but that it would first need to take Singapore and NEI. Only after securing Port Moresby and other bases to Australia's north would it be possible for them to attempt to invade Australia. The Japanese as we now know had reached a similar conclusion in January 1942 and abandoned any attempt to take a part of the Australian mainland, which had briefly been among four options under consideration. While Port Moresby held, Australia was safe. Dr H.V. Evatt, the Attorney General, further argued that with the USA involved in the war, Allied victory was certain in the long term.[23] Even some Australian-Japanese believed Japan could not win. When two prosperous merchants interned from Thursday Island were asked why they had not sold off their stock but instead had paid a year's rent in advance and locked up the shop before their arrest they replied:

> No could replace, stock get dear all the time, me back here [in] four five months [time], war over then,
> Japan all b------d up, can't fight England and America.[24]

Despite the assessment by the Chiefs of Staff and the War Cabinet, nothing was done to change public perception of the events. Instead, moments of panic coloured Curtin's speeches on radio and reports in the press through 1942. In some instances Curtin, who anxiously paced his backyard in the night, made alarming radio speeches before he had received up-to-date information on the actual situation to the north. In his broadcast to open Australia's Austerity Campaign on 3 September 1942, long after any likelihood of an invasion attempt had passed, Curtin stated that Australia's fate was in the balance in the Battle of the Solomons: "it represents a phase of the Japanese drive in which is wrapped up invasion of Australia". If Port Moresby or Darwin, which were the Singapores of Australia, fell then inevitably Australia would be faced

> with a bloody struggle on our soil, a struggle in which we would be forced to fight grimly city by city, village by village, until our fair land might become a blackened ruin.

Curtin had added the phrase "invasion of Australia" himself to the assessment given to him by the Chiefs of Staff. Later on 4 October, he added a further embellishment to the situation in New Guinea. His radio speech stated that: "The enemy strikes now at Moresby. We are staging a holding fight." He did not read until 5 October an operations report written on 30 September that "there was every reason to look forward … to the removal of the *threat* to Port Moresby." The Japanese had not reached Port Moresby at all and the Chiefs of Staff knew this.[25]

Such differences between what the War Cabinet knew and what the people of Australia were told through press and radio and believed (from under-reporting the actual number of casualties at Darwin and overstating the current danger in New Guinea) shaped popular memory of the war. This contributed to the climate of fear of sudden attack or invasion at the time and left a legacy of belief, which persists in popular memory of the war today, that an invasion was planned but failed, despite evidence to the contrary from Japanese and Allied sources. We must also not overplay the extent of the belief in invasion at this time. Not everyone believed that an invasion would occur and many gave up on preparations (especially when backyard trenches filled with water), which made the government step up its campaign to obtain better co-operation. In recent times these beliefs about the war, especially in a totally terrified Australia, have found expression in the concept of a 'Battle for Australia', a phrase, which Stanley demonstrates is very recent. These memories and concepts are expressed through five main beliefs about Japanese activities in Australia before the war (which are explored in this book) some of which have become embellished in the telling over the decades.

Placing blame for the raids

The most common popular belief about who bears most responsibility for the raids is that Japanese people in Australia prepared for the attacks along the north, and for an invasion that failed, over many years before the bombing of Pearl Harbor. Wurth claims to know of the existence of a militant Japanese party in Australia by 1940,[26] a claim that needs careful investigation against the evidence provided by security services' records and those of the Japanese trading companies in Australia, which he has not examined. Patrick Lindsay in his study of Kokoda writes that when Japan entered the war, "Australians immediately recalled in a new light the many visits Japanese naval ships had made to Australian ports ... with their swarming crews and their ever-present cameras."[27] Even the final report on the bombing of Darwin blamed the Japanese residents of NT. But although Japanese immigrants were continuously resident right around Australia from the 1870s, there were no Japanese in Darwin after 1 January 1942 when they were shipped to Sydney for internment.[28] If these two groups of Japanese could not have assisted in the raids, what part did Australian-Japanese people play in the attacks?

The second popular belief is that Japanese residents, diplomats and business people spied in Australia from the 1920s to provide Japan with the information that it needed to conduct a war against Australia and that the information was used in World War Two. The evidence provided for spying needs careful re-examination. Many stories of spying developed during and after the war. Even reputable historians continue to repeat largely unsubstantiated post-war stories and allege that large Japanese companies, the *zaibatsu* like Mitsubishi and Mitsui, controlled the Arafura Sea in the 1930s while Japanese lugger captains charted reefs for the Japanese navy. Fear of Japanese espionage in Australia was often expressed, particularly in Queensland, during times of international uncertainty. But what is the evidence for actual spying of a useful military nature? Further, 'spying' in the stories is often defined as collecting any information whatever for any purpose. Buying a tourist map or postcard at a shop becomes an act of espionage under this definition and such incidents were often reported to the authorities by over-zealous citizens in times of international tension. These stories need careful assessment against the information in security records for the pre-war period. Most of the stories presuppose that Japanese people in Australia had no other use, apart from preparing for an invasion, for the information that they gathered over decades.[29] How useful as a preparation for the raids was the information that Japanese gathered in Australia?

A third view is that there was a terrible lack of security in Australia when it came to Japanese activities. Wurth, in a very selective use of Australian government records, argues that the Japanese First Minister in Australia, Tatsuo Kawai, gathered critical information on Australia's economy and defence from his arrival in 1941 and throughout his internment within the Consulate in Melbourne from December 1941 to his repatriation in August 1942. He further maintains that Australian security services permitted Kawai and his staff: "to take complete information about conditions in Australia and her territories to support Japan". He argues that this terrible lack of security existed in large part because the Attorney General Dr H.V. Evatt had so trusted the Japanese that he unwittingly compromised Australia's security. This is a very serious allegation indeed. In support of this view, Wurth states that Evatt had defended people who were friendly with Japan from the late 1920s. Further, Evatt received 305 cases of seized documents from the Japanese Consul-General in December 1941 and knew of the top-secret fund administered by the Consul-General for undercover work and to attempt to influence Australians in positions of power who might be receptive to Japanese propaganda. Wurth's allegations do not distinguish between information gathering for non-military purposes and true espionage. He gives no examples of the information they gathered or of the work of the security services that watched the Japanese.[30] Much more careful investigation is needed before claims can be substantiated that Australian security was woefully inadequate and contributed to the raids.

The fourth view is that Australia was so fearful of Japan from 1905 when it defeated Russia in the short Russo-Japanese war of 1904–05 (at which Australia was an observer) that a policy of appeasement dominated national policies and diplomacy from that point on and made Australia vulnerable. Further, it is argued that even members of the War Cabinet, including the Attorney General in 1940–41, did nothing about Japanese activities for fear of provoking Japan into war. Recently two historians have alleged that wartime fear of invasion was the result of the 'terror' that Australians had felt about Japan since 1905. No distinction is made between appeasement and an ongoing policy of promoting genuine trade and co-operation between the two nations. One argument that is often suggested as an example of appeasement is that Australia went so far as to consider giving Japan a foothold on Australian soil at Yampi Sound's rich mineral deposits in Western Australia in 1938. This project failed. But the example ignores the rich context of the existing, legitimate and long standing trading arrangements between Japanese and Australian companies and government bodies from the 1890s, such as the contract worth approximately £74,000 in the 1930s between Mitsubishi and

BHP for minerals at Mount Isa and contracts in 1939–40 to supply the Australian army with cloth for parachutes and uniforms. Japan had supported Australia in World War One and Mitsui and Mitsubishi had traded in Australia since 1901 and 1911.[31] Was Australia appeasing Japan by allowing BHP and other companies to trade with Japan for decades before the war? What was the role of the *zaibatsu* in Australia in the decades before the raids?

In a contradictory fifth belief, the Australian government is accused of being too lenient on Japan in the operation of the immigration laws of the time, even though this argument conflicts with the belief that in 1901 Australia put up the 'great white walls' against Asian immigration despite vigorous protests from Japan.[32] The knowledge that Japanese people had of Australia was, it is argued, the result of exceptions to the White Australia policy, which allowed them to enter after 1901. Which is correct? What special arrangements were made for the Japanese to enter Australia after 1901 and what security risk did this pose? Was fear of Japan or a desire for appeasement behind relations with Japan in the administration of immigration law or were other factors at work?

In view of these five beliefs about the Japanese presence in Australia, it is a simple step to blame pre-war Japanese residents (if indeed there were a significant number remaining under the White Australia policy as some doubt) especially along Australia's north for the raids during the war. However, an immediate problem in blaming the Japanese is that the raids were not one front but three separate operations. How is this fact to be reconciled with blaming Japanese immigrants? If the records of what Japanese people and trading companies actually did in Australia are considered alongside the overlapping diplomatic, business, social and personal relations throughout the country then these issues can be properly addressed. These beliefs about the war and the preparation for the bombings by Japan rest on contradictory understandings of Japanese immigration to Australia and activities within Australia, which are partial and distort the full and more remarkable story of what actually happened before the raids. The commonly understood picture leaves out crucial sections of the overall narrative that we now have available to us. Much of it was buried with the war and like the records stored unnoticed for decades. After all, given the horrors of World War Two, it was not wise to admit friendship with Japanese people until much more recent times.

The missing story of the Japanese in Australia

On both sides of the Australia–Japan relationship today, Australians and Japanese still tend to remember the bad things and hold to simple images of the threat of invasion in Australia and the insults of the White Australia policy in Japan. The most commonly understood story of Japanese immigration to Australia can be narrated briefly as follows. Australians closed their minds and doors to Asia when concepts of race came to dominate in the lead up to federation. Thousands of Japanese had arrived in the 1890s to work as pearlers along the north coast of Australia and as cane cutters in Queensland. Calls for a White Australia led to severe immigration restrictions in 1901, when the White Australia policy prohibited Asian immigration. However, under exceptions to the laws, Japanese still entered for pearling and trade and gathered an enormous amount of amorphous information about Australia. Japanese harboured ill feeling about the policy throughout the period to World War Two. By 1940, cordial relations such as that between Prime Minister John Curtin and the Japanese First Minister in Australia, Tatsuo Kawai became, as Wurth states "islands of tolerance in a sea of hatred". Australians who had been terrified of invasion since the Russo-Japanese war of 1904–05 became increasingly fearful of a Japanese invasion particularly from the late 1930s, which led Australian governments to take steps to appease Japan. The presence of large Japanese combines in the seas to Australia's north, and spying within the country, threatened Australia's security and had an influence in Australian affairs before the war. The information that the Japanese gained contributed to the raids on Australia. In this way, it is argued, the fears of 1905 were realised when Japan appeared ready to invade in 1942.[33]

This current, popular and simple story omits a lot of the narrative. The picture of Japanese people working in isolated settlements along Australia's north, pearling along the coast with the opportunity to map the coast and prepare for invasion with immigration restricted to a trickle after 1901, is far from accurate. It leaves out the complexity of the Japanese networks, which were present and active from the 1860s until 1942. The popular story also leaves many questions unanswered. Are we seriously to believe that Japan engaged in an awful lot of wasted effort in decades of diplomacy, trade and Australia research for nothing if it did not intend to invade? If Japanese were not living in Australia after 1901, or were largely confined to the north, how did they spy and gain enough knowledge to raid and bomb around much of the Australian coast? If Japan had such good knowledge of Australia and prepared years in advance for an invasion as some argue, why did that invasion not take place? Why did they fail to land or take territory early in the war? If Australian authorities knew about Japanese spies before the war, why did they not act to stop them at the time? Most importantly, if Japan did not plan to invade Australia, what did the Japanese want?

The early chapters of this book restore the missing parts of the Japanese story by piecing together the settlement patterns and development of networks Australia-wide between the 1860s and 1941. This puts 1942 in a context. On the Japanese side they examine why Japanese people were interested in the particular areas in which they settled, what information they collected and how they used it. Was the choice of location strategic in terms of Japan's expansion policies, or haphazard? On the Australian side it asks why Australia was prepared to continue Japanese immigration in a changed but controlled form and how this contributed to the situation in 1941–42.

These first chapters also look at two results of Japanese immigration. First, the large multinational Japanese trading companies, the *zaibatsu*, virtually ran Australia's trade with the east, especially with Japan, from the 1890s and, by the 1930s, controlled 95 per cent of Australia's trade with Japan. These were the same *zaibatsu* that supported Japan's war machine and caused the Allies in World War Two such enormous concern that they forcibly broke them up straight after Japan was defeated.[34] What did the *zaibatsu* want from its involvement in Australia? What influence did they have on Australian business and government policies before the war? A secondary result of the strong business immigration was the development of positive relations between Japanese and Australians at all levels of society. The networks supported hundreds of small Japanese businessmen and forged partnerships with Australian firms. Japanese families integrated into local Australian communities. They knew Australia well. But was this integration genuine? How did Australians respond to the Japanese in their midst?

Later chapters examine questions raised by the Japanese presence in Australia. First, what was the role of the White Australia policy in Australia's security? From the Japanese perspective, writers often argue that Australia's exclusion of Japanese people was a 'running sore' which contributed to a series of events that put the two countries on a path to war.[35] However, from the Australian perspective, did the policy play a part in keeping Australia safe from invasion, and, were the exceptions to the policy for Japan part of an attempted appeasement? Second, in the light of the largely positive relationships between Australian and Japanese people at all levels within Australia, when, how and why was the undercurrent of suspicion manifested? Was it justified? Do we know if the invasion theme of popular fiction was universally supported as factual in any way by the media or the general population? Third, how effective were Australian responses to external threats during the dangerous years of 1937–41? How alert were Australian security and defence forces to the risks from outside Australia, when a militaristic Japan was at war with China? Fourth, how effective was Australia's internal security? What measures did Australian authorities take to assess the threat within the country from the Japanese networks, which had been interwoven into Australian business and society at all levels for over 40 years? What was the actual nature of the threat from espionage? What did the security services find and how did they respond to this? Is the allegation valid that a desire to appease Japan resulted in lax security measures that actually endangered Australia?

Conclusion

Beliefs about what happened before the raids are coloured by two traditions. The one based on fear and suspicion survived the war and has been magnified. The other, balanced with friendship and a competently defended Australia, was buried and struggles to surface sufficiently to be considered seriously. To admit one had a Japanese grandfather and a white grandmother or a Japanese neighbour or friend was not possible in the decades immediately after the war, but it is now. Japanese people also can remember a grandfather who lived in Australia or an aunt born in Australia. This other story needs consideration to balance the theory of 50 years of fear of Japan before 1942 and enable us to see a wider context for our relationship with Japan today. The story of Australian security services' actions before and during the war in the face of the possible threat has also been neglected. The restoration of the older tradition of friendship, which balances the narrative of fear and suspicion, allows us to address successfully many key questions about the possible connections between Japanese residents and visitors and the bombings of Australian shores during the war. What did Japan want in Australia and why did it not invade? How can we better understand the raids of 1942? Where does the truth lie about what fate our troops saved Australia from?

The raids and Japanese settlement

Three major locations that suffered Japanese air raids in 1942–43 are now prime tourist destinations: Broome, Darwin and Townsville. All had early Japanese connections. Broome's museum and Japanese cemetery commemorate its pearling heritage and the loss of Japanese lives in that industry. Darwin and Townsville have heritage sites that memorialise the bombings and record Japanese trading activity in the area. In all three places, some allege that sinister activities lurked beneath legitimate Japanese endeavours. Australia's war memorials, particularly in Canberra and Melbourne, also document Japanese wartime activities. Inland at Cowra in NSW, the graves of Japanese prisoners of war who died in an attempted escape in 1944 testify to the Japanese as the enemy.[1] But if we look carefully at the information on the three main northern bombing sites, any attempt to connect Japanese settlement to the war raises more problems than it solves.

Broome, the best-known area of Japanese settlement, experienced the second worst raids of 1942. Its adventurous pearling history began in 1861 when Aboriginal people were forced to collect mother-of-pearl shell in the shallow water of Roebuck Bay, which supplied 75 per cent of the world's needs by the mid-1860s. The romantic Broome of the history books began when E.W. Streeter, an English businessman, built a rough jetty near a well-worn path in the mangroves. A motley collection of bush camps, tents and corrugated iron sheds erected near the jetty formed the beginnings of a town. Proclaimed in 1883, Broome became home to thousands of Japanese divers brought from Singapore and Hong Kong by pearling masters like Streeter. About 900 of them died in the decades before World War Two. They are buried in the largest Japanese cemetery in Australia.[2]

After the war, Broome's pre-war Japanese residents, who outnumbered white Australians, were depicted in a sinister light. As Sarah Yu writes:

> Romantic Broome … the locale of exciting novels! White-sailed luggers skimming across the azure seas …. Colourful Asiatics jostling in Sheba Lane – the famous street 'o pearls … wild riots, treacherous storms, … Japanese spies, the pearling masters in their whites on the shaded verandas. All this has been recorded in writings and photographs of Broome.[3]

Today, Broome's tourist web pages are kinder to the pre-war Japanese population and celebrate the friendship that Japanese and Australians shared. In December 1941, Broome residents were suddenly faced with rounding up and interning Japanese friends and employees, many of whom had been born and raised in Australia and no longer had ties to Japan. As the website says:

> Although they complied with the internment policy, Broome residents tried to make life as easy as possible for the Japanese, bringing food and presents to the camp and allowing regular visits to town to go shopping.[4]

The Japanese were later blamed for Broome's wartime suffering. The raid on 3 March 1942 destroyed 24 aircraft and left the town's buildings, vehicles, boats and the ocean on fire. Seventy people died. The bombers attacked 15 Dornier flying boats anchored in the shallow bay, which were filled mainly with refugee women and children from NEI. Many of these died from swimming through burning oil on the sea surface. But why bomb Broome? It could boast a good harbour and a cable connection to the northern hemisphere but was not a good invasion point. Was the stable Japanese population spying as novels claim, or friendly as the website maintains?

Darwin, the site of Australia's worst bombings, was first settled as Palmerston in the 1870s. Exotic stories of the port's pearling fleets date back to the first Japanese arrivals in 1883. C.L.A. Abbott, the Administrator from 1937–45 and his wife, Hilda, often sat on the verandah of government house to watch the beautiful white sails of the luggers as they entered port. The Abbotts entertained Japanese naval and civilian visitors to Darwin. As a keen photographer, Abbott left a large collection of photographs of the visiting fleets that took on fuel and supplies at Darwin's harbour facilities as the closest port on the Australian mainland to Timor and New Guinea. But it was not an advantageous place for an invasion. The NT Japanese population, although influential, numbered only a few hundred. The local photographer and a pearling agent were thought to be spies. Many people in Darwin today still believe that they were. A strong belief also remains that the visiting captains and crews of Japanese ships, some of whom were entertained by Abbott, were naval agents on missions.[5] What connection did Japanese visitors and pearling operations have to the air raids? Considering that the official report on the bombings blames a Japanese population that was interned in Sydney at the time, this is an important question.

Townsville, the third site of bombing raids of any note, was never a major Japanese settlement although it rightly boasts that it had small Japanese importing firms and the first paid Japanese consul (who was not an Australian) between1896–1908. The first party of settlers set up camp in 1864 where a town was proclaimed in 1866. Townsville's first

Japanese arrived in 1892 to work on cane fields at Mourilyan. About 3,000–4,000 Japanese people were spread all over Queensland with the largest population living on Thursday Island.

Townsville suffered three minor bombing raids in July 1942. Rod Cardell, who was 10 years old at the time, recalls:

> Townsville was caught unawares as two giant four-engine flying boats leisurely flew around for half an hour while late-nighters enjoyed themselves in the brightly lit streets below. A couple of suspicious searchlights ... caught the raiders in their beams. An American light anti-aircraft battery opened fire to no avail. ... A small group of prison warders from Stuart Prison were playing a game of cards at home at the time of the raid. They heard some loud bumps in the distance and felt the ground shake slightly. At the time they had no idea that the Japanese had attacked Townsville. They heard about it in the news the next morning. Slit trenches were hurriedly dug in back yards for use during any further raids.[6]

Japan gained propaganda value out of the raids on Townsville, calling them "the largest raids ... since the fall of Singapore". They were not. Locals who received Japanese short-wave broadcasts, felt an exhilarating sense of satisfaction because Japan, which had so vocally threatened the city for months, even addressing inhabitants and businesses by name, had been forced to exaggerate grossly when they finally penetrated Townsville's anti-aircraft cover. Townsville received an advance party from the USA Army Airforce (USAAF) on 5 January 1942, and although Allied troops were based in Townsville, it was not a major target but perhaps useful for Japanese propaganda purposes. But what connection does its slim Japanese heritage have to the war?[7]

Stories of the pearling centres and the more sinister wartime accounts of the raids form today's familiar picture of Japanese settlement in Australia. The men of the pearling fleets are indentured labourers, now often depicted as transients returning to their native land after a short stay, or, less often as long-term resident friends of the white population. It is an idyllic vision of Japanese immigration to Australia with a sinister side, perhaps overly influenced by the events of the war. In popular imagination, Japanese pearlers and labourers have become government agents collecting information, making maps and spying out the best landing sites for an invasion. What truth is there in this well-known and accepted story? What relationship do the idyllic and sinister sides of the coin bear to the raids on Australia?

Recent research into Japanese immigration to Australia has not disturbed the popular story or addressed the questions that it leaves unanswered. When the story of Shigeyoshi (Sam) Hirodo surfaced during an exhibition at the Museum of Sydney in 2004, it highlighted publicly for the first time Sydney's substantial Japanese merchant community, which later featured on ABC TV's *Asia Pacific Focus*. Sam arrived in 1907 to study wool classing. "How was that possible under the White Australia policy?" asked the presenter, Michael Maher. Sam rose to become managing director of F. Kanematsu (Australia) Pty Ltd and raised a family in Mosman. New studies of the merchants and trading companies that opened in major centres like Sydney or in towns like Geelong in Victoria or Cossack in WA are often seen as additional uncovered histories. They add to stories published in 1996 about Japanese people who lived in Australia for 30 to 50 years before their internment in World War Two. Further stories of mixed relations between Japanese and other races in Australia's north add the personal touches of family life. For example, in Broome, Steven tells of his mother's relations with Okumura a top diver while other Japanese at Mt Isa and Thursday Island report liaisons with Aboriginals and Chinese-Australians. These additional stories do not alter the popular view that Japanese people lived in unconnected settlements particularly along Australia's north. They only add to the list of places in which Japanese lived before Federation.[8]

The enduring popularity of the prominent tourist locations that were bombed means that other places where Japanese lived are still not given much attention. When Japanese are mentioned, it is assumed that their major connection was always to Japan and not to other Japanese settlements in Australia. Without an overall picture of Japanese connections within Australia, it is not possible to see why the Japanese came to Australia in the first place or what Japan's real interest was in Australia as a whole. Neither is it possible to support or refute the belief that Japanese visitors and settlers bore some responsibility for the raids by gathering the intelligence needed for the events of 1942. Is the assumed connection between Japanese visitors, their ever-present cameras and spying, as Patrick Lindsay writes, correct?[9]

This chapter introduces a totally new way of viewing the Japanese in Australia. It explores how Japanese *networks* in Australia (rather than isolated settlements) built on individual, official government and business activities that were interconnected from the arrival of the first Japanese visitors and settlers to create an influential Australia-wide Japanese presence by the 1910s with links to the Asia-Pacific region and to Japan. As Map 1 shows, the settlement was so widespread by 1942 that Japanese people lived in most larger coastal towns and cities and many inland rural towns well beyond the areas that were bombed.[10]

How did Japanese people first become interested in Australia? What factors determined the character of the early immigration? Was it officially planned as part of a Japanese expansion or simply haphazard? Was the choice of settlement location strategic?

Japanese expansion and emigration

Scholars place Japan's desire to expand and emigrate southwards at various points in history. Certainly, if the Japanese settlement of Australia was a prelude to the raids, then it began very early indeed in the 1860s. Australia settled about 10,000–15,000 Japanese people from the mid-nineteenth

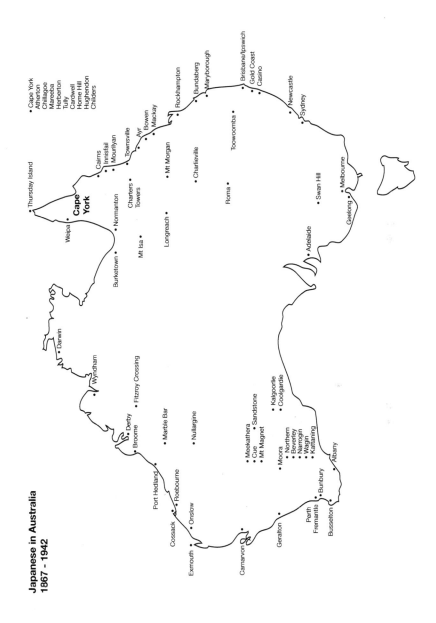

Japanese in Australia
1867 - 1942

Cape York
Atherton
Chillagoe
Mareeba
Herberton
Tully
Cardwell
Home Hill
Hughendon
Childers

Thursday Island

Cape York

Weipa

Cairns
Innisfail
Mourilyan

Townsville

Ayr

Bowen
Mackay

Rockhampton

Bundaberg
Maryborough

Brisbane/Ipswich
Gold Coast
Casino

Newcastle
Sydney

Normanton

Charters
Towers

Mt Morgan

Charleville

Toowoomba

Burketown

Mt Isa

Longreach

Roma

Darwin

Wyndham

Fitzroy Crossing

Adelaide

Swan Hill

Melbourne

Geelong

Derby
Broome

Marble Bar

Nullargine

Kalgoorlie
Coolgardie

Meekatharra
Cue   Sandstone
Mt Magnet

Moora
Northern
Beverley
Narrogin
Wagin
Kattanning

Albany

Port Hedland
Roebourne

Bunbury

Cossack
Onslow

Perth
Fremantle
Busselton

Exmouth

Geraldton

Carnarvon

century to 1941. Approximately half were indentured labourers who lived in Australia for between three to 50 years. Compared with total Japanese emigration in the nineteenth century, this is a small number. Japanese immigrants to Brazil, for example, numbered 11,868 in 1913 and 110,191 between the two world wars. In 1914, official Japanese figures placed the number of emigrants at 359,716, 122,000 of them in Manchuria and China and 117,000 in the USA but provided no figures for Australia. The majority immigrated through employment contract arrangements negotiated between the governments of Japan and the host nation, although many individuals travelled abroad before formal arrangements existed. Japan's interest in Australia in the nineteenth century was a marginal part of a general interest in voyages of discovery to search for unsettled islands and new trading posts where Japan could 'plant the flag' as the European powers were doing.[11]

Many scholars argue that the nineteenth-century period of emigration and exploration resumed an earlier policy of southern expansion before 1635, (often called *nanshin* or *nan'yō*), when Japan became a 'closed' country through passing acts that practically ended contact with Europeans. This view of Japan as a clearly defined country that acted in the 1860s on a desire that it had harboured for over 200 years to expand south and take territory makes it appear particularly threatening to Australia. But other scholars date the *nan'yō* policy much later at 1890s, 1910s or 1935. Frei assesses this view.

> ... it would be easy to concoct a conspiracy theory to suggest that Japanese indeed had long wanted to encroach on Australian territory ... pick a stray sentence from Yoshida Shoin's writings about colonizing Australia in 1854, combine it with Japan invasion stories that flourished on and off in Australia since the mid-1890s, add ... Australia-bashing books that appeared in the early stages of World War II, ... It would make a splendid plot, though one far from the truth.[12]

Japanese strategic writings on *nan'yō* were never seriously analysed until quite recently to understand beliefs about Japan's intentions for Australia. Japan's actions *within* Australia have *never* been examined to assess exactly what Japan's plans were for Australia and how early they were developed. As Frei argues, we need to look extremely carefully at the evidence before assuming that Japan had a long-term intention to attack Australia.

It is true that the nineteenth century emigration was not the first in Japan's history. Before the 1630s, tens of thousands of Japanese traded abroad and about 7,000 emigrated. This period has been called the first period of Japan's advance towards the area where Australia lies, although it is mistaken to see this as an intention toward Australia, which at that time was not even mapped. Instead, the period from 1580s–1630s was a time of unprecedented Japanese participation in trade in SEA. Japan initiated this expansion to take advantage of the *entrepôt* function of ports where they could exchange exports for Chinese goods and overcome the ban on direct China–Japan trade. At that time also the frontiers of Japan were not even fixed. Japan as we know it today did not yet exist under the semi-feudal central government run by the Tokugawa shoguns from 1603. This government, with the emperor largely as a figurehead, had varying degrees of control over the territory held by the daimyo (or feudal lords) that surrounded its seat of power in Edo. Only in the nineteenth century was Japan forced to grapple with a western idea of a frontier as a line marking the boundary between one nation and another. Before that, Japanese authorities thought in terms of a concentric circle of increasing strangeness or foreignness and a decrease in real control. These foreign areas included parts of modern Japan such as the Ryukyu Islands and the northern island of modern Hokkaido.[13]

Until recently, scholars believed that from 1630s–1850s Japan was a closed country. We now know that when Tokugawa passed a series of maritime prohibitions in the 1630s (also called the Seclusion Acts) that restricted foreign traders' access to Japanese markets, these did not 'close'

Japan nor were they intended to do so. The aim was to avoid foreign influence in Japanese affairs. Initially, Japan banned Christians, expelled the Portuguese and confined Dutch merchants to Nagasaki. Foreign travel by Tokugawa subjects was also greatly restricted. Recent research shows that what is called the seclusion is better understood not as a set of measures applied to the outside world but a means of centralising the control of foreign trade under the Tokugawa shogunate to enhance its legitimacy and security *within* Japan. Japan continued its overseas trade and retained a distinctive policy for virtually every country. Although the measures excluded all Europeans except some Dutch merchants on the tiny island of Deshima, Japan was not closed to Asians. Chinese merchants at Nagasaki, the Ryukyu Islanders at Satsuma, the Koreans through Tsushima and the Matsumae in what is now Hokkaido conducted most of Japan's overseas trade as agents abroad, enabling Japanese merchants to remain prime players in the world economy. This arrangement gave Japan continued access to scientific developments during this period.[14]

For the Japanese people, the prohibitions meant that many emigrants at the time either chose not to return to Japan or were prohibited from doing so. They integrated into their host countries. In NEI, for example, wealthy Dutch merchants married Japanese women and Japanese men wed local women. The majority were respectable citizens and traders who were prosperous enough to afford large houses and servants. Even women became entrepreneurs like the widow Cornelia van Nijenroode of Batavia, the daughter of a geisha and a Dutch merchant. This meant that generations of Japanese descendants lived in exile abroad with their links to Japan dissolving over time.[15]

The end to Japan's seclusion is portrayed as being just as sudden as its beginning. In fact it was gradual. Japan had ongoing disputes with Russia in the eighteenth and nineteenth centuries. The Dutch and the USA had tried to obtain trading arrangements with Japan in the 1830s and 1840s. Japan was aware of European activities in China and did not want the problems that China had experienced. By the 1850s, increasing external pressure finally forced Japan to open its doors. European exclusion ended after 1853, when Commodore Matthew Perry, Commander of the East India Squadron of the US Navy, sailed into Tokyo Bay with a letter of demand from President Fillmore to the Emperor of Japan to open the country to international trade under threat of attack. His four black-hulled steam frigates fired at buildings onshore to reinforce the message, unnerving the Japanese. As a result, the Treaty of Kanagawa (Yokohama) of 1854 opened Shimoda and Hakodate to US ships for provisions and permitted a consulate and some extraterritorial rights. In 1858, under the Ansei Commercial Treaty with the USA, Holland, Russia, Britain and France, Japan agreed to open five ports to international trade: Hakodate, Niigata, Yokohama, Nagasaki and Kobe. With this new openness, some scholars argue, Japan 'resumed' its southward advance this time with Australia eventually in its sights.[16]

Despite Japan's interest in resuming overseas trade with the west, it was not Japan that initiated interest in Australia but Australians who took advantage of the opening of Japan to initiate contact with the Japanese in the 1850s. This set up the early mechanisms for Japanese networks in all parts of Australia. The opening of treaty ports encouraged Australian merchants to join European nationals, particularly at Yokohama. Two Victorians, Alexander Marks of Melbourne and T.A. Tallermann of Kilmore, were among the first Australians to settle in Yokohama in the late 1850s. Marks arrived straight after the treaty was in operation in 1859 and did not return to Melbourne until 1872. Marks was shipping substantial quantities of merchandise by 1862 and engaged in auctioneering and storekeeping. By 1870, they advertised that they were selling out in Yokohama. Tallerman traded in Yokohama from 1869 and later added an Australian branch in Sydney to his Japanese-based importing and exporting business, which survived into the twentieth century. Edward C. Kirby, who was born in England and spent some time in Australia during the 1850s, took advantage of the treaty to expand *within* Japan. From 1865, as a retailer and entrepreneur in Yokohama, he opened the first small-scale department store in Japan in which he sold a variety of imported groceries and clothes. He imported the first bread oven and opened a bakery. He expanded to Kobe to import foreign goods for the western residents. He operated an abattoir, which used Kobe beef. In the 1870s and 1880s, he expanded into shipbuilding for the Japanese Imperial Navy.[17]

The resumption of travel from the 1850s led to an extension of trade into the areas where Japanese trade had flourished before the 1630s. From 1866, a new Japanese passport system permitted travel abroad for study and commerce. In 1868, after considerable internal struggle, the Tokugawa shogunate ended and Japan became a more unified state under the Emperor Meiji, which placed it in a better position to meet the new challenges. Japanese could now follow their desire to learn what opportunities lay beyond Japan's shores from where the foreign merchants had come. If employed by foreigners, Japanese were now able to apply for a passport from the governor of any treaty port to live and work overseas. However, Australia barely warranted a mention in the 1860s when a few Japanese articulated the quest of southern expansion, or *nanshin*. This concept had not existed before the seclusion era but many Japanese books written in the nineteenth century depict the Tokugawa period in heroic terms as an era of expansion. Tsuneya Seifuku, a prominent economist, when advocating this policy contended that Japanese penetration of the South Seas and NEI and some colonisation were essential to check Western expansion and to compete with Britain in the region. The development of a navy and particularly the training squadron (depicted on the cover of this book), which sailed through the South Seas on a regular schedule, helped to promote awareness in Japan of further opportunities. The Japanese mistakenly believed that uncolonised islands remained in the Pacific, partly because they were convinced that Europeans did not have enough immigrants to colonise hot climates. 'Colonisation' did not necessarily mean territorial acquisition, although unclaimed islands were sought after, but often just working and settling abroad, trading, fishing and engaging in any activities considered necessary for the livelihood and growth of Japan as a nation. To achieve these aims, Japan needed to develop strong companies to place its foreign trade in Japanese hands and end the dependency on overseas agency arrangements.[18]

Although Japanese people initially travelled to the Asian mainland or to the North American gold fields to seek opportunities, some adventurers were attracted by the exotic stories of the South Seas. Japanese fiction did more than anything else to create fevered excitement about this romantic area. The main characters of these ocean melodramas are often young naval officers who stumble across a pristine island. Komiyama Tenko's 'A hazardous enterprise or the great king of the Pacific' (1887) centres on a naval officer travelling to Australia to become a trader. He makes his fortune as a freebooter in a fictitious war between France and China and then discovers an uncharted island on which he becomes king. Such literary wonders inspired young men like Mizutani Shinroku who set off for Micronesia on a small schooner loaded with goods. However, the dream turned sour. Spanish officials arrested him for trading illegally in the Caroline Islands. He was forced to leave and sailed for Micronesia to Guam and Truk. Such voyages did not bring riches and Germany soon gained control of the territories. Impelled by the dream, a few isolated traders created a small, tenacious but often imperilled, Japanese presence in Micronesia in tiny outposts until World War One. Frequently their vessels were overloaded with cargo and sank at sea. They operated under severe restrictions and harassment from Spanish and German colonial regimes. But limpet-like they established a commercial foothold, which only bore promise after Germany's defeat in World War One. The difficulties in Micronesia did not exist further south in Australia where Japanese were welcomed and even invited.[19]

How Japanese settled in Australia

Just as Australians had initiated trading contact with Japan in the 1850s, Australians also brought the first Japanese settlers to Australia with the assistance of their countrymen who traded in Japan's treaty ports. By 1867, entrepreneurs involved in entertainment took advantage of the new passport arrangements to hire troupes of acrobats and theatrical artists for the delight of their patrons. As a result, the first Japanese arrivals were entertainers in 1867, who thrilled audiences in dozens of colonial cities and country towns. The *South Australian Register* wrote:

> There is such an endless variety that instead of being one performance it is a series of performances ... each a thorough success. ... Risk and danger are robbed of their alarming aspects by the quiet matter of fact way in which the hazardous task is performed ... the applause was genuine, general, and hearty. Adelaide has never before seen an entertainment of the kind which would bear comparison with it and those who have had an extra-colonial experience would have great difficulty in recalling to memory anything to surpass it. [20]

These performances introduced thousands of Australians to Japanese culture and raised interest in Japan. Later entertainment events like the Japanese Village, which toured in 1886–87, also drew large crowds. It was a major event in the history of colonial popular culture. [21]

In the 1880s and 1890s, Japanese visitors to Australia published influential books and reports. These gave Japanese people their first glimpses of possibilities in Australia. These early writings, sometimes authored by sailors, stimulated people's imaginations and dreams of wealth but contained fictionalised impressions more like those in the ripping yarns of popular Japanese novels. Their information had dubious value and contributed perhaps to some misinformation about Australia. Better reports came from the few individuals who actually managed to travel in Australia rather than just call at a port or rely on hearsay. Travel to Australia was not easy before 1896 when the first direct shipping service between Yokohama and Australian ports began. Kazuo Mishima, for example, aged 23, was an employee of the Japanese newspaper, *Mainichi Shinbun*. He travelled from Japan to Samoa on the Pacific Ocean training cruise of the HIJMS *Hiei* in 1889 and from there caught the SS *Lubeck* on 18 December 1889 for the remainder of his voyage to Australia.

A stream of trade visitors, researchers and government representatives wrote more accurate reports. Australia was considered a more hospitable place to do business than the German territories in Micronesia. The Inter-colonial Exhibition in Melbourne in 1875–76 and the International Exhibition in Sydney in 1879–80, which showcased colonial and foreign products, provided a vehicle for Japanese and Australians to explore the possibilities for trade. By the 1870s, Japan had undertaken preliminary investigations into markets in Australia for Japan's developing manufacturing industries. Ōkuragumi, a large *zaibatsu* firm and a major participant in the Sydney and Melbourne exhibitions, employed Australian agents in the wool industry in Sydney and Melbourne. It was responsible for obtaining wool for the new Senju Seijyūsho woollen mill, opened in 1879, that was founded to improve Japan's position in the international wool trade. Wool became important for uniforms in Japan in the 1870s. An attempt to establish a sheep industry in 1875 was abandoned by 1880 but the wool mill was a success producing 22,406 yards in 1879 and 273,754 yards by 1889 (one yard equalling 0.914 metres). It mostly relied on Chinese wool but purchased some Australian wool from London. It began importing wool from Victoria in 1888. The Japanese government also commissioned Masato Hashimoto and Haruo Sakata to report on the exhibitions. Robert Page, an English-speaking resident of Tokyo, was their guide and interpreter. They were wined and dined by local politicians and toured the University of Melbourne and Mr Thomas Mort's meat preserving company. Their books contained detailed descriptions of the products available in Australia's six colonies. Sakata concluded that Japan needed to let Australians know quickly what Japan produced, "lest the white people get all the trade". He envisioned a prosperous two-way trade where Japan would sell tea, rice, soybeans, paper, silk and ceramics and buy coal, wool and, possibly, meat. Other influential and accurate books followed which encouraged Japanese to explore trade in Australia.[22]

Kazuo Mishima's 300-page book written in 1891 gave a Japanese perspective on Australian life and trade. Mishima stayed in Melbourne in 1889 from 27 January to 22 September, after a short stay in Sydney. He predicted accurately that Australia would become Japan's future trading partner but lamented the lack of mutual trade at the time of his visit. He found Australian shops exciting and particularly liked the way that they advertised and presented their products but only a few Japanese articles were for sale in Elizabeth Street, Melbourne. Mishima recommended Japanese products that would sell in Australia and urged Japanese businessmen to establish good credit ratings through sound references and hard work.[23]

Kanjuro Watanabe completed the first exhaustive Japanese government study of Australia in 1893, which included daily life and employment. Watanabe gathered his material by roaming Australia incognito and visiting major towns throughout the country to talk to immigrants. The report was aimed at Japanese businessmen, officials, journalists and prospective immigrants. It provided accurate data for future government talks on immigration policy. Watanabe's positive comments about the opportunities in industry and agriculture made Australia attractive to Japanese who were planning commercial ventures. Unintentionally it strongly encouraged some Japanese to emigrate.[24]

Officially, except for a short period in the early 1890s, the Japanese government actively discouraged emigration. However, individuals caught the new frontier spirit fostered by developing organisations such as the

Tokyo Geographical Society and the Colonisation Society. Hattori Toru's enticing description of Thursday Island in *A New Colony in the Southern Hemisphere* could have provided some incentive for people wanting to escape the poverty of a Japanese fishing village. As Frei remarks:

> We can only guess at how many Japanese were induced by their pamphlets to emulate frontiersmen who already in the 1870s had sought glory and fortune in the shell-beds on the Australian coast.

While individuals emigrated for their own reasons, the Japanese government increasingly sought to develop overseas trade. Australian individuals and companies were also keen to capitalise on this new interest and pursue the trade that they had initiated with Japan since the 1850s without much support from colonial governments. In 1879, Kihachiro Okura the founder of Ōkuragumi, invited the Sydney based Smith Brothers, who had entertained Japanese visitors in Australia in the previous year, to a banquet. The Smiths were visiting Japan at the time to promote good commercial relations on their way to the USA with the expectation of generating great profits from personal contact with Japanese traders. At the banquet, the Smiths met Tsugumichi Saigō and Kaoru Inoue, high-ranking officials in the Meiji government, who were interested in developing trade with Australia.[25]

Despite Japan's trade efforts, in 1874, foreign agents and merchants still controlled 99.9 per cent of Japan's foreign trade. Japanese merchants lacked the deep knowledge of western markets and economic practices that foreign merchants possessed. To overcome this problem, Japan needed large, home-grown firms to compete internationally. Japan's two largest companies developed in the 1870s with government subsidisation. Mitsui, a very old family business, was formally established in 1875. It acquired strategic information and trading expertise through relationships with British firms in London. It opened its first overseas branch in

Shanghai in 1877. Mitsubishi Shoji Kaisha (MSK), founded in 1870, obtained a leading place in services, finance, trade and shipping. It established Nippon Yusen Kaisha (NYK), which pioneered the first direct shipping route from Japan to Australia in 1896. As the fortunes of Mitsui and Mitsubishi grew, they diversified. By the 1880s, the term *zaibatsu* was used to describe large family-owned concerns with functionally related enterprises in commerce, mining, finance and industry. These firms performed essential services by importing raw materials and industrial equipment and exporting light industrial products such as raw silk, matches and cotton yarn. Despite this progress, 80 per cent of Japan's foreign trade remained in foreign hands in the 1890s.[26]

Japan gained treaty arrangements with other countries in the 1890s to improve its position. In 1894, it signed the Treaty of Commerce and Navigation with Britain, which included reciprocal immigration rights. Because all Australian colonies were implementing restrictive immigration provisions for non-white peoples, most chose not to ratify the treaty. To obtain good trade arrangements with Japan, Queensland was the exception. It negotiated to limit the Japanese population to the 1900 level of 3,264. Japan's victory in the Sino-Japanese war provided a new confidence and gained some respect for Japan as an emerging power through the Treaty of Shimonoseki of 17 April 1895. Japan obtained great power status in China, secured Formosa, the Pescadores, Port Arthur, the Liaotung Peninsular and a promise of a large indemnity from China. It also settled the question of the control of Korea over which Japan and China were in dispute. However, intervention from Germany, Russia and France saw Japan's hold on the peninsular slip, a situation that led to war with Russia in 1904 over control of Manchuria and Korean ports. The treaty provisions in 1895 accelerated Japanese activities in Manchuria, particularly in textile exports that made inroads into Chinese and Manchurian markets along with the expansion of commerce, banking and transport. This helped Japan's trading companies, especially Mitsui,

Mitsubishi and Okura, to grow. Okura traded in mining, forestry, agriculture and metallurgy. Mitsui expanded in 1890 from its Shanghai branch and benefited from the freight trade along the South Manchurian Railway.[27] These companies also investigated trade with Australia.

Closer to Australia, Japan's Treaty of Commerce and Shipping with the Netherlands in 1896, granted European status to Japanese immigrants in Dutch territory including NEI in 1899 and freed them from pass laws and residential restrictions. Under this new arrangement, Japanese people gained the freedom to establish industrial and commercial undertakings wherever they liked. Employees of these new firms travelled to India and Australia to study western business practices and especially to seek trade opportunities in minerals and foodstuffs.[28]

Australian merchants in Sydney also took early steps to expand into Japan. In 1878, they approached visiting Japanese authorities for opportunities to export to Japan when the first Japanese naval training ship, the HIJMS *Tsukuba,* visited Sydney. The merchants sent a petition via its Captain Matsumura to the Japanese Minister for Foreign Affairs, Mr Terajima. Trade between Sydney and Japan was patchy at that stage. NSW's exports to Japan for 1869 had amounted to £1,309 and fell in 1870 to only £52. Most of the trade in the year of the adventurous petition was exported coal in return for rice. In comparison, Victoria's imports from Japan were minimal reaching £10 in 1870. Exports were at their highest point of £60 in 1877. After 1877, trade volumes were improving. As Kanematsu Shoten records, Australian imports from Japan in 1877 amounted to ¥26,356 when one yen was roughly the same amount as one US dollar. Clearly there was room to investigate ways to increase mutual trade.[29]

Australians' fascination with the east and Japan in the 1880s presented a growing retail market for Japanese exporters and Australian importers. After the 1885 performance in Sydney of Gilbert and Sullivan's *The Mikado*, interest in Japanese curios sky-rocketed. When the Japanese-owned import and retail firm Akita & Co. closed in Melbourne at the death of its owner from tuberculosis in 1884, this did not end the Japanese retail trade in that city. Messrs Gemmell, Tuckett & Co., Auctioneers of Collins Street, opened a shop of very fine Japanese art ware including bronzes, ivory plaques, carvings, inlaid work, cabinets, embroideries and paintings and held a public auction in October 1890. An exhibition of novelties also took place in Sydney in August 1888. Bush hawkers travelled inland successfully selling Japanese curios, especially fans and silk handkerchiefs, even through the great depression of the 1890s. This interest was not confined to the southeast of Australia. Even at Palmerston (later Darwin), V.L. Solomon & Co. imported Japanese curios and advertised in the *Northern Territory Times* from 1882. The firm marketed Japanese goods throughout the 1880s. In Queensland, Finney Isles & Co. of Brisbane advertised 140 packages of useful, unique and ornamental 'Japanese novelties' as ready for inspection in November 1884. In April 1889, James Murdoch displayed Japanese goods on behalf of some Japanese merchants in Willard's Town Hall Auction Mart in Brisbane in May 1889. By the end of the 1880s, the trade figures had improved to a total of ¥486, 396 in imports from Japan to Australia and ¥267,085 in exports from Australia to Japan.[30]

As Japanese and Australian individuals and businesses took advantage of new opportunities, Japanese individuals seeking adventure or a better life, often aided by Australians, swelled the numbers of people immigrating to Australia. This real settlement was multifaceted, mostly individual, sometimes accidental and quite independent of any government agenda. The information that Japanese people gathered about Australia at this time whether they were officials or travellers was generally for an immediate purpose. Why people chose a particular location to settle in Australia varied as much as the individuals, officials and companies who came. But was there any particular pattern in the arrival and settlement of Japanese in Australia, which might suggest a long-term agenda?

Why Japanese settled Australia

Early written impressions of Japanese emigrants, that were often speculative rather than accurate, have influenced Australians' popular picture of Japanese settlement consisting almost entirely of pearlers and prostitutes and confined to northern Australia with few if any Japanese people settled elsewhere. The traveller, Muraoka, wrote unflattering descriptions of Japanese in the South Seas that were repeated in newspapers such as the *Japan Times* and never questioned by Australian historians (except Sissons). Muraoka believed that if a brothel opened anywhere in the South Pacific, a store soon followed and clerks arrived to eventually open independent businesses. In effect, Japanese people took up an amazing diversity of work all over Australia and were extremely mobile before federation in 1901. If we start with what existed in a particular locality in Australia before the Japanese arrived, and study the stories left by the Japanese people who immigrated, a very different and more haphazard settlement picture emerges.

Briefly, in colonial times, Melbourne received the colonies' first Japanese visitors in 1867 and settlers in 1871. The first two Japanese merchants opened Akira & Co. in 1881 in Melbourne. Melbournians first brought domestic servants from Japan in 1883. But the city's first prostitutes did not arrive until 1887. Sydney's first Japanese visitors came in 1878. Sydney's earliest known settler, Mr Yasuda of Hunters Hill, a shell carver, arrived in 1883 and was wealthy enough to have Japanese servants. Independent merchants opened businesses in 1886. Sydney's homes and small businesses employed Japanese workers by the 1890s. In WA, Geraldton is credited with the first Japanese laundries and tailors along with Port Hedland in 1888. The first Japanese residents of Fremantle were laundry men in 1891. These travelled inland when gold was discovered along the railway and dirt road tracks to Kalgoorlie by 1894 and on to Mount Magnet and Coolgardie. Broome, the best-known area of Japanese settlement, which experienced the second worst raids of 1942, began its adventurous pearling history in 1861 as we saw before.[31] Cossack's Japanese merchants opened stores from 1888. The coastal steamer made it easy to travel to other towns such as Roeburne and Onslow, which also had Japanese labourers and domestics by the end of the 1880s. Queensland towns first saw the arrival of Japanese in 1874 as free labourers and as merchants in 1889 on Thursday Island.[32]

Opportunism was the hallmark of early settlement and it took place almost simultaneously in great variety all around Australia. Sixteen years after Japanese people arrived in Melbourne, the first pearling workers arrived on contract to European master pearlers on the north and west coasts where the practice of employing Japanese indentured labour spread quickly within five years in the 1880s. E.W. Streeter of Broome, also employed Japanese for pearling at Port Darwin in 1884. In 1883, Fearon & Low hired the first Japanese indentured pearling workers at Thursday Island. A number of other pearling masters had Japanese workers at Cossack from 1885 and at Broome in 1886. The northern settlements were not isolated but connected by coastal steamer and developed a complicated network of colonial businesses, some of which were owned by master pearlers. For example, prostitutes in pearling areas arrived slightly later in 1888 at Darwin and Cossack, 1889 at Wyndham, 1890 at Broome, 1894 at Derby, Carnarvon and Marble Bar with Roeburne following in 1896, and Rockhampton in 1898. Non-indentured work for free settlers or former indents, who had worked out their contracts, also flourished. Japanese boarding house keepers opened businesses at the same time that pearlers and prostitutes arrived. Some of these men also had stores to provide goods to the pearling fleets and local inhabitants. Stores undertook a certain amount of importing so the larger northern towns had constant contact with trading ports in SEA and around the Australian coast via the coastal steamers. This also drove employment in the towns, which was largely fortuitous, and meant that the Japanese population along the north was often more concentrated than in other areas. Queensland's sugar cane areas were dependent on indentured labour in a similar way.[33]

Official Japanese government interest in the Australian colonies at this time partly followed the pattern of settlement. Where Japan established consular services and in what order reflects the areas that Japan considered the most important. Here, two facts are striking. The first consulates were all in the southeast of the country and the first consular representatives were not Japanese people but Australians. Alexander Marks, the former merchant in Yokohama, became the first Honorary Consul for Japan in Melbourne in 1879 with consular responsibilities for Queensland, NSW, Van Dieman's Land and SA by 1889. His role was reduced in the 1890s as services expanded.

In 1896, Marks no longer had responsibility for Queensland when the first professional Japanese consul, Tsunejiro Nakagawa, was appointed to Townsville, an area with many indentured workers and some substantial trading businesses and stores. However, Nakagawa was transferred to Sydney the following year after the direct shipping line run by NYK opened from Yokohama. The southeast corner represented areas that the Japanese thought were increasingly important. Kisahichi Eitaki succeeded Nakagawa as Consul in 1906 and the Sydney position was upgraded to Consul-General with the appointment of Kisaburo Ueno in 1908.

Marks' responsibilities for SA also ended by 1898. At that time, John Langdon Parsons, the former SA Trade Commissioner for Japan was appointed Honorary Consul for that colony including its northern territory, which was not separated and placed under Commonwealth control until 1911. Darwin, however, did not have one single person in the town to help Japanese until about 1928. It never had an official consulate. WA, with its enormous pearling industry, large Japanese population and reliance on Japanese labour, had no consular representation of its own but relied on Melbourne and Sydney until the Australian, Archie Male, businessman, pearling master and Mayor, was appointed at Broome in 1910, to be succeeded at his death in 1923 by his brother Arthur.

Consuls played an important role in assisting Japanese immigrants from the very beginning. The Japanese in Melbourne were in need of such a service. *The Argus*, 5 August 1878, reports that Japanese in Melbourne instituted criminal proceedings against ships' captains for ill treatment. Marks also investigated the cases of Japanese domestic servants. Work in domestic service was not always satisfactory for the young Japanese men involved. In November 1891, Marks drew the attention of the Japanese Foreign Ministry to cases where Victorians had engaged domestics from Japan under contracts that provided wages at a much lower rate than those prevailing in the colony. One example was A.H. Chalkey, an auctioneer, who had engaged a cook, laundryman and houseboy on three-year contracts. Under one of these contracts, the cook's wages for three years would have been £82-10-0d but the prevailing wage in Victoria was at least £52 per annum. Marks warned that this kind of treatment could only lead to trade union pressure on government to impose a poll tax (or entry tax) on Japanese immigrants.[34]

The network of consular services, which were staffed mostly by Australians with connections in Japan, oversaw the settlement of Japanese people in all colonies. Gradually at each port Japanese people had someone to whom they could refer for help. Normally a Japanese resident or Australian with connections in Japan met them, helped them with documents, accommodation and work. The consuls also promoted bilateral trade. However, it is important to realise that from 1896, for Japan and the Australian-Japanese, Sydney was the most important port and trading centre of all the colonial ports. Sydney became the hub of all Japanese networks, not just the place of residence of the Consul-General. Although Japanese were connected throughout the country, different areas had special characteristics that interested Japanese people.[35]

Regional developments

Australians initiated the movement of people back and forth to Japan to take advantage of the new developments in the 1850s and 1860s. The south east of Australia showed interest in Japan first and attracted the first true Japanese settler, Dicinoski or Rikinosuke Sakuragawa. His life epitomises the varied and colourful nature of many of the first Japanese. He arrived as a member of a visiting acrobatic troupe in 1871, which performed at the Princess Theatre in Melbourne for five weeks. Although he married Jane Kerr, a barmaid, in Fitzroy, Melbourne, on 10 February 1875 at age 20, he did not remain in Melbourne. His troupe of performers travelled through Queensland in the 1870s and 1880s. He naturalised in 1882 by which time he had a house, garden and three children 11 miles from Herberton in Queensland. He resumed his travelling circus in 1883 and was still in show business in 1917.[36]

Prominent Victorians were among the first to bring out Japanese men for domestic service as gardeners, butlers and houseboys. Mr A.H. Tuckett and Mr Gemmell Tuckett, partners in Messrs Gemmel Tuckett & Co. Auctioneers in Melbourne, hired Nakamura who arrived in 1883, and Harry Nitobe in 1895. Dame Nellie Melba also had a Japanese butler, Thomas Nagai, at her Coldstream home before she left for London in c. 1917. Nagai had arrived in 1899 and first worked as a butler for John Ettershank at his Bridgewater property. His other notable employers were Judge Gaunt in Melbourne's St Kilda Road, Melbourne Grammar School and Scotch College. Japanese men took domestic service positions generally as a first step to more lucrative occupations. All three of these men eventually opened their own laundry businesses.[37]

Melbourne was not the first overseas or even Australian destination for some immigrant Japanese. Individual businessmen often travelled and worked overseas before coming to Australia. George Nakamura, a laundry keeper in Malvern, arrived in Melbourne about 1903–04. He had left Japan in 1892 for America employed on the sailing ship *John A Karia* as a seaman, cook and steward. He left the ship at New York and travelled to South America. He was discharged from the *Senorita* at Sydney in July 1901 without a passport and sailed to Melbourne by steamer. A few days later, he went to Geelong where several Japanese had laundries and obtained work in one of them. He then returned to Melbourne and owned a succession of laundries in South Yarra, Richmond and Armadale. Other Japanese men, like George, found their own way to Australia and their own work on arrival. Often the availability of work spread by word of mouth leading to employment in Australian small businesses. For example, Mrs Elder had a Japanese cook at the Sorrento Hotel. Mrs Twomey of Heidelberg employed several Japanese in her laundry from the early 1890s until 1911.[38]

The Japanese who were already living in Victoria helped new arrivals. In Geelong, for example, several families established laundries but also interpreted for customs and local officials at the port and engaged in some importing. George Taro Furuya, who arrived in 1897 with others who became laundrymen, played an important role at the port and in finding work for young Japanese men who had wandered from as far away as Queensland's cane fields in search of work. Toyo Kashima who worked for Furuya in 1910 had deserted the *Kasuga Maru* in Melbourne in November 1901. He went straight to Geelong to his countrymen and worked in a Japanese laundry for four months before taking a position as houseboy to Mr McGlashan at Brighton Beach. After a brief but failed attempt to run his own laundry in St Kilda, he worked in a succession of short-term domestic and laundry positions for Australians and Japanese as far apart as St Kilda and Bacchus Marsh.[39]

Japanese small businessmen brought out their own countrymen. For example, Mr Kojiro Nakamura, a tailor in 'The Block' in Collins Street Melbourne in the 1890s hired two men, Sakai Kunakichi, or Ku Sakai, and Ichiyo Sato. Ku Sakai trained as a tailor in Japan. During 1886 and 1887 he worked in Seattle, USA, and then returned to Japan where in 1900 Nakamura arranged for him to come to Australia. Ichiyo Sato was a tailor in Yokohama from 1895 to 1901. He accepted the position in Melbourne in March 1901 because he had heard that there were good prospects in the tailoring industry in Australia. He worked for Nakamura during 1901–02 at 'The Block'.[40]

Japanese women in Melbourne display the same varied travel patterns and mixed occupational lives as men. Kami Kagame and her sister, Minnie, had touring theatrical parents. Kami was born in Italy in 1882 and her sister in England. The family arrived in Melbourne on 15 November 1891 for an Australian tour. Kami attended a private school in Sydney and then trained as a tailoress at Buckley & Nunn in Melbourne. She tried to naturalise but could not because her parents were Japanese. The father died in St Kilda in 1900 and the mother in 1916.[41]

Sydney had a wider range of work available and a larger commercial population particularly as it surpassed the previously booming 'Marvellous Melbourne' from the 1880s. The descriptions of Japanese in Sydney in the 1880s are far less flattering than those of the community in Melbourne. In 1886, Shigetaka described Sydney's Japanese as 40 or so of the lowest class of Japanese actors, tea girls and impoverished geishas with two or three Japanese traders doing petty business on the third floor of a Sydney hotel. This impression soon proved to be very misleading. The central participants who were responsible for Sydney's development into a major Japanese trading centre in the southern hemisphere arrived shortly after Shigetaka left. Hideo Kuwahata, a landscape gardener who arrived in 1888, imported the first Japanese plants. He opened the earliest independent Japanese trading firm in Sydney, Kuwahata & Sons. He pioneered providoring for Japanese ships from his thriving store. From 1890, Kuwahata supplied Burns Philp & Co.'s ships, the British-Australian company that traded throughout the Pacific region. Another business compatriot, Hideichiro (Henry) Ide arrived in 1890, aged 28. He married an Australian, became a Presbyterian and was naturalised in 1902. He pioneered the silk trade. A major business figure, Fusajiro Kanematsu, first visited Sydney in November 1887 and opened F. Kanematsu (Australia) Pty Ltd in April 1890, with the head office in Osaka.[42]

Kanematsu was the first *zaibatsu*-like company to establish in Australia. It opened as Kanematsu Shoten under the management of

Toranosuke Kitamura who developed what was to become the company's multimillion-pound import–export trade. Founded by Fusajiro Kanematsu, the firm was the product of long-term planning. Kanematsu founded Nichigō Bōeki Kanematsu Shōten in Kobe in 1889 after an intensive three-year study of the potential for trade between Australia and Japan. Kanematsu became interested in Australia as an export market for rice as early as 1876 and as a source of pastoral and mineral raw materials. Kanematsu sent Itoh Yatiro a former officer of the Japanese Mines Bureau to Australia and New Zealand to investigate the extent of their mineral resources. He opened the Sydney office in April 1890 and shipped the first consignment of wool to Japan in May 1890. The firm imported porcelain and lacquer ware, copper, bamboo curtains, parasols and other oriental objects that were in vogue at the time. Most of the merchandise was handled on a consignment basis for Mitsui & Co. in Japan and the Yamanaka Curio Shop in Sydney. The opening of the firm in Sydney and the importation of Japanese rice ended the long monopoly of E.J. Hunter & Co. of Kobe. In this way Japanese firms began to claw back Japan's export trade from Europeans.[43]

Kanematsu's early years were very difficult. It managed seven shipments to Japan in the first year, which included wool to the Osaka Woollen Yarn Spinning Mill and tallow and hides. Kitamura hired Einosuke Ogawa, a resident of Sydney and brought out Mannojo Matsuzaki from Kobe. Their attempt to open a branch in Melbourne in September 1890 failed within two months. The great depression, drought and the financial crisis of 1893 placed the firm on the verge of bankruptcy. Kitamura, in debt to the Bank of NSW, approached its manager for a postponement of the payments that he owed. He argued that although the Australia-Japan trade was insignificant at that time, it would gradually develop into a substantial trade. If they had to close the Sydney office, trade between Australia and Japan would be abandoned without accomplishing anything. The bank granted the extension and the firm thrived. Kitamura registered the firm in Sydney on 30 June 1903 as an importer of western merchandise and exporter of colonial produce, particularly wool. Its future was secured.

Despite this for many months after the loan that rescued the firm Kitamura had a daily struggle to keep the doors of the export office and retail shop open. For a time Kanematsu's store was the only Japanese store remaining open. As the company history records, there was almost no money in the office at that time and Kitamura could hardly afford to have meals from day to day. Kitamura had to go out of town carrying on his back sundry goods from Japan for peddling to earn his daily bread.[44]

Although Kanematsu was the most important Japanese firm in Sydney, Hideo Kuwahata became a key contact for Japanese arrivals in that city. He met all Japanese ships at the port and found work and accommodation for new immigrants. This role became semi-official over time. By 1931, shortly after Kuwahata died, the Consul-General acknowledged that Mr Kuwahata's actions had relieved him of some responsibility for arriving Japanese. One early visitor whom Kuwahata met was Komakichi Tomiyama. In December 1891, he was a passenger on the Japanese naval training squadron ship HIJMS *Hiei* and wrote a report on Australia that recorded Kuwahata's entry into providoring and Kitamura's establishment of F. Kanematsu (Australia) Pty Ltd. He recorded the activities of residents including the Nihon Shōten or The Japan Store run by Okamura, and tattooers like Yoshisuke Kudo who had arrived on the *Miike Maru*, the first trial voyage of the shipping line NYK. Tomiyama also reported on important visitors to Australia and the South Seas such as Yoshiro Kawagoe, a civilian and member of the colonisation society (*Shokumin Kyōkai*).[45]

Sydney attracted young men who came to work as houseboys for Japanese residents and used the position as a first step to bigger things. Hirokichi Nakamura and Sentsuchi Suyenaga were hired in Japan for the Yasuda family of Hunter's Hill, who had arrived in 1883. Nakamura arrived in 1897, aged 17, with his abacus, determined to start a business. He studied English at Ashfield Primary School during his two years of domestic service, continuing at Darlinghurst Night School after he left the Yasudas' employ and obtained a position with Farmer & Co., a large Sydney retailer and importer. Suyenaga worked for Yasuda for 13 months in about 1896–97. He also attended public school evening class. He then worked in hotels and restaurants in Paddington, Point Piper, Manly, Neutral Bay and at the Caresbrook Hospital. After a short time participating with Sawada, a laundryman, and Nakamura in the lease of six acres of land at North Botany, which was rented out to the NSW government, Suyenaga moved to Victoria where he worked as a cook at the Queenscliff Hotel in 1903 and subsequently in other Melbourne hotels and coffee palaces.[46]

By federation in 1901, Japanese business development in Melbourne had all but stalled compared with Sydney, which had the advantage of the direct shipping line to Japan and professional consular services. Melbourne's Japanese population was stagnant at 55 but Sydney's Japanese population increased as work in service positions, laundries, trading companies and stores became available. Sydney was the hub of the growing Japanese networks and other parts of the country referred to it.

Japanese arrived in west and northern Australia shortly after white settlement as coastal towns developed possibilities for employment. Pearling areas, as we saw, had the most work but that was not all that attracted Japanese people. Like Europeans, Japanese benefited from the ease of travel provided by the coastal steamers and developing road and rail networks and used them to advantage. However, Perth and Fremantle, like Melbourne, attracted only a few Japanese people who tended to work as hotel cooks, laundrymen, storekeepers and prostitutes. The earliest known arrival in Fremantle was F. Fukuda in 1891, a cook and laundryman. Other early arrivals were a fisherman, M. Fujiki in 1893 and T. Fuji, a shopkeeper, in 1896. Business people such as T. Yoshida, an importer of fancy goods, arrived in Perth in 1894. However, population numbers vary according to different sources. For example, Mr Aiba clerk of the Japanese Foreign Ministry in 1901 stated that 53 Japanese lived in Perth and six in Fremantle, but the Japanese residents at Coolgardie wrote to Honorary Consul Alexander Marks in 1897 that there were 70 engaged in prostitution in Perth, a number that cannot be substantiated from entry records.[47]

Japanese men and women were highly mobile before Federation. Su Jane Hunt reports travelling madams in the 1890s and women moving inland for other work. One example of a Japanese man who moved across the north for work was Otomatsu Yamaguchi.[48] He arrived in 1897 and had spent eight years in Cue, one at Mount Morgan in Queensland and 20 years in Geraldton district as a tomato grower by 1928. Others did not move far for example, Kumazo Asari who arrived in 1897 spent three years at Cossack and then moved to Broome. He worked as a laundryman and barman. [49]

Japanese settlement followed town development. In WA, the site of Geraldton was surveyed for town lots in 1849. Japanese market gardeners arrived in 1891 and established a small but stable community of tomato growers who continued until 1941. Laundrymen followed them in 1893 and by 1894, residents of Geraldton petitioned against Japanese brothels. Geraldton also had laundries run by Japanese from about 1893. Japanese moved inland from Geraldton to Kalgoorlie where 1894 was the peak year for the establishment of laundries, some of which were also brothels. Other Japanese worked as cooks and as tailoresses.[50]

Japanese were attracted to small towns. Roebourne, a pastoral area settled in 1864 and centre for the copper and gold of the Pilbara, had a Japanese cook in 1888. By 1896, the town had a Japanese village. Port Hedland records a Japanese laundryman in 1888 followed by further laundries and cooks in the period from 1893–97. Onslow had Japanese settlers in 1889 and female housekeepers from 1895 who were without husbands. Derby was settled in 1885 and reported prostitutes by 1894–95. Other towns to report Japanese were Marble Bar in 1894 and Nullargine in 1898. Between 1890 and 1901 Japanese arrived to work in Kalgoorlie, Coolgardie and Cue.[51]

The larger pearling centres of Cossack and Broome had much bigger Japanese populations and greater activity. Cossack was the only port on the west in the 1860s when pearling began. In 1888, Sakutaro Muramatsu, a businessman, arrived to establish a chain of stores and settle with his three sons, one of whom, Jiro, attended Xavier College in Melbourne, naturalised in 1899 and became a master pearler.[52] In Broome, where Muramatsu also operated, the Japanese population in 1901 was at least 303 males and 63 females out of a total population of 576 Japanese in the northwest, although Hunt states that there were 110 women at this time.

European pearlers dominated the industry and by 1890, Streeter owned one-eighth of the pearling fleet. He also took up pastoral leases at Broome where he ran cattle and dairy herds. The stock supplied a dairy managed by pearlers' wives. He employed two clerks, Archie and Arthur Male, in his business by 1899 and also worked luggers at Thursday Island. By the end of the 1890s, pearlers from Thursday Island, for example V.J. Clark and Ancel Clement Gregory arrived with Japanese crews to work the rich pearl grounds that brought sufficient wealth to build Broome. However, these pearlers were not confined to the colonies. With overseas-based pearlers such as Captain Hilliard and Alexander Chamberlain from Kupang, Australian pearlers before *c.* 1905 moved back and forth across the Arafura Sea between Aru Island, Kupang, Darwin and Thursday Island.[53]

Broome's early Japanese had a wide variety of businesses and employment. Married Japanese women worked as dressmakers and tailoresses from 1883. In the 1880s men worked as carpenters, cooks or general hands. Sail makers and a billiard maker arrived in 1884. Records for 1890 list a restaurant keeper and the arrival of one of the partners in what was to become the biggest business in the west, Tokumaru of

Tokumaru Bros. Other businessmen opened large enterprises, for example, Toyosaburo Mise in 1891 and Enomoto in 1894. In 1891, Mise, aged 26, sailed to Singapore as a deck hand but finding no work he sailed to Broome in 1891 and obtained work painting and cleaning luggers. By 1894, he was a cook and pump tender. By 1898, he had settled in town with his companion, Hatsu. He had 11 children over two marriages during his life in Australia and NEI. Although men and women arrived separately, married men tended to arrive first and then bring out wives after about 12 months in Australia as Nakeji Minami did arriving in 1896 with his wife following in 1897. People who initially worked in one occupation such as pearling later moved on to other work in laundries or as gardeners. Eizo Asari, for example, arrived in Broome in 1893 for pearling. He later worked on shore where he was well known by white businessmen of the town and Archie Male, the pearler, Mayor and Honorary Consul.[54]

In the northern territory of SA, Europeans first settled Palmerston in 1869. After a commercially unsuccessful first attempt in the 1870s to harvest pearl in Port Darwin, the first shipload of Japanese indentured pearl labourers, engaged in Hong Kong, entered the Territory to work new pearl beds in 1883. In 1884, Palmerston capitalists including Streeter and V.L. Solomon floated the North Australian Pearl Shell Company to exploit the newly found beds but met with little success and wound up by 1885. However in 1892, one diver 'Charlie Japan' or Hamaura from Cossack successfully raised shell again at Port Darwin. Hamaura equipped his own boat and employed some of his countrymen from Broome. This attracted other Japanese to Palmerston in the 1890s from the industry in Cossack and Broome, increasing the population to 30. In 1893, Watanabe reported this successfully revived industry with Australian-Japanese playing a direct role in its development.[55]

When Watanabe visited Palmerston in 1893, he met 21 Japanese men and 14 Japanese women. Three of the 21 men were pearling masters. The

Japanese, he noted, were engaged in individual occupations and "could look whites in the face" unlike the Japanese in California where restrictive legislation was having a prejudicial effect. The Japanese population averaged about 10 per cent along the north and roughly a little less than half of the Chinese population. By 1900, Consular records list 213 Japanese in Palmerston out of a population of approximately 1,300 of whom 374 were Europeans. However, the Japanese population fluctuated because people constantly moved across the top in the course of their businesses, often owning stores or holding pearling licences in more than one location or working under contract for an employer with several business locations on or off shore.[56]

Although pearling was the mainstay for employment for Japanese with most of the 166 Japanese of Darwin in 1900 engaged as divers and seamen, it was not the exclusive avenue for earning a living. People often had more than one job at any given time. Sixteen Japanese men worked in mining. Yonesichi Mori, for example, spent his whole Australian stay from 1898 to 1929 in the Territory. He mined at several places including Pine Creek but also worked as a tender on luggers, as a baker and as an employee of R.E. Holmes from 1924 to 1929. Other early settlers include 18 Japanese who engaged in businesses or employment on shore. For example, Mr Takada ran a brothel from about 1889. Inouye Hidematsu lived in the Territory from 1895 to 1932 and worked as a diver, butcher and cook.[57]

Japanese women arrived in 1888 when Palmerston had five Japanese brothels with 25 women, but they were not confined to prostitution. A woman named Omaki worked in mining areas from 1898 to 1914. She is listed as a cook, but may also have been one of the early travelling prostitutes or madams. She was still in NT in 1924 and retained the right to return to Australia after travelling to Japan in that year. Another woman named Shio arrived in 1895 at Thursday Island where she stayed for 18 years, moving to Broome in 1913 where she met Jiro Muramatsu. When she moved to Darwin in 1930, she listed her occupation as boarding house keeper and domestic. She was one of hundreds of Japanese who had contacts across Australia.[58]

Queensland's rich mineral deposits, fishing and agricultural opportunities led to the development of its east coast settlements. Rockhampton was founded in 1855 and gold was discovered there in 1858. Cairns, settled in 1875, was an outlet for gold, tin and later sugar. Charters Towers on the Burdekin River, settled during the 1870s gold boom, became known for its schools. In 1864, Robert Towns, a merchant and pioneer cotton grower, settled Townsville as a suitable place for a port. Towns also pioneered the use of South Sea Islander labour in Queensland. From the 1860s, a thriving pearling industry developed in the Torres Strait as Robert Towns, Charles Edwards, James Paddon and William Banner set up island stations. By 1877, Merriman & Co. had 21 boats registered at Thursday Island. Burns Philp, incorporated in 1883, followed in 1884 with the procurement of Malays from Singapore. By 1895, they were the largest concern on Thursday Island with 34 boats. Carpenter & Sons followed in the 1890s. Japanese began to arrive into this situation from 1874. By 1883, 15 individuals worked on shore as free labourers and in business. In that year, 37 indentured labourers arrived to work for Captain Miller, at the same time that free Japanese settlers arrived in Sydney and Broome. In 1884, more arrived under pearling contracts to Fearon & Low. In 1885, Alexander Marks visited to investigate complaints of poor contracts and conditions.[59]

Although pearling accounted for over 80 per cent of the work of Japanese at any one time on Thursday Island, other Japanese ran their own businesses. Yamashita Haruyoshi, who arrived in 1899, had a small soy sauce factory. He married Tei who was born on Thursday Island and they had seven children. He was the Secretary of the Japanese Society. Sumioka, who arrived in 1900, owned a general store. He had worked in Innisfail as a cook. Seiichiro and Tojo Mori were watchmakers. Other Japanese worked as caretakers of boathouses, ran boarding houses or worked in tailoring and prostitution.[60]

Thursday Island had the first Japanese settlers in Queensland and the greatest population of Japanese over time, but it was also a first step to a life on the mainland. In 1893, Watanabe wrote that although 264 Japanese arrived to work on Thursday Island that year, over 100 moved to the mainland in 1894 because of unemployment on the island. In this way, important business settlements occurred in towns such as Cairns, Townsville and Brisbane. Mackay also became important for the sugar industry where many Japanese worked as indentured labourers. Japanese spread to inland Queensland following the rail and road network that developed as people opened up the inland areas across to the Gulf of Carpentaria. They travelled to Burketown and Mount Isa from Townsville and Ayr via Home Hill, Burdekin, Charters Towers, Hughendon and Richmond. From Rockhampton they moved to Mount Morgan and Longreach. The population was mobile with individuals spending several years in one town and then moving on to others. This kind of movement meant individuals were known to each other and heard of work by word of mouth. It also gave an impression of organised networking, which might be sinister in intention especially as most towns along the coast had at least one Japanese resident.[61]

Cairns and Townsville had the most important settlements in Queensland in terms of connections to other areas of Australia, especially Sydney, by the steamer. They became important ports for Japanese mainland arrivals and for business. Townsville had three well-known businesses, Y. Tashima & Co., the Ebisu Co. and a laundry run by N. Mirakawa. Ebisu Co. employed a number of Japanese over time who then moved on to other Queensland towns. Y. Tashima & Co. was a large business with international connections. At Cairns, Nakashiba, who had first arrived on Thursday Island, was the most important storeowner and business in the town shortly after federation. He moved to Darwin in the 1930s. Other residents had worked in many other towns and colonies before arriving in Cairns. For example, Gyogi Ujita was a cook at Atherton. He had arrived in 1895 at Mackay where he stayed for three years and then visited Victoria and NSW for four years spending 14 years in Sydney before living in the Cairns district for 25 years. However, some residents lived in Cairns for their entire Australian stay like Utaro Murakami, a gardener, who arrived in 1893 and lived in the Cairns district for 48 years. Japanese businesses flourished in Cairns, for example K. Ishikawa & Co. Yorokuro Hayami arrived in November 1916 as a merchant's clerk to work for Ishikawa and enter into partnership with him. Ishikawa also had a cane farm.[62]

Conclusion

Before 1901, Japanese people settled all over Australia, often assisted by Australians rather than by the Japanese government. These settlements were served by a network of consulates staffed mostly by Australians with the most important consulate in Sydney. People knew each other and were very mobile. Early settlers helped new arrivals establish themselves. Those who came for work in pearling often moved on to other work or to their own businesses. These networks had a practical, personal and trading purpose and were connected to SEA and Japan. The networks served the fledgling Australia–Japan trade well but Australia was only one small piece of a developing worldwide trading and modernisation venture begun by Japan in the 1860s which included the development of its navy, the advent of naval training voyages into the Pacific and Australia and new treaty arrangements with European powers. Australian businesses were integrally involved in these developments and especially in the trade, which held great promise. The choice of settlement location was dictated by its prospects for trade and business to support a new life. The only possible strategic advantage was the existence of Australian networks that could provide information of a detailed but general nature like that gathered by Watanabe for immediate use. There is no evidence that this played any part at this early stage in any preparation for the conflict that occurred in 1941.

The sites that were bombed and are now famous were only three among dozens of locations in which Japanese had an interest before the raids. Unlike the heroic literature that accompanied Japan's exploration into the Pacific and SEA in the late nineteenth century, the official Japanese position lacked any cohesive policy of expansion for territorial conquest.

Dick, Harold George, Lac. Arthur Ewings RAAF of Townsville, Qld, and "Min" the donkey mascot of a RAAF unit. "Min" has her tin hat and a turtle shell back protector for protection in air raids. She eats everything including newspapers. Black and white photograph Northern Australia, 13 - 08- 1943 (Date taken) Australian War Memorial (015551)

"Darwin has been bombed —but not conquered"

"We must face with fortitude the first onset and remember that whatever the future holds in store for us we are Australians and will fight grimly and victoriously.

"Let us each vow that this blow at Darwin and the loss that it has involved, and the suffering it has occasioned, shall gird our loins and steel our nerve.

"We, too, in every other Australian city can face these assaults with the gallantry that is traditional in the people of our stock."

John Curtin

Commonwealth Aircraft Corporation; Northfield James, A united 'fighting mad' Australia can never
be enslaved. 1943 (Date printed); 1943 (Date published) photolithograph 76x49.2 cm
Australian War Memorial (ARTV09053)

Hirokichi Nakamura, wife Bessie and daughters, Mosman, Sydney, 1938
(Courtesy of Nakamura family)

Wedding reception of Elizabeth Gerard to Hirokichi Nakamura 1917 (Courtesy of Nakamura family)

Nakamura family at Woy Woy, 1922 with T. Kitamura of Kanematsu on right.
(Courtesy of Nakamura family)

Mrs Iida (left) and daughters at Consular event 1930s
(photograph by I Kagiyama, courtesy of Mrs Iida)

Above: Hirodo family on HIJMS Asano
(Courtesy of Mrs Iida and Kenji Hirodo
– photograph by I. Kagiyama c1936)

Right: John Iwamatsu Nakashiba and his
adopted European son, Peter, 1937.
(Courtesy of the National Archives
of Australia, NAA: M119, 74)

Jiro Muramatsu, 18 March 1920 (Courtesy of NAA: K1145)

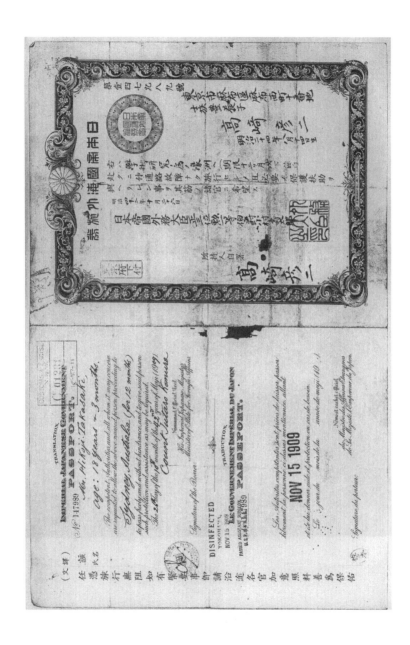

Passport of Hikoji Takasaki (Courtesy of National Archives of Australia, NAA: B13/0, 1911/5281)

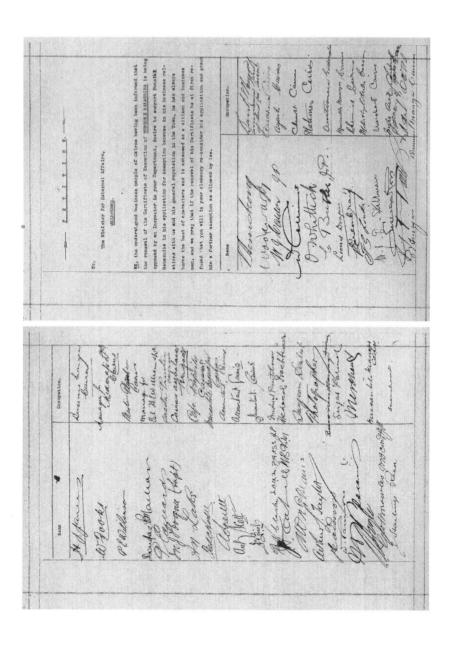

Petition of citizens of Cairns on behalf of Bunsuke Nakashiba, February 1921.
(Courtesy of National Archives of Australia, NAA: A1/15, 1921/24441)

After a terrible decade of depression and continuing drought, on 1 January 1901, Australians celebrated the federation of the colonies to form the Commonwealth of Australia with renewed hope. But despite Japan's alliance with Britain, the Japanese-Australian networks faced additional uncertainty about their legal status under planned federal immigration laws. Since 1897, colonial immigration restrictions had given Japanese people a taste of what might happen after federation. However, even in NSW, where there was a dictation test aimed at excluding 'people of colour', Japanese people had managed to continue to enter, reside in, leave and return to the colony without any difficulty, particularly with the assistance of the official consuls, who could negotiate for them, and of the customs officers at the ports who knew the regular travellers. The great variety of regulations and individual circumstances under which people had been permitted entry in the different colonies made the future of the networks precarious.

In the late 1890s, Henry Ide in NSW and Jiro Muramatsu in Victoria naturalised in anticipation of restrictive federal immigration provisions. Ide had no difficulty with his application and continued to live in NSW with his family, importing silk as usual after 1901. Muramatsu's application was first refused in Victoria in 1899 in expectation that new federal laws would restrict the entry of non-white people. Alexander Marks, the Honorary Consul, intervened on Muramatsu's behalf, and testified to his good character and commitment to life in Australia. Muramatsu then returned to Cossack in WA where he was living in 1901. With immigration laws proceeding through the new federal parliament, it was uncertain whether he would be recognised as a naturalised person beyond Victoria. What would happen to the rest of his family, who were not naturalised, and the business in Cossack and Palmerston?

Hirokichi Nakamura was not naturalised but was still working for Farmer & Co. in Sydney at the time of federation. Like the majority of Japanese people, he had been consistently resident since his arrival. Nakamura was one of hundreds of single men in business or domestic service who intended to stay if permitted to do so. Many, like Keiji Shimada, had moved freely from colony to colony for work in the 1890s. Shimada first travelled from Japan to China to investigate the prospect for straw products. He roamed through Queensland, SA and its northern territory looking for lucrative work in 1897. He hoped to mine for gold but found the work was too onerous and instead decided to open a laundry in Sydney. Would Japanese people enjoy such freedom of movement after the new laws were passed, if they were even permitted to stay in Australia?

Streeter, Carpenter and other Australian and European employers in pearling and cane cutting wondered if new Commonwealth legislation would permit them to continue to hire indentured labour from Japan. Would their workers have to leave Australia? What would be the effect on the shore businesses that Japanese and Australian people had established in coastal towns that depended on pearling? What would be the fate of Queensland's special arrangement with Japan on immigration, which kept the numbers to 3,246?

The proposed new immigration laws were of particular concern to men such as Kitamura, Kanematsu, Kuwahata and Muramatsu, who benefited from the great opportunities for international trade that Australia presented. These Japanese businessmen had put down roots in Australia and invested large sums of money in the import and export trade. The series of networks and trading hubs that they had established across the country linked them to SEA, the Pacific and Japan. Between 1901 and 1904, Japanese networks, particularly in business, were just developing, assisted by the new direct cargo and passenger shipping line from Yokohama run by NYK. The trade figures for imports from Japan to Australia had risen to ¥2,530,524 in 1900 or approximately £260,878 Sterling and exports to Japan were worth ¥2,455,939 or approximately £253,189 Sterling.[1] Japanese-Australian firms dominated the trade. F. Kanematsu (Australia) Pty Ltd was successfully exporting wool and tallow to Japan and importing Japanese products to sell in its Sydney store. Kuwahata & Sons was expanding imports in plants and fancy goods. Melbourne had two local merchants of note, Nakamura and Ozawa. Western Australia had five times the number of merchants and stores than Sydney by federation. Queensland's Japanese were widely spread and sported two important general stores, which also imported, Matsushita on Thursday Island and Y. Tashima & Co. in Townsville. Palmerston (later Darwin in 1911) had prominent Australians and a few local Japanese who sold Japanese goods and supplies for the pearling industry. How could firms continue to run the trade and deal with Australian business if Japanese merchants could not leave and re-enter the country or if representatives of Japanese industries could not visit? What would happen to wool buyers who came to buy from Australian farmers? In addition, hundreds of ex-houseboys, labourers and pearlers owned small businesses such as laundries, brothels and boarding houses all over the country. A few had farms. What was their future? It was clear that the Australian networks would be greatly affected by the restriction of immigration at a federal level.

When the Immigration Restriction Act, or White Australia policy as it is familiarly known, became law on 1 January 1902, the great white walls designed to keep Australia white and British, and 'people of colour' out, went up.[2] No Japanese person could enter the country. However, those who had lived in Australia as a primary place of residence gained domicile status. Naturalisation was not recognised beyond the boundaries of the state in which it had been granted. This greatly relieved domiciled men such as Hirokichi Nakamura and Keiji Shimada but if they left the country for any period of time, they required a Certificate of Domicile to re-enter, a provision which also applied to those who were naturalised. The pearling lobby obtained permission to continue to employ indentured workers, an exception which applied north of the 23rd parallel for hiring 'coloured' workers. However this did not help merchants like Muramatsu and Kitamura of Kanematsu, who although domiciled in Australia needed to travel overseas. Neither did it help clerks and assistants, who did not qualify for domicile status. After protracted negotiations between the Australian and Japanese governments, who remained allies under the new Anglo-Japanese Alliance of 1902, Japanese merchants, tourists and students were granted entry on passport from 1904 for one year. After that period, a person needed to apply for a Certificate of Exemption from the Dictation Test (CEDT), which permitted them to stay for a designated period of up to three years. With this certificate people could leave the country and re-enter while it remained current. Multiple extensions of stay were not difficult to obtain, particularly if the person applied first through the Japanese Consul.

On paper, the new laws appeared straightforward but because of the variety and complexity of individual cases, the day-to-day administration of the laws became critical. Even in Sydney, it was difficult for Henry Ide, who needed to travel to New Zealand frequently, to establish which provisions in the law related to his particular situation. Because of the case-by-case approach, the actual *administration* of the new provisions changed the nature of Japanese immigration to Australia and shaped the networks for the following 40 years. Effectively, the CEDT system gave Japanese people permanent residency. As Atlee Hunt, the Secretary of

External Affairs who was responsible for administering the Immigration Restriction Acts until 1922, pointed out to the Japanese government, "passport[s] only give temporary privilege whereas C.E.D.T. admits to permanent residence". Select Japanese people in good standing not only entered through the great white walls but also gained the right to do business and to reside with their wives and children within them.[3] Australia permitted this because Japan was an ally and the trade between Australia and Japan was relatively small in the 1900s. Immigration restriction existed more to control who entered rather than to exclude certain people absolutely. How did the changes in immigration laws and the discretion to make exceptions on a case-by-case basis affect the nature of the networks throughout Australia? And, why, despite the new restrictive, and somewhat insulting, legislation did the Japanese still wish to come? What did Japan want in Australia?

White Australia and southeast developments

Melbourne did not fulfil its pre-federation promise as a major trading centre. Apart from Teiji Akiyama and Toshihiko Tokuta who set up Akita & Co. between 1880–84, small operators, like J. Numashima, an importer from 1887–89, and Mr Nakamura, the tailor who set up shop in 'The Block' in 1883, no large enterprises opened in Melbourne. After federation, Daijiro Ozawa of Ozawa & Co., who had been at the 1880 International Exhibition, established one of the earliest large firms to enter Melbourne in September 1902. Ozawa was a manufacturer and exporter examining trade prospects. He had a partnership in Sydney until about 1907 with Henry Ide. The Japanese community of whom Ozawa was a part consisted of a small number of stable families, who had mostly lived in Melbourne prior to federation. These people now had domicile status but no longer travelled interstate or overseas because returning, particularly by ship, required proof of domicile, which could be difficult to establish.

Melbourne did not benefit much from the 1904 provisions until the 1920s when firms in Sydney opened branch offices. From 1905, a small number of merchants entered Victoria with money to invest but development stalled. There is little information on trading houses in Melbourne from 1905–15, but Japanese businessmen came with capital to invest. They either did not stay in Melbourne for long or moved on to other areas of work. One example is Jo Takasuka, a silk merchant, who arrived on 27 February 1905. He lived with his family at 136 Queen Street, Melbourne, and was involved in Takasuka, Dight & Co. Manufacturers' Agents, Indentors and Importers for the East. In 1906, Jo, his wife, son Sho aged six, and daughter Aiko aged three, moved to Swan Hill to experiment in rice growing, where a second son Mario was born. However, Melbourne's true development did not take place until Sydney's medium sized firms like T. Nakano & Co. and *zaibatsu* firms such as Mitsui & Co. (in 1913) travelled south to open branches.[4]

World War One boosted Japanese business in Australia. It was almost impossible to obtain goods from Europe. Larger firms,[5] many of which were registered and approved as importers and had already succeeded in Sydney, were looking to expand to other state capitals.[6] Many initially investigated co-operative relationships with Australian firms before opening branch offices. As a first step, agents of Japanese firms were attached to Australian importing and exporting concerns. For example, H. Dawson & Sons had Japanese agents for Iwai & Co. Osaka and Iwai Shoten and assisted wool buyers and merchants. H.C. English, Indentors, of Flinders Lane, had agents from Maitachi Kaisha of Osaka. In effect agency arrangements were essential in cities where Japanese trading houses did not have branch offices, like Adelaide and Perth. The tradition of Australian traders operating in Japan or through Japanese people continued as it had in the 1850s and 1860s. Messrs T. Smith and Duff, Indentors, of Post Office Place were agents for Summers Trading Co. of Kobe. Similarly, Australian firms were integrally involved in the network of trading companies run by Japanese firms in Australia and Japan. Some Melbourne residents opened agencies for Japanese companies. For example, Moshichi Jingu worked in Melbourne from 1917 where he lived with his wife and Australian born children. He managed the Melbourne branch of T. Nakano & Co., Merchants of Sydney based at 5 Royal Arcade in Bourke Street. In 1919, the firm in Melbourne changed its name to Omiya. In 1922, Jingu purchased this fancy goods business from T. Nakano & Co. It remained a small concern with only one other manager by 1925.[7]

Many of Melbourne's pre-federation immigrants remained in small business. Ichiyo Sato, who had worked for the tailor Nakamura at 'The Block' in Collins St, moved to 51 and 97 Toorak Road, South Yarra, as a sole proprietor when Nakamura left. He married Elizabeth Eva Chu on 26 November 1921 who had an Australian mother and Chinese father. Sato became a ladies' tailor and also registered as a merchant in 1916. Ku Sakai, who was also brought out from Japan by Nakamura, worked in tailoring for four years and then became a gardener in Melbourne. The Kagami sisters continued in business. Kami ran her own dressmaking business in High Street, Armadale. Minnie married a Japanese laundryman, Kajime Furusawa, whose business was in the same street.[8]

Sydney's development was much more extensive and firms that were established before federation fulfilled the promise of great trade with Japan. Aided by Australian businessmen and the NSW government, they pursued trade with Asia to a greater degree than any other business centre in Australia. In 1903, the NSW government appointed J. Suttor as Commercial Commissioner for New South Wales in the East. Stationed in Kobe and reporting annually, Suttor provided a unique perspective on the development of the Australia-Japan trade. He lamented that Australian firms were not taking advantage of the opportunities that the developing trade with Japan presented. He complained that Australia took the trade for granted and ignored Japanese requirements at its trading peril.

Local merchants have often remarked to me that Australian people seem to think that anything will do for the East but such is a mistaken policy. America, India &c., place their products on this market exactly in accordance with the tastes of the Japanese, and give local agents as little trouble as possible in connection with samples, bagging and weights. The extension of our grain traffic vitally concerns the producing interests of Australia, future success would appear to be in our own hands, and all this is asked is, to pay close attention to suggestions made from this end.[9]

In 1906, Suttor argued that bad reports in the Australian press hindered the trade.

I can assure you that … criticisms and untactful interviews appearing in our newspapers are taken some notice of in … Japan and form a serious impediment to commercial expansion as well as a handicap to the endeavours being made to improve the commercial relations between the Orient and Australia. This solid fact should not be lost sight of; that … the Japanese … are possessed of very highly sensitive natures, and do not easily forget unkind remarks that from time to time emanate from Australia.[10]

By 1905, Suttor noted that Japanese exports exceeded imports for the first time. Japan was doing her utmost to encourage direct transactions without the assistance of foreign merchants. Japan was producing so much of its machinery, and had even set up commercial museums to educate its people about foreign tastes and requirements, that foreign merchants were worried about their future. In 1900, 4,896 factories had engaged in the wool industry in Japan with 403,474 operatives. In 1906, there were 5,500 factories with 600,000 operatives. Suttor concluded that because of Japan's lower wages, Britain could not compete with such development. Japan's economic and trade progress and the failure of Australian merchants to provide what Japan required assisted the growth of Japanese merchant business in Sydney. By 1907, Suttor reported that Japanese mills and buyers were paying greater attention to Australia and were establishing agencies. By 1910, Australian traders struggled to remain competitive in the Japanese market. Australians remained complacent in dealing with Japanese firms and even failed to supply his office with sufficient wool samples, although Japanese firms' purchase of Australian wool increased dramatically from 933,836 lbs in 1901 to 55,827,121 lbs by 1921–22.[11]

The trade expansion brought an unprecedented increase in Japanese shipping. NYK's activities particularly angered foreign shipping companies when one of their directors remarked that it was "the duty and object of the Nippon Yusen Kaisha to check the arrogance of foreign steamers to the East of Suez".[12]

Japan's aim to run its own foreign shipping and trade and Australia's neglect of the trade meant that Australian-Japanese did very well in setting up import and export businesses. Large firms joined pre-federation arrivals, leading to a rapid expansion. By 1911, Suttor reported that Japanese imports from Sydney, where every Japanese firm of any standing had established the necessary agencies to expand commercial relations, had increased 560 per cent since his office opened in 1903.[13] These firms of standing, as Suttor put it, included Japanese-based *zaibatsu* like Mitsui and Mitsubishi that arrived and worked with Australian firms and existing Japanese traders such as Kanematsu, Kuwahata, Ide, Nakamura and Komura to build a multi-million pound trade.

The 1904 provisions of the Immigration Restriction Act assisted existing businesses. The trading conditions after 1904 permitted Kuwahata & Sons to expand. Kuwahata purchased a 22-acre farm at Guildford in 1908, and where he propagated his imported Japanese plant stock for sale in the shop at 183 George Street in Sydney. With the expansion of shipping, his providoring business supplied the steamers of NYK, Osaka Shosen Kaisha (OSK) and the Japanese navy. His farm provided an address for Japanese seamen on shore leave. It also had a steady stream of commercial and naval visitors. He purchased the business of Mr Ochi in Watt Street, Newcastle, which had been associated with Japanese shipping to Newcastle for some years. Kuwahata kept that association and sold fruit, vegetables and groceries.[14]

Hideichiro 'Henry' Ide, the pioneer of the Australia–Japan silk trade, born in 1863, was described as "the grand old man of the silk trade" and the oldest Japanese resident in Sydney by 1941. He arrived in November 1890 on the *Ruhbeck* at Sydney, married Clare, an Australian, became a Presbyterian and was naturalised in 1902. The couple had seven children, four boys and three girls. Ide & Co. began after the partnership with T. Komura & Co. and D. Ozawa & Co., formed in 1902, dissolved by 1907.[15] However, despite his naturalisation, Ide had difficulties with the Immigration Restriction provisions. Six years after the passing of the Act and three years after the 1904 amendments, Ide wrote to the Department of External Affairs to inquire what was required for him to travel back and forth to New Zealand. He was naturalised but still uncertain of his re-entry status, even though he had been a well-known resident for over 15 years. Ide inquired if it was safe to go to New Zealand on business because he was not a subject of the new Commonwealth under the Act. Atlee Hunt replied that merchants were now allowed to leave Australia for three months and return without difficulty. This permitted easy travel to New Zealand, South Africa and Pacific ports.[16]

Hirokichi Nakamura learned importing through his work at Farmer & Co. and set up his own import company in 1907. He later told his daughters that it was very easy to start a business, as it needed only an office, a telephone and a secretary. Nakamura developed good relationships with other Japanese traders in Sydney, particularly T. Nakano & Co., and traded through World War One importing cotton piece goods, silk fabrics and other goods required by department and drapery stores in Sydney. He socialised with Japanese men and visiting ships' personnel when they came to Sydney. He knew Kuwahata and the managers of other Japanese firms well. By 1917, he was established enough to build his own home in Mosman and marry Elizabeth Gerard from Jennali. By the 1920s, Nakamura was one of the largest independent owner-operators in Sydney with such extensive contacts that even large firms from outside that city sought his advice and used him as their sole agent to secure orders from Japan. He had important and profitable agency arrangements with Y. Tashima & Co. of Townsville and with the large wool exporter, Nosawa & Co. By the 1920s, his annual turnover was £200,000. His family lived very well in Mosman with a maid and chauffeur.

Before 1901, only F. Kanematsu & Co. (Australia) Pty Ltd even approximated the structure of the *zaibatsu* firms in its first three decades. It was a recently established firm based on one family with only one office in Japan at Kobe. It struggled to establish an export wool trade in Sydney in the depression of the 1890s but when economic conditions improved after federation, Kitamura, the firm's manager, trained in wool buying. He was the only Japanese to do so in Australia before the Russo-Japanese War of 1904–05. Between 1907 and 1912, business increased dramatically. At Kanematsu's death in 1913, the company became a joint stock venture unique among Japanese firms at the time, with the family owning only half the shares. The company's Memorandum and Articles of Association stipulated that all employees (many of whom were Australians and the rest Japanese who entered on 1904 provisions) hold shares, usually allocated after 10 years' service. Shareholding in the Australian company was divided in a complicated fashion between Japan and Australia. Shareholders employed in Australia held the same share capital in the Japanese parent as Japanese workers held in the Australian company. The firm was registered in Sydney in Kitamura's name on 30 August 1918, but he continued to trade under the name of F. Kanematsu (Australia) Pty Ltd. In 1922, the Sydney branch was separated from the Kobe office and registered in NSW with £100,000 subscribed capital, which was fully paid up by 1929.[17]

The 1904 provisions permitted Kanematsu to expand into the Australian wool industry before World War One, and to train young Japanese men as wool appraisers, auctioneers and wool buyers. In 1907, for example, Shigeyoshi Hirodo, aged 17, came to Australia to work at the suggestion of an official in the Ministry of Agriculture in Tokyo and learned part of his trade first-hand in the shearing sheds at Bell Trees Station in country NSW. Once back in Sydney, he started at 7 am before the auction each morning to assist the chief wool buyer on the show floor in inspecting and appraising the rows of bales on offer for that day. He became a familiar figure at the auction rooms and was called Sam for ease of pronunciation. After the day's auction he returned to Kanematsu to work in the office. After two years he was also appointed as foreign correspondent for the *Mainichi Shinbun*, which had once been owned by Fusajiro Kanematsu. He reported on the Japanese expedition to Antarctica in 1911.

Extensions of stay on CEDT eased movement for employees of Japanese-run firms and particularly helped them to adjust to the challenges of World War One, which brought an increased demand for wool and consequently a rise in its value. Firms like Kanematsu were placed advantageously because they had access to direct shipping arrangements where Europeans did not. They were also well known in the Australian importing and exporting community and had good working relationships with Australian firms that traded overseas. However, their trade suffered after November 1916 when the Commonwealth government under Prime Minister Billy Hughes suspended wool buying and selling under wartime regulations allowing the British Imperial government to acquire all available wool. Kanematsu could no longer buy wool in Australia, which caused shortages in Japan's textile mills. The firm sent Sam to Kobe to take responsibility for wool buying. In 1918, he travelled to South Africa to buy as much wool as he could. Before sales of Australian wool resumed in 1920, Sam and other Japanese wool buyers had also made purchases in South America, through connections, which were later used by the Australian firm. From 1922, after the peace settlements, Sam Hirodo became a director of the firm and returned to Sydney. His standing in Australia gained him permission in 1923 to return to Sydney as chief wool buyer with his new bride and child, the beginning of what became a dynasty of Hirodo family members in Australia. By the 1920s, the Japanese firms in Sydney had a majority share in the wool market and dominated the prominent front row position at the auction rooms. By the end of the 1920s, Kanematsu was Australia's biggest wool buyer.[18]

The 1904 regulations allowed new *zaibatsu* to enter the market. Firms that had set Japan on the path to independence in foreign trade in the 1870s, MBK and MSK, along with two smaller *zaibatsu*, Iida & Co. and Okura Trading that had retained agents in Australia during the years since the International and Intercolonial exhibitions of 1879 and 1880, entered Sydney. Mitsui & Co. investigated trade in Australia from federation and opened for business in 1907. Iida & Co. opened in 1909. Okura Trading officially operated in Sydney from 1916 although it had had an agent since the 1870s. It was a small *zaibatsu* branch managed by S. Sawada of Mosman, which was attracted to Australia by the availability of wool, barley, wheat, flour and hides. By 1917, it also imported goods such as barbed wire and brass wire cloth for Australian firms like Haughtons in Sydney. Okura bought a wide variety of goods for sale in Japan such as sulphate for fertiliser from T.M. Goodall & Co. Ltd. It collected information on Australian conditions beginning in 1916. Large news cuttings books organised by topic contain detailed information on wool, agriculture, Australian industry and foreign trade. Okura also notified its Japanese head office when goods were up for sale in Australia. For example in January 1917, the Australian government placed sheep skins out to public tender to approved buyers who were exporting to other parts of the British Empire or allied countries.[19]

The activities of Mitsui provide a picture of Japanese operations in Australia straight after federation, which aimed at achieving a steady and growing mutually beneficial trading arrangement with Australian companies. Mitsui sought the resources in Australia (as it had in China) that Japanese industry needed. It also looked for markets, no matter how small, for Japan's manufactured goods. To achieve these aims it took no end of trouble to build personal relationships with corner stores, large department stores, farmers and agricultural companies. When Mitsui began its formal trading business in Sydney in 1907, it employed seven Japanese people and three Australians. Two of these Australians were still working for Mitsui in 1940. The firm hired more Australian staff and increased the size of the office with new partitions and furniture arriving regularly. Newly arrived Japanese, who were sent to night school if their English was not up to standard, travelled a great deal with Australian staff as they sought business in other cities and in rural Australia. The pay was good and overtime plentiful. The senior Japanese manager, Mr Nishimura, was paid £58 a month in 1912 and Mr Pickup, the senior Australian, £16 a month. The stability of staff meant that personal business relationships developed with heads of other firms. Australian businesses had confidence in exchanging contracts with Mitsui because of the certainty about whom they were dealing with. On Mitsui's part, the head office in Japan expected branches to make their own profit and decisions. They could not rely on the head office in Tokyo for financial assistance. This meant that they needed to establish long-term relations with customers in Australia and look after them well. The Myer Emporium, David Jones and Foy & Gibson were regular customers and obtained yarn and cloth for their clothing factories from Mitsui. No order was too small for Mitsui and they supplied local drapers stores with cloth, and grocers with small quantities of canned salmon and matches. In this way it made small profits on extensive transactions and developed a loyal customer base.[20]

Mitsui became so big by 1910 that it reorganised into departments according to products, which is known as the Japanese *bu* system. Silk, general merchandise, sundries, cotton goods, oils, matches, jute and timber were import departments and wool, grains, tallow and coal were

among the export departments. In 1920, the Sydney branch expanded
its trade starting a 'foreign to foreign' section. This exported Australian
flour to countries other than Japan. For example, it bought 1,200 bags of
malt barley in Tamworth in June 1920 to sell in Auckland, New Zealand.
It also sent Australian produce to the UK, USA and South America.[21]
In this way, Mitsui & Co. became an Australian export company even
though it was one part of the worldwide MBK *zaibatsu* network.

Mitsui believed in cementing good relations locally and in hosting
overseas visitors. It entertained lavishly and spent large sums on gifts
and functions. One major event was the periodic arrival of the Japanese
Training Squadron in Australia. These biennial events involved five days
of civic receptions in each state capital city that the squadron visited.
Mitsui arranged to entertain its crew and provision the ships. It paid
£1,300 for coal for the ships at Perth and Melbourne in 1913. It also
arranged for a representative of the company to travel to meet the
ships at each port of call. The Japanese Navy also received its supply
of cigarettes free of charge. Other regular entertainment expenses
often cost as much as the month's office rent such as a dinner party for
Captain Homura in November 1907 and a picnic for F. Kanematsu
(Australia) in April 1910, which cost £40.[22]

Mitsui was also generous to its local customers and presented whiskey
and boxes of cigars to regular clients at Christmas. During the year large
customers such as Farmer & Co. were entertained at a cost of more than Mr
Pickup's monthly salary. Mitsui also attended social events in Sydney such
as the testimonial dinner at the Bank of Australasia for its retiring manager
in January 1914. The firm was generous to charity including the Red Cross
and made donations to the wool samplers' picnic. Its extensive membership
of Australian organisations such as the Merchant and Traders Association
from 1913 to 1940 and Chambers of Commerce from 1913, its activities
within the business community of Sydney and contact with the Japanese
communities around Australia cemented its position as a leading company

and gave it an Australian flavour.[23] It was part of the first wave of growth in Japanese-run trading companies in Sydney as Table 1 shows.

Between 1914–19, a further nine companies were founded, eight by Japanese and one by three Australians, Nippon Trading established in 1914, which lasted only three months as it was unable to compete with resident Japanese who had the advantage of speaking Japanese fluently.[24]

In World War One Japan seized the opportunity to supply Australia with manufactured goods and increase its purchase of primary products that were not restricted under wartime conditions. Australian department stores benefited because their supply line from Britain was cut by the war. By the early 1920s, both the department stores, particularly in Sydney and Melbourne, and the Japanese companies were entering a boom time. But the trade extended beyond the Sydney hub to all states and territories, aided by the smooth working of the immigration acts and close relationships between Australian and Japanese business houses.

White Australia and the northern network

From the beginning, the central Sydney hub had links to and agencies in other parts of Australia and overseas. Before federation, the northwest had formed its own hub with its connections to southeast Australia and SEA. These supplied the pearling industry and provided Japanese goods within the towns to Japanese inhabitants. Townsville was a third hub connected to other parts of Queensland, the Pacific Islands and New Guinea. After the passing of the Immigration Restriction Acts, these three hubs became more closely integrated by necessity with Sydney as the centre. In effect, the restrictive legislation hastened the consolidation of Japanese networks in Australia.

Individuals, rather than existing Japanese firms established Japanese business in the northwest. Many Japanese businesses in WA, whether run by men or women, were multifaceted, combining enterprises such as boarding house keeping, store ownership, tailoring, barber shop work,

Table 1: Japanese trading companies in Sydney listed by opening and folding dates, with name changes

Company	Opening	Folding / name change
Kuwahata 1888		c1950s
Kanematsu 1892	J Gunton 1941	Kanematsu 1997
Mitsui 1901		1941
Ide 1902		1936 Wiltshire
Osawa 1902		1927
Komura 1902		1920
Nakano 1909		1921
Nakamura 1907		1941
Iida 1909		1941
Chiba 1910		1920
Matsui 1911	1915	
Fukushima 1913		
Nippon Trading 1914		
Horikoshi 1914		1940
Suzuki 1914		1941
Yokohama Specie Bank 1915		1941
Yonei Shoten 1917		
Mogi 1918	1920	
Meiji Trading 1918–19		
Okura 1917		1941
Murakami 1919		
Mija 1919		

cooking, commercial photography, banking, importing or consular and trading company agency work. Because business owners engaged in diverse activities often in more than one town, the formation of partnerships between early arrivals for one aspect of their endeavours became a feature of Japanese business. This reduced competition to a manageable level. Toyosaburo Mise (1867–1945), for example, amalgamated his banking services with those of other immigrants to form the Western Australian Ehime & Co. Partnership Bank in 1901. Federation gave Mise domicile status that enabled him to open an importing business and store. In 1903, a further merger between Mise, Eijiro Yamazaki, Takuzo Izumi and others formed the Western Australian Farming Savings Company.[25] Yamazaki and Izumi had arrived with their mutual friend, Kametaro Yamamoto (1866–1915) after initially working their way to India, Singapore and Broome. Yamamoto founded a store in Broome in 1902, after the 1901 Immigration Restriction Act gave some stability to his domicile. Yamazaki was one of his three Japanese partners. Yamamoto also ran a boarding house for prostitutes with Tada Tsudad. Such complex relationships extended into social and civic life. Yamamoto founded the Broome Japanese Society with his partners. He died in Japan in 1915 but Izumi remained in Broome.

Aided by the 1904 provisions, good business conditions also prompted the Japanese to expand, to move overseas or establish links to SEA, particularly in Java and Singapore. Yamazaki moved his business interests to Singapore by 1910 where he had a rubber plantation. Mise expanded to open a new business in Surabaya in 1927 with Kaichiro Saumi and his wife. He moved back to Japan, then to NEI and on to a Darwin laundry in 1936. He exported beer to Indonesia. However, true merchants who imported into WA were in the minority, a pattern of endeavour that was mirrored to a lesser extent at Cossack and Onslow.[26]

The administration of the 1904 amendments on a case-by-case basis over time resulted in business immigration developing a cooperative pattern of procedure involving companies, merchants, the Consul-General and the department. This assisted business growth. The department almost never refused an application for an extension of CEDT that was made through the Consul-General. The department investigated the activities of each applicant in the preceding period. If they were satisfied that the merchant had continued to work within the import–export trade, the extension was granted. Although the Consul-General had an important role in recommending the person, the department retained the final say. This process also allowed merchants within Australia to take on other roles in their local areas. The story of Tokumaru Bros illustrates this process.

The 1904 provisions allowed the largest Japanese company in WA to develop. It originated with Shingoro Tokumaru, who immigrated in 1890, and became an importer, indentor, moneylender and store founder. He expanded from Broome to Perth, Melbourne and Singapore. In 1910, he employed two assistants from Japan, Yasaburo Miyata and Shintaro Nobutaro Umeda. Miyata had a short four-year stay originally landing on Thursday Island on 24 May 1910 and journeying through several states to his intended port, Broome. He left for Japan on 22 June 1913. Umeda arrived in June 1910 via Thursday Island and Sydney, where he deposited his passport with the Consul-General. He began as a store assistant hired for four months. His stay was extended to experience English commercial customs and trade. By 1915, he was the firm's bookkeeper, Customs Clerk and acting manager in Tokumaru's absence.[27]

Umeda's rapid rise in the firm led to appointments beyond the store. He accepted important, unofficial, consular and international positions. In 1924, he was appointed agent of the Tokyo Overseas Industries and Emigration Co. Ltd to watch the interests of indentured Japanese at Broome. The indents had come from Singapore for some years but it was now proposed to hire them from Japan. Japanese emigration laws required the appointment of an immigration agent at the port of indenture to look after immigrants.[28] He also became Honorary President of the Japanese Society at Broome and respected in the town.

Umeda remained manager of the firm until its founder and his wife died in 1923. Although Mrs Tokumaru's brother, Tsura Mihara, worked in Broome, he was due to return to Japan in February 1924. Umeda was charged with winding up the firm. Umeda received an extension of stay in Australia in December 1924 in recognition of the family circumstances and because he was respected in his other capacities.

Not all sizeable Japanese businesses merged or expanded. J. & T. Muramatsu took on a local Australian character between 1888 and 1942 in Cossack, Broome and Darwin. It was the biggest independent Japanese business in the west and north of Australia. It was well connected to Melbourne and Sydney Japanese in its early years but bought most of its stock from Australian firms which it then supplied to pearling luggers, some owned by Muramatsu and others by local people in the towns. Founded by Sakutaro Muramatsu in 1888, it was run by his son Tsunetaro, after Sakutaro's death in 1898 while Jiro was still at school in Victoria. By the time Jiro joined his brother to run the firm in 1898, he already knew and had visited the managers of F. Kanematsu (Australia) Pty Ltd in Sydney. He naturalised in Victoria in 1899. Early after federation, the third brother, Saburo, arrived and soon brought out his wife, Aya. The couple lived in Cossack until the mid-1920s.[29] Jiro moved to Darwin in the late 1920s with his wife, Hatsu, and his daughter, who attended Rose Bay convent in Sydney. During the 1920s, he travelled constantly back and forth between his stores and pearling operations in Western Australia and Darwin.

Muramatsu did not trade with Japanese firms in Sydney, Perth and Singapore but used local Australian firms or British and German firms. For example, he sold pearl shell to Otto Gerdau Ltd, a firm based in Singapore and New York, which realised £340 in November 1923. He placed orders during the 1920s for small quantities of shoes, clothes, food items and large quantities of meat probably intended as goods for the store and provisions for crews. His business brought increasing wealth until his internment in 1941.[30]

Family firms like Muramatsu often had wide connections. One of the biggest and most influential was situated in Townsville, Queensland. Particular individuals and firms linked Queensland to the hub in Sydney. Yoshimatsu Tashima and Mrs Kame Tashima of Townsville opened Y. Tashima & Co. Ltd in *c.* 1897. It imported and sold Japanese fancy goods, silk and curios and traded with towns along the coast and even with Yamato Co. of Melbourne, Importers of Japanese Goods. In 1905, the stock at the store in Townsville was listed as worth £1,303, with the wages totalling £8 per week. Tashima's policy was to obtain any stock that was profitable, and during 1907 that was *bêche-de-mer*.

The Tashimas were respected citizens of the town and considered 'of good birth'. An application for extension in 1913 described Tashima as conducting his extensive operations

> in an up to date manner with a reputation for honesty and attention to his business. He participates in the various social functions of the city and both he and his wife are undoubtedly good citizens.

From 1910 onwards, Tashima employed a number of assistants from Japan. Saisaburo Ishikura first arrived in 1909 to assist in the fancy goods store, to gain further insight into business methods and obtain a thorough knowledge of suitable goods for the Townsville trade.[31] Several members of the Tashima family came from Japan to assist at the main store in Townsville and beyond: Yosaburo or Yezaburo, Yoshitatsu and Eizaburo, the younger brother of Yosaburo, who was an indent merchant and acted as assistant manager for the Brisbane branch in 1916. Eizaburo was in such good standing that he gained permission for his wife Miyo and infant son to live in Australia.[32] Tashima used a mix of Japanese and

Australian agents beyond the family. Mr S. Sadokane not only worked at the Townsville store but acted as agent in Cairns. Mr Humphreys was the agent for Cooktown in 1903. Hirokichi Nakamura became the agent in Sydney in the 1910s.[33]

In the 1920s, the nephew of Tashima senior, Toyosaburo Araki, entered an agreement with Tashima of Townsville and the other family firm in Japan, Yoshimatsu Tashima & Co. of Kobe. Araki lived in Sydney from 1916 with his wife and children, and earned £416 per month by 1923. In 1924, C. Tashima & Co. Ltd formally appointed Y. Tashima & Co. Ltd as sole agent for the sale of Japanese products in Queensland such as silk and cotton piece goods. They were the sole buying agent for Kobe, commissioned to purchase Portland cement, tallow, wheat and other agricultural products. Tashima purchased from dozens of large Australian firms such as G. Myers & Co., Edwards Dunlop & Co. and Finney Isles & Co. of Brisbane (an early department store involving drapers, tailors, furniture, furnishings and hardware with branches in Rockhampton and Gimpie) and traded with Japanese firms in Sydney, for example Jano & Joko, Z. Horikoshi & Co., H. Nakamura, and Mogi & Co.

The arrangement between Tashima of Townsville and firms in Japan was formalised in 1928 and the entire Australian operations became part of Araki & Co., a large *zaibatsu* firm.[34] Y. Tashima & Co. Ltd was never a small operation, even before it became part of Araki & Co. Profit and Loss accounts for the year ending 31 December 1912 list assets valued at £5,126. In 1914, the net profit was £2,562 and assets valued at £7,299. Net profits and assets grew steadily each year. The trial balance at 31 December 1923 lists capital in hand at £11,083 and a turnover of £242,803.[35]

Apart from Y. Tashima & Co. Ltd, which traded into NT, Nakashiba Bros of Cairns, which traded in Queensland towns and Brisbane, Japanese people in Queensland were dotted in small numbers all over the state and mostly owned or worked in small businesses. Many had arrived on Thursday Island or at a major coastal town. For example, John Iwamatsu

Nakashiba arrived as a houseboy on Thursday Island in 1890 and married a European woman. After failing in his own business, he moved to Cairns in 1906. He and his brother Bunsuke, who was the brains behind the business in Cairns, were respected citizens of the town. In his early years, John diversified and the white people in the town did not resent his growing prosperity. In effect, his reliance on importing Japanese goods for sale to locals and to tourists off the coastal steamers brought business to the town, which did not compete with Australian businesses. He also provided some banking facilities. In 1912, he opened a fancy goods' store in Brisbane in partnership with Mr Asajiro. He became a partner in a registered firm of boat builders at Cairns and was employed as an interpreter by the Customs service. He had a seven-year lease on a 45-acre sugar farm on the Mulgrave River. This prosperity was Bunsuke's work but in 1921 he was threatened with deportation for bringing his brother-in-law, Warkichi, from Aru Island to the port on the family boat without proper customs clearance. This pending deportation sparked a public outcry as the town businessmen realised that if Bunsuke left then the firm would collapse. It was too important to the town to let that happen. The major residents of Cairns petitioned the Commonwealth government and prevented the deportation.[36]

The 1904 regulations brought about the centralisation of Japanese business in Australia and connected people throughout the country. The official roles of local business people, and their involvement in Australian and international trade, connected businesses in all states and territories to the worldwide Japanese trading company network. By the 1920s, Sydney could boast more than 40 Japanese-Australian firms and the head offices for Australasia of *zaibatsu* such as Araki & Co., Mitsubishi Shoji Kaisha, Mitsui & Co., Okura Trading, Kiku Gumi, Japan Cotton Trading Co. and Iwai & Co. With F. Kanematsu (Australia) Pty Ltd, the Yokohama Specie Bank and Yamashita Shipping Co., these multinational companies engaged in millions of pounds worth of trade and commerce annually for the import and export market in co-operation with hundreds of large Australian firms such as Broken Hill Pty Ltd, Dalgety Pty Ltd, Myer Emporium and David Jones Pty Ltd.[37] The tight administration of the restrictive immigration laws under which the companies operated meant that the Japanese networks in Australia were very well organised and integrated. White Australia policy provisions, which included the Immigration Restriction Acts and additional state acts, both assisted and limited the trade. However, the interpretation of the provisions through the administration of the laws and regulations by state and Commonwealth officials, with the direct assistance of the Consul-General for Japan in Sydney, was critical. The manner in which policy was administered decided who entered Australia and what they could do while resident. Japanese people were very adept at working within the administrative framework of White Australia and at expanding their activities at the same time to mutual advantage. The good standing in which Japanese people were held meant that they could also bring their families through the great white walls and marry Australians achieving *de facto* permanent residency.

Negotiating the detail

Henry Ide and hundreds of other merchants benefited from the changes to the Act in 1904 but the working out of the detailed administration of the act in each case was critical. Ide, a naturalised British subject in NSW before 1901, had needed to clarify his position about travel to New Zealand even though he had domicile status and was a homeowner with an Australian family in Sydney. The situation for other aspects of merchant activity and life was also unclear. Could a businessman like Muramatsu, a naturalised person, continue to obtain pearling licences? Could firms bring out assistants who were not technically merchants in their own right? Could all employees of firms bring their families, maids and governesses to Australia or would only those in high positions such as directors and managers like Hirodo be granted that privilege? What would happen if a person could not prove the date of first entry to one of the former colonies? What kind of proof would people need? The 1904 amendments gave Japanese people some rights of entry and a form of permanent residency but the terms and conditions were far from clear.

Despite the goodwill between the Commonwealth, the Honorary Consuls and the Consul-General in Sydney, Japanese people did not have an easy time doing business under the White Australia policy. Difficulties included obtaining English-speaking assistants from Japan needed to deal with Japanese visitors and to import Japanese goods, arranging for families to enter and stay in Australia, obtaining licences, buying or leasing property, and dealing with changing Commonwealth criteria for extensions to CEDTs. Satisfying the changes to regulations challenged individuals and businesses and required good legal knowledge.

After federation, the relationship between Atlee Hunt, as Secretary for the Prime Minister's Department and later for the Department of External Affairs, and the Consulate played an important part in the administration of the Immigration Acts in relation to Japanese entry.[38] The personal correspondence with consular officials particularly E.M. Foxhall, shows a different side of the policy. Hunt and Foxall corresponded at least from 1905 onwards. Both men recognised the importance of personal relationships and the ability to speak to each other 'off-the-record'. As Foxall said, he valued the wise discrimination of the Department. Hunt explained that when Foxhall wrote to him privately, "I ... shall take advantage ... to speak a little more freely than I could in an official communication". Both considered this unofficial correspondence, as they saw it, a means to resolve situations that might prove very difficult if addressed in official correspondence through the normal channels. The two men were familiar enough to use first names.[39]

In 1916, Foxall and Hunt discussed a longstanding problem faced by Japanese merchants who wished to bring their wives to Australia. In 1905, the provision permitting wives to accompany husbands was abolished for fear that too many Asiatic families would arrive and give birth to children in Australia. These children would be eligible for British subject status, which might change the character of White Australia. As Hunt explained to Foxhall in 1908, this provision, which irked the Japanese, was basically aimed at the Chinese, who had taken advantage of the clause in the original Act that allowed wives to accompany merchants.[40] The Commonwealth ameliorated the harshness of the provision on a case-by-case basis for Japanese when the Consulate-General requested this. The letters of 1916 illustrate two applications from merchants for their wives to enter Australia. One man, a sub-manager, was granted his request but the other, a clerk, was refused. The sub-manager approached the Consul-General but the clerk applied directly to the Department, which Hunt did not appreciate because External Affairs valued the Consul-General's opinion of the applicant. The status of the applicant and the manner in which he applied mattered in White Australia. Higher-class people received better consideration. Those who went through consular channels and obtained consular approval were more highly regarded than those who sidestepped the consular service. In other words proper procedure and references mattered.

These criteria extended to small businessmen. The Consulate-General's personal relationship with the Department became important in the case of the laundryman, Denzo Umino, who could not prove that he arrived in 1901 before the Immigration Restriction Act was passed into law. This made it impossible for him to obtain a Certificate of Domicile to re-enter Australia should he travel overseas.[41] Umino had married Violet, an Australian girl, in Brisbane in 1918. In 1921, Denzo was accused of being a prohibited immigrant and the family faced deportation. His white, Queensland-born mother-in-law wrote to the Consul-General to ask his help. Her daughter had a three-month-old son and neither mother nor baby was in good health. Their problems developed when a rival laundryman reported to Secretary J.G. McClaren (Hunt's successor at the Department of External Affairs) that Denzo was in Australia illegally. In fact, in 1912 Denzo had stowed away on a steamer for a trip to Hong Kong, returned to Thursday Island and then sailed to Brisbane on a coastal steamer. He had no passport but because local officials knew him, his movements were not challenged. Although in January 1921, the Collector of Customs in Brisbane supported Denzo, he had to take the Dictation Test in French. He failed. He deposited £100 as surety to secure three months to wind up his affairs and to leave with his wife and child who were counted as Japanese subjects under Australian marriage and naturalisation laws. At that time, Australian women who married a man of another nationality lost their British subject status. Umino's solicitors objected that Mrs Umino, who spoke no Japanese, would not adjust to life in Japan. Moreover, if she and her infant son remained in Australia without Denzo they were likely to become a "charge on the state". The Minister refused to consider these circumstances or to reverse the deportation order.

Acting Consul-General Tamaki, in response to Mrs Umino's mother's plea, wrote to Secretary McClaren. He stressed the value of the personal relationships that operated between Japanese and Australian bureaucrats. Tamaki argued that the practice of unofficial correspondence since 1901 was the most effective way in which to resolve difficult cases like that of the Umino family and hoped that McClaren would continue the practice. Tamaki stated that Violet and her baby were not Japanese subjects under Japanese law despite the fact that under Australian law she had lost her British subject status when she married Denzo.[42] Further, he argued that although it was "no part of my duty to intercede on behalf of Australians, the broader question of humanity comes in". McClaren welcomed the continuation of the unofficial correspondence and accepted the Acting Consul-General's word that a jealous business rival in Brisbane had reported Umino. He changed his decision and the family was granted a 12-month CEDT. The degree of trust that had built over the years between the Consul-General and the department enabled the Umino family to stay. By the mid-1930s, the Department informed Denzo that he did not need to reapply for an extension to his CEDT. He had in fact regained his domicile status.

Compared with the case of Ichiro Kagiyama (1891–1965), Umino's case was straightforward under the law. In about 1907, Kagiyama sailed to Australia as a teenage merchant seaman after graduating from high school. He tried various jobs, took up photography in 1913 and married an Australian in 1917. He became an influential member of the NSW Photographic Society where "it is certain that his mastery of photographic technique and expression must have helped him to find a place in society amid the privations imposed by the white Australia policy". He had a shop and sold photographic equipment, opening his own studio in 1927. By 1936, the journal *Home* published his photographs (alongside those of Cazneaux and other famous Australian photographers of the time). In 1937, he had a studio in Kings Cross at Minton House. This was not the career of a merchant, tourist or student with permission to enter under the 1904 amendments.[43]

Why Kagiyama came to Australia in 1907 is uncertain. His relationship with trading firms, particularly Okura Trading, and the Consul enabled him to enter and live in Australia until he left in 1938. The 1904 provisions and the case-by-case administration allowed people like Kagiyama, who associated with trade but were not directly engaged in importing or exporting, to enter the country. Kagiyama photographed the official functions at the Consulate-General and produced family albums for trading companies and their employees although he mostly worked as a laundryman. His work for the Consulate-General and trading companies no doubt helped him to stay in Australia. Even after his divorce in 1934, he was permitted to bring out a Japanese wife.[44]

Although many firms had no difficulty bringing out maids, just as Okura Trading had no trouble keeping Kagiyama in Australia, firms who wanted to bring assistants from Japan to work in stores or as representatives, where no suitable Australian was available for the position, did experience difficulties. Jiro Muramatsu's first attempt to bring his brother Saburo back from Japan as an assistant struck trouble. On 14 August 1912, Jiro applied to the Department of External Affairs through his white Australian solicitor A.J. Davies of Roeburne for permission to employ two shop assistants from Japan. Davies argued:

> Muramats is one of the best, and best known business Japanese in the NorthWest and I am assured can be depended on not to abuse a permit if the same is granted. I may say that there is considerable difficulty in obtaining suitable white assistants I am informed that some understanding exists between the Govt [*sic*] of the Commonwealth and that of Japan to meet such a case as this.

The accompanying testimony hailed Jiro as a "good citizen & of sound financial standing, & manager & Part-Owner of 8 boats with 51 permits [who] has always been ready to give every assistance to the Department".

Atlee Hunt refused the request without giving a reason although another officer in the department had been inclined to grant it. Jiro then applied for Saburo to visit on passport for 12 months. Hunt felt that Jiro was attempting to circumvent the law, but finally agreed because Saburo was a merchant employed by Kanake & Co. in Osaka. However, Saburo worked as an assistant in the store on arrival "to gain knowledge of the trade". Saburo's arrival aided the firm's importing and exporting efforts. From 1913 onwards Saburo's stay was extended each year, through application by the Consul-General to External Affairs. He worked mostly in Cossack but travelled in WA, visiting Kalgoorlie and Broome on business. In 1915, he returned from a trip to Japan with his wife Aya, who also worked in the store until 1921. By that year, the firm was so important to the people of Cossack that its leading citizens petitioned the Minister for Home and Territories to exempt the couple from the Immigration Restriction Act. They wrote:

> Mr Saburo Muramats also represents some of the principal Manufacturers of Japan. It is desired that permission be granted them to become free Persons, that is free from Immigration Restriction Act, ... The above Persons are well known and respected also good Citizens, speak the English language fluently. [*sic*]

Home and Territories refused the request on 18 October 1921 because it was impossible to exempt anyone from the Act, but stated, "whilst he retains his present capacity in the firm of J. & T. Muramats, no difficulty will be raised in granting exemptions in favour of himself and his wife".[45] As a result, Saburo and Aya continued to receive extensions of stay until they left on 18 August 1924. However, in 1932 their Member of Parliament who had inquired about permanent residency for them was informed that if Saburo intended to return and engage in trade as before, they would received "due consideration". Saburo did not return.

It is interesting that the Muramatsu family could enlist such support from the white community and have its business and local trading climate seen as British enough to qualify as one in which a merchant from Japan could learn the Australian trade. It is also interesting that the policy was applied individually to each case. Jiro clearly knew how to manipulate the regulations and did so staying strictly within the law.

State governments also passed White Australia legislation. After 1901, each state enacted laws to define and limit the rights of non-citizens. WA laws affected Jiro's operations within that state. Jiro operated his business in pearling activities and onshore general merchandising in a similar manner to that of white businessmen. He was the only Japanese master pearler in Australian history and one of the bigger store operators along the north coast. He employed Japanese indents for his pearling luggers but also hired white Australians like E.M. McKay to manage part of his operations. Jiro's business was based initially on the store in Cossack, but in 1906, he obtained a Master Pearler's licence at a time when the industry at Broome was increasing steadily. By 1908, Broome had the same predominance of Japanese indents as Thursday Island. Jiro gradually purchased more pearling boats and permits to hire indentured labourers who included Japanese and Kupangers from the Celebes. He owned 10 boats by 1912 when WA law prevented Asiatics from obtaining any further licences. By 1915, Jiro's influence in pearling at Cossack became so extensive that white pearlers saw him as a threat. In 1909, there were 113 pearlers in WA of whom 48 owned one boat and approximately six owned eight or more luggers.[46] With 10 boats, Jiro was a major player. There is no evidence of any other Japanese person resident in Australia who actually owned luggers. Western Australian law aimed to limit the size of pearling firms in non-white hands. When Muramatsu's competitor, Geoffrey Taylor, left to serve in World War One, he had not fully paid for the boat *Ivy* that he had bought from Jiro, although he held six permits for the Japanese divers. During the war, the ownership of the boat reverted to Jiro. He attempted to claim the six permits but failed. The permits remained in Taylor's name but the department ordered that should he fail to return from the war, the permits were to be re-issued to a white pearler or cancelled. Jiro applied again in 1920 without success for the permits and for the £150 still owing to him from the sale of the boat. To avoid the restrictive legislation in WA, Jiro then extended his pearling operations to Darwin where he purchased further boats and obtained more licences.[47]

Before World War One, Jiro's on shore operations followed practices more representative of European traders. As a point of comparison, small Japanese concerns in Sydney, Townsville and Cairns, for example, while selling some general goods, imported Japanese specialty items and in this way complemented rather than competed with white storeowners.[48] Jiro's activities place him in direct competition with white owners and pearlers although the arrival of his brother Saburo introduced an element of importing from Japan over time.

The state-based White Australia laws also systematically reduced the political rights of naturalised non-white British subjects. In 1923, Jiro appealed to the High Court for the restoration of his right to vote in Commonwealth elections. Under Section 41 of the Federal Constitution of 1901, a naturalised person who was eligible to vote before 12 February 1902 could enroll to vote in a Commonwealth election if they were on the electoral roll for the more numerous House of Parliament of the state in which they lived. Further, Section 39 of the Commonwealth Electoral Act stated that no aboriginal native of Australia, Asia, the Pacific or Africa could vote unless eligible under Section 41. But WA passed further legislation under the Electoral Act of 1907 to prevent non-whites from enrolling as voters even under Section 41. However, the Police Magistrate at Roebourne approved Jiro's enrolment for state elections in 1922. Consequently, Jiro claimed that he was entitled to Commonwealth enrolment under Section 41. But, the Commonwealth Electoral Officer, H.R. Way, dismissed Jiro's application under the 1907 WA Act. Changes to the Nationality Act in 1920 meant that non-whites could naturalise if they were already British subjects, but under the Electoral Act they could not vote.[49]

Jiro argued in the High Court that because he was registered on the WA electoral roll he had the right to vote and to register for Commonwealth elections. Further, although he was born in Japan, Jiro argued he was not an aboriginal native of Japan, an Ainu. The High Court ruled that Jiro was an aboriginal native of Japan even though the Perth Magistrate had ruled that he was not. 'Aboriginal', the High Court argued, was properly defined as one who lived in the country before Europeans settled. It was used from a "European perspective". Ainu were only aboriginal natives of Japan from the Japanese perspective. Therefore, although Jiro was a naturalised British subject he was also an aboriginal native of Asia. His case was dismissed but he remained on the electoral roll in Darwin into the 1940s even though he did not vote.[50]

Attitudes to land ownership and leasing property also varied between states. NSW was accommodating and permitted merchants to own or lease land. People like Nakamura and Kuwahata bought homes and farms. Kinjiro Onishe of Kanematsu purchased over 20 acres of harbour-side land in Sydney in 1922. In Queensland Japanese had to lease farms.[51]

Minerals and merinos

Sam Hirodo's time at Bell Trees in 1907 was a harbinger of the development of good relations between rural Australia and Japanese companies. The administration of the White Australia policy provided a climate that opened up markets for Australian primary products. To 1922, firms such as Kanematsu and Mitsui dominated the sheep and wool export trade to Japan. They were also involved in New Zealand and South Africa, which were close enough in ship travel time for merchants based in Australia to visit and return within the permitted three-month period. Like Sam, merchants such as Ken Shimada of Nosawa & Co., travelled to Jerilderee and Forbes to see first-hand the sheep and wool that Australian farmers had for sale. Such wool trips were regular and often organised by companies like Dalgety's and Eastern Australian. Kagiyama took photos of Hirodo's car trips into country Victoria and NSW. Nosawa & Co. organised the early sale of live Australian sheep to Japan's northern island of Hokkaido for a sheep-breeding programme. From 1918, tens of thousands of corriedales and merinos were transhipped to Japan.

Large firms were attracted to Victoria's primary produce, especially wool, dairy produce and wheat. Mitsui investigated business in Victoria in 1913.[52] It was instrumental in substantially increasing Victoria's wool exports. Victoria produced 50 per cent of Australia's cross-breed wool but before 1919, 99 per cent of wool exported to Japan came from NSW. With Mitsui Melbourne's efforts that figure decreased. NSW had a predominance of fine merino wool for sale but Mitsui recognised the potential for other wool types and exploited that. They had to contend with stiff competition from Kanematsu and Nosawa & Co. in Sydney. By diversifying into different areas of the wool trade, each company was able to grow. A letter of 1922 to Mr Urabe in Sydney that reported on Victoria's wool industry shows the intensive market research that Japanese always undertook in any business expansion. Australians often thought in the light of the war that this research was sinister in purpose but in fact it was normal business practice whether for selling teacups or looking for new sources of iron ore. Mitsui Melbourne also had to bear in mind that Victoria was at a disadvantage when positioned against Sydney in trade with Asia. Ships from Sydney took a week less to travel to Japan than those from Melbourne. Additional research and credit checks were made on every potential customer in Melbourne and throughout Victoria. Each year, all Japanese firms obtained credit and general histories on all their customers through Dunn and Co., the equivalent of today's Standard and Poor's.

Japan also sought minerals in Australia. The iron ore deposits at Yampi Sound were known from 1907. Minerals at Mount Isa mines and deposits worked by Broken Hill Pty Ltd attracted Mitsubishi and Mitsui. Minerals became more sought after and a more contentious issue in the late 1920s.

Conclusion

The groundwork developed by Japanese *zaibatsu* companies and small firms that were an integral part of the Japanese network in Australia paid huge dividends in the Australia–Japan trade in the late 1920s and 1930s. The *zaibatsu* came to dominate the trade and brought Japan much of what it wanted from Australia. Australian government departments watched Japan's trade development. What it meant and where it fitted in Japan's intentions in the Pacific was a matter of interest and speculation from about 1908. The 1904 amendments to the Immigration Restriction Act had set the parametres that enabled Japanese people to enter and leave the country, even to reside and raise families. Australia was not only attractive because passage through the white walls could be negotiated but also because the untapped resources were promising and what Japan needed. The wool, minerals and the markets for an increasing volume of goods meant that by 1922 the immigration was almost entirely trade based. Such a situation was attractive to Japanese people and gave Australia a sense of control under the immigration policies. However, the developments after 1922 with the World War One peace treaties in operation, led to an explosion of business growth. What did the expansion of the *zaibatsu* in Australia mean? What were Japan's intentions in Australia at this stage? To answer these questions it became critical to obtain an assessment of Japanese activities in the South Seas and its possible intentions towards Australia in the long term.

Chapter 3

Undercurrents: Japan — an uncomfortable ally, 1901–20s

Japanese people's attraction to Australia's untapped resources and growing markets led them to negotiate their way through the great white walls. Although they developed networks, raised families and worked hand-in-hand with Australians right around the country, the case-by-case administration of the immigration policy kept Australian society overwhelmingly white and culturally British. Despite the good relationships with Japanese people at local and national levels, there was a degree of mismatch between some Australians' concerns about Japan and the actual intentions of Japanese in Australia between 1902 and 1922. The Anglo-Japanese Alliance of 1902 contained uncomfortable undercurrents for small sections of the Australian press and defence forces. But today in some books on this aspect of Australia's history, there is an even greater mismatch between what actually happened before the 1920s and current Australian beliefs about Australian fears at that time.[1]

Since the 1990s, many books that discuss the invasion question argue that Australia feared Japan in the decades before World War Two. David Walker's description of this conjectured fear in his groundbreaking work

Anxious Nation in 1999 is in stark contrast to the positive experiences of Australians and Japanese that we have already seen. He writes:

> It was not until the 1890s that Japan's military capacities and territorial ambitions began to induce some anxiety over a looming 'yellow peril' ....
> Australia came to nationhood at a time when the growing power of the East was arousing increasing concern. As 'rising tide' or 'flood' the East threatened to overwhelm boundaries ... Entire peoples and nations might be submerged. This was a vision of drowned cities, lost kingdoms and defeated races tossed aside by forces too powerful to resist. This was the fear of racial annihilation.[2]

Walker studied the literature of the late nineteenth and early twentieth centuries for attitudes to Asia rather than archival sources. Imagined invasion stories and lurid cartoons from those times depict a fearsome yellow peril in support of an immigration policy designed to keep Australia white and British and prevent it from being 'swamped by Asians', a catch cry we are familiar with from One Nation's Pauline Hanson in the 1996 election campaign. Neville Meaney's more balanced arguments in 1999 are based on defence documents more than on fictional stories. These show that Australia added Japan to the list of possible threats from 1905, which already included European powers such as Germany and France that possessed colonies in the Pacific. But by 2008, Australians are not only portrayed as having been 'anxious' since the 1890s or as having considered Japan a possible threat from 1905, but terrified of a Japanese invasion for 50 years before 1942. Fictional stories and anecdotes dominate the first third of Peter Stanley's popular book *Invading Australia*. He writes: "By 1910 there was little doubt that Japan was Australia's greatest threat." He makes the remarkable claim (to counter arguments by those like Bob Wurth who argue that Japan planned to invade Australia but failed) that this historic fear of Japan still clouds our judgment about what actually happened in 1942.

My argument is simple. Australians had feared invasion by Japan for half a century before it seemed to become a reality in 1942, and that apprehension affected how they saw the real crisis. In 1942, the Japanese did not invade – indeed, they decided not to – and they never had a chance to change their minds. The depth of anxiety Australians felt – rightly, because no one knew that invasion would not occur – colours the memory of the invasion threat: memory has turned 'could' into 'virtually did'. Since 1942 Australians have never quite confronted the fact that they were not invaded as they had feared – there is even a persistent fantasy that the Japanese did arrive but that the truth has been concealed.[3]

Over a 10-year period since the late 1990s, the belief in a terrified Australia in the years before federation, indeed an Australia terrified of Japan between the wars, has come to acceptance, to either explain a fear of Japanese invasion that turned out not to be real or a fear of Japanese invasion that was real but was stopped by force. This *belief* in Australians' fear of Japan did not always exist and was certainly not shared by many Australians living between 1890 and 1941.

Back in the 1950s and early 1960s, when Japan's wartime actions were still very raw and vivid in Australian minds, the very dark days of the Cold War brought the prospect of a nuclear conflict between Russia and the USA that might kill us all as the book and movie *On the Beach* explored. During this period, D.C.S. Sissons (who had enlisted and been sent to learn enough Japanese to become an interpreter in the war) was Australia's legendary and most eminent scholar of the Australia–Japan relationship. He studied Japan at its best and worst. He was expert on the Japanese atrocities, war crimes trials, wartime cryptography, the occupation and reconstruction of Japan and of Japanese emigration, particularly to Australia, from the 1860s. In his exhaustive study of the written views of Australian politicians, media and defence forces from 1890–1923, he wrote that in 1910–11:

Although conflict with Japan was considered as not unlikely there was little animosity towards her. The struggle was seen as the product of inanimate and largely economic forces – not of viciousness. Japan was still more often than not the object of admiration for the speed and the thoroughness of her industrial, cultural and administrative development. … The prevalence of this attitude is indicated by the comments on Japan's final annexation of Korea in August 1910.[4]

Sissons showed that Australians at that time believed that Japan's annexation of Korea lessened its chances of moving south. In 1911, the entire press hailed the renewal of the Anglo-Japanese Alliance with relief and confidence that Japan would keep the terms of this friendly agreement. However, all but three papers in the country spoke of a future danger when the Alliance expired in 1921 and of the need to complete Australia's defences by that date. None of these reports was alarmist. Unlike English press reports on German naval programmes, the Australian press did not search for news about Japanese naval construction with which to scare the public, but barely mentioned it. To Sissons, before World War One, Japan was one possible future enemy among several including Germany, but no threat was likely while Japan remained a formal treaty ally of Britain. Even Japan's acquisition of Asian territory after its war against Russia, whom Australia did fear, was greeted with some relief because it acted as a check to Russian aggression. This is a very different picture from that painted by Stanley and other recent writers and is based on far more evidence.

An Australia afraid of Japan from the 1890s, if real, might explain a lot, as Stanley advocates, but it is far from accurate. We need to examine the large body of Australian archival evidence which writers have not used and ask the following questions. When did Australia begin to see Japan as a threat? What prompted this? How widespread was this sense of threat? What evidence is there that the threat was real? Did fear of Japan lead Australia to engage in appeasement of Japan, as Bob Wurth maintains, through the administration of the White Australia policy and other accommodations? Did we let them spy on us? Did they spy on us before 1922? What were Australian defence responses to Japan's actions?

Understanding fear is important because, as Stanley says, it is a factor in how we interpret what is happening or what has happened. As Frei wrote, it is easy to concoct a theory to suggest that Japan had long wanted to invade Australia. In effect, belief about fear of Japan and invasion in recent books in Australia has become so complex and contradictory that any one of the versions could, as Frei said, "make a splendid plot, though one far from the truth".[5] The question is: what do we believe? How does an understanding of this fear help us understand the raids on Australia? And, if Australians were so terrified of the Japanese, why did they befriend them and even marry them? Why are we hearing now so many stories of friendship, which are borne out by archival material?

All the historians who say that Australians feared Japan and possibly an invasion before World War Two (or even before federation) look at the tradition of the ripping yarn to support their views. Horror stories, they say, reflect a deep unease in the Australian psyche. For example, Dixon argues that such writings reflect a mood of crisis that characterised the pre- and immediate post-federation eras.[6] Was there a real fear about Australia's security at this time? And how did Australians at the time understand the fictional stories that other books about the war rely on?

Defence concerns

Before 1901, Australia was a collection of colonies without much defence. Concerns over defence arose every time European powers with colonies in the Asia Pacific region were at war or likely to be at war in Europe. The Australian colonies had a concept of the land beyond the northern borders, as an empty 'no man's land', ready for the taking, and so posing a threat to their security. The rivalry of colonial powers such as Germany, France, Britain and the USA for that 'no man's land' in the Pacific in the late nineteenth century was of urgent concern to Australian colonials. If good harbours in the Pacific Ocean were developed by foreign powers, Australia was at potential risk from naval attack. In the 1870s, Britain withdrew its troops from the Australian colonies leaving local militia to take over. Australia wanted a rampart from New Guinea to Fiji to protect its northern border. So concerned were the colonies that defence spending was never higher than in the 1880s. In 1883, Queensland even took East New Guinea but Britain refused to sanction the action believing that Germany was not interested in the territory. When Germany did annex that territory in 1884, Australia was furious. Britain then took South East New Guinea, which was handed to Australia in 1906 as Papua. The colonies constantly pushed Britain to annex more islands in their back yards, including the New Hebrides, but without success. Australia's experiences of attempted diplomacy at this time made it aware that it needed its own defence rather than relying totally on Britain whose interests did not coincide with Australia's. However, in the 1890s, Australia only expected coastal raids from any enemy and still had the protection of the British navy. Sissons shows that during 1889–91, Australia believed that Japan was "merely a casual acquaintance whose friendship cannot make us and whose enmity cannot mar us". True apprehension was centred on China, not Japan. From 1885–1901, defence planning gave no indication of any apprehension of an attack from Japan, "although in the later years the French in Noumea appear to have been a source of worry".[7] The possibility of the invasion of Australia from New Caledonia became a recurrent theme and was alive and well in 1942. In effect, Australian colonial and early federation fears of other nations surfaced from time to time but the projected sources of threat were many and varied and certainly not focused on Japan.

Japan's defeat of China in 1895 resulted in increased discussion about Japan in Australia but Sissons and Meaney find no evidence in government or press records for the fear that other historians argue developed towards Japan at this time. The *SMH* and *The Age* said it was better to have the rising Japan as a friend than as an enemy but their reports contained no hostility towards Japan. The *SMH* thought Japan had engaged in a "just war fought on fair issues" and that her peace terms were reasonable. *The Age* thought it was better to have Japan dominate in Korea rather than Russia and hoped a firm alliance would result between Britain and Japan because Russia was the greater threat to Australia. A large number of newspapers were unconcerned about Japan. Even the *Bulletin* saw no threat from Japan at this time. Sissons concludes that the Sino-Japanese War made no profound impact on the press. The British Colonial Defence Committee envisaged a possible attack from France but gave no consideration to Japan because its navy was inferior to the British navy at that time.[8]

The Boer War of 1899–1902 heightened Australian fears of Russian, French, German, Japanese and Chinese ambitions in the Pacific but the major fear was of a coalition of European powers. Britain was foremost in seeking good relations with Japan and hoped that the mere existence of the Alliance would dampen Russian ardour. However Britain still did not believe there was any threat to Australia in 1904 and Australia decreased defence spending at this time. General J. Hutton, the General officer commanding the Australian Military Forces, was more afraid that the Pacific might become an arena of old world strife than of a war involving Australian territory. Indeed a substantial number of speakers during the debate on the Defence Bill in 1904 rejected all talk of danger and invasion. There was no British plan for any defence for Australia before 1904–05, although plans existed for India and Canada.[9]

The Russo-Japanese war of 1904–05 changed perceptions in Australia. Japan met Russian encroachment in Korea with war and won decisively in the great naval battle at Tsushima. Britain then permitted a Japanese protectorate over Korea. Sissons argued: "It is fantastic to suggest, ... that Japan at this time saw in the Alliance a means of luring the British

Navy away from the Pacific." Rather, Japan wanted Britain to maintain its fleet in the east just as Britain wanted help in India but both provisions were dropped. Had this part of the negotiations been published, it might have reassured those in Australia who were apprehensive about Japan's immediate intentions. Japanese victory did not alarm Prime Minister Deakin's ministry as Deakin held the view that the development of the Korean territory adjacent to Japan would tax all its resources for a very long time and encourage Japanese expansion in a direction away from Australia. It is clear from the type of defences Australia put in place that invasion was not seen as a threat: marine defences, torpedo boats and destroyers. In May 1905, the Director of Commonwealth Naval Forces still supported the view that Australia needed to provide against raids and commercial destruction. Although politicians, the navy and the press felt Japan was not a present danger Australian soldiers, for example Major J.G. Legge, were concerned at the relative strength of British sea power compared with a possible combination of powers, particularly Japan and Germany. A reorganised China in alliance with Japan could in the future, the *SMH* argued, reconstruct the map of Asia. Sissons in the main found the apprehension about Japan in the papers as limited and argued that such fears may have been to a degree the product of enthusiasm about improving Australia's defences.[10]

Reactions to the Russo-Japanese War in Defence records show that the Japanese and British shared good relations in the 1900s. British naval officers accepted invitations on board Admiral Togo's flagship *Mikasa* during the war and Australia's Colonel (later, Major General) John Charles Hoad acted as an observer and official attaché with the Japanese army among a number of foreign observers at the land battles. Hoad made drawings, which are unfortunately lost, of the troop manoeuvres especially at a battle at Liao-Yang on 27 August 1904, which involved 70,000 Japanese troops. In a further battle in the area on 3 September, Japan suffered 15,000 casualties. Hoad reported that it had involved the "heaviest fire that the world has ever seen". Far from being concerned about Japan's military might as a result of his observations of the war, Hoad thought that its army had made terrible military mistakes in the campaign. To him, the Japanese did not show enough initiative or originality, nor did they follow up properly during a battle because of the weakness of their cavalry in manoeuvres. Despite not making the Russians fight to the finish, he believed that Japan had methods worth studying and copying. He became a great friend of the Japanese and received the Order of the Rising Sun. His relationship with the Japanese navy, which so distinguished itself at Tsushima, was longstanding and led to a very heavy involvement in the regular visits of His Imperial Majesty's Naval Training Squadron to Australian ports. Needless to say, Hoad was an enthusiastic supporter of the Alliance with Japan.[11]

Hoad was clearly not worried by Japan's defence capabilities despite Japan's territorial acquisitions from the Treaty of Shimonoseki at the end of the Sino-Japanese conflict in 1895 and the Treaty of Portsmouth at the end of the Russo-Japanese war in 1905. All of these places were a world away from Australia. American historians writing much later, like H.P. Willmott, disagree with Hoad and believe that Japan had wanted since the sixteenth century to expand and place Asia under Japanese rule starting with Korea and China, but had never had the means to do so. There is no evidence for this. Historians of the Tokugawa era point to a ripping yarn tradition in Japanese writing of the nineteenth century that romanticised the heroes of the earlier times. Some Australian historians take this heroic literature as factual evidence, like Willmott does, and use it to support the theory that Australians feared Japan in the period before World War One. Japan, according to Howe who does cite hard facts, demonstrated that Japan's treaty rights allowed it to develop *economic* activities in parts of Manchuria. The South Manchurian Railway (SMR) joined the Japanese-Korean rail line. Between 1905 and 1914, Japan intensified the Manchurian economy including mining, steel works, banking and the cotton market. The now well-established trading companies, MBK, MSK and Ōkuragumi experienced a boom, particularly in the freight trade from the port along the SMR. Japan was clearly after trade expansion and resources. The Australian naval report of 1914 said that the Japanese were extremely busy and had "more outlets ... than they require". Japan also displayed a desire for international respect but was there more to this as Willmott and others later maintained? Could Australia truly rely on Japan for defence or was it a prime potential enemy? Only a major war would tell.[12]

Opinions changed 1907–14, when Japan increased naval and military spending. Australia speculated on what would happen when the Anglo-Japanese Alliance ended in 1912. Rear Admiral Sir William Rooke Creswell, (who had been Director of the Commonwealth Naval Forces since 1904 and had worked for the establishment of an Australian navy from 1899), mentions Japan directly in discussions about the need for coastal destroyers. However, he felt that the worst scenario was the possibility of a German-Japanese alliance with Germany acquiring NEI. The Committee of Imperial Defence from 1906–07 gave most of its attention to the danger of a major war that would require the defence of Britain against Germany and defence of India against Russia. The Committee reiterated the policy that Australia should rely on the British navy to prevent attacks. Britain's concentration on North Sea defence with the rise of German sea power stepped up Australian proposals for the development of local defence. In this way, the Committee influenced Australia independent of events in Japan.[13]

Deakin accepted the Admiralty scheme for Australia to control Royal Navy Cruisers in 1907 but nothing happened. He then invited the USA fleet to visit Australia in 1908. In 1909 at the Imperial Conference, the Admiralty accepted a Pacific Fleet with an autonomous Australian unit, "a navy within a navy" and the Royal Military College of Duntroon was founded. From this time onwards both naval defence documents and the more extreme publications assess the threat from Japan. This paralleled the continuation of celebratory reports in the daily papers and women's magazines about the Anglo-Japanese Alliance.[14]

The *Lone Hand*, which often demonstrated in its stories, articles and cartoons that today would be considered a racist and alarmist bias towards national issues, expressed suspicion of Japan. Its articles by eminent people accompanied fictional stories on the same theme. In the June edition of 1907, an article on 'Building an Australian navy' argued that an (unnamed) invader would seize a first-class base in the empty north, fortify itself and pour in supplies for a gradual advance over the continent. The following quote from the article hardly matched what was happening with Japanese or any other immigrants at the time.

> [Australia] can only be conquered by a country peopling each tract of territory as it wins it. Against that sort of attack an Australian army would take years to make an impression. But if it were backed by an Australian fleet, which could hold the sea and cut off the invader's communications and supplies, the invading force could be isolated and ground to powder.[15]

What better argument could there be for an Australian navy?

An assessment of potential threat was an essential part of planning for the degree of military and naval strength that Australia required. An attack from the north, the most popular hypothesis, featured in naval reports in 1914 but not all navy brass supported the concept of a northern invasion. On 14 January 1915, one Vice-Admiral argued that the NT was the last place for an invasion because any enemy would "simply fritter away their strength there and do no material harm to Australia". Rather, by taking Tasmania, he argued, an invader could best impress its will on Australia and use it to bargain for concessions. He was obviously unaware of the extensive concessions Japanese people already had under the White Australia policy when he wrote:

I am no believer in the idea that the Japanese wish to colonize Australia. They have more outlets already than they require in Manchuria, Corea [*sic*] and Formosa. But Japanese sentiment and *amour propre* might be so wounded by the Continuation of the White Australia Policy with regard to them, that popular opinion might drive their Government to attack Australia in order to force her to give Japanese equal rights with other civilized nations.

One major concern for Australia, if war broke out in Europe as expected, was the need to defend the nation in the event of the annexation of enemy territory in Australia's back yard by any power other than Britain. At that time, Germany and the Netherlands were the nearest neighbours in New Guinea, Micronesia and NEI. The French held small islands in the Pacific, New Caledonia being the nearest. The Australian government discussed possible threats to Australia's security at great length between 1901 and 1919 and, uncertain about what reliance it could place on Britain in the event of a war, established a navy in 1910, an Intelligence Corps in 1911 and an Air Corps in 1913 to augment the existing armed forces.[16]

Fear of Japan eased in 1911 when the alliance was renewed. But from July 1914, Defence paid close attention to Japan. This was part of the reason why Australia seized German New Guinea early in the war to prevent Japanese occupation. Attention turned to improving defences in case Japan obtained southern territory after the war and the Alliance was not renewed in 1922. As we have seen, the operation of the Immigration Restriction Acts controlled entry of Asians into Australia and worked well for both Australians and Japanese, which also alleviated any fear of being swamped. What part then did the fictional stories play and how do we read these? Truly if people believed them, Australia would have been a much more anxious place than the evidence outside the stories suggests.[17]

The place of ripping yarns

From 1871, when Germany was at war with France in an unsettled Europe, a new form of fiction emerged, which became very popular in Europe, Britain and USA. Its purpose, according to I.F. Clarke who wrote the most comprehensive study of this literature, was to warn people of the dangers of remaining unprepared in a warring world. The nineteenth century had seen plenty of wars including the Napoleonic Wars and the Crimean War involving Russia in 1854. As literacy increased in Europe at the end of the nineteenth century and inventions permitted news to travel faster by telegraph, eminent persons wrote appeals to the public in the press through the medium of future war tales to draw attention to defence needs. Increased armaments and new technologies were seen as the key to winning wars. The science fiction writer, Jules Verne, saw these inventions as a deterrent to war.

Such fiction was so popular because of the general expectation of progress at the time. Literature forecast the future conditions of mankind. Anything seemed possible for science with the invention of wonderful, imaginary machines like the submarine *Nautilus* in *20,000 leagues under the sea*. The Victorians, Clarke argued, had a tremendous interest in war, which was seen as profitable, natural and romantic. In imagination it was an affair of brief battles and heroic individual deeds that underestimated the scale of real war. Readers had not yet experienced the horrors of the trenches of World War One. Paradoxically, none of the flood of imaginary wars or eminent articles foresaw the total devastation that would actually happen when the major industrial nations decided to fight it out. Also relevant to Australia and the Japanese was the development of the popularity of spy stories which sky-rocketed between 1903 and 1909 with the publication of *Riddle of the Sands* when serialised spy stories (mostly about German spies) were stock in trade for British newspapers. Australian readers of English magazines and papers became familiar with this type of literature and just as hungry for it.[18]

Before federation, when the actual sense of threat was amorphous and its source a matter for speculation, different nationalities featured as potential invaders in these vivid narratives. In *The Battle of the Yarra* in 1883 it is the Russians, while in William Lane's novel, *White or Yellow? A Story of Race-war in A.D. 1908*, which appeared in serial form in *The Boomerang*, the plot turns on a projected Asian aggressor. It joined *The Big Five*, which appeared in the *Lone Hand* in 1907 and featured a colony of Chinese and Malays deep in the NT that was mining and exporting Australia's mineral wealth. Frank Fox's story, *The Commonwealth Crisis* of 1909 (relied on by Stanley) was a late version of this type of literature and came at the height of invasion literature especially in Britain. Fox's story, set in 1922, featured Japanese. In this story Thomas Burt and his friend are on a hunting trip. They observe the landing of Japanese troops at Junction Bay. They find a colony of over 6,000 people of mixed Asian origin in the NT. After a long and complicated story, the British government accepts the allegiance of this colony under the Alliance against Australia's wishes. With diplomatic and legal measures ineffective (which Australia had usually found with Britain and was doing so over naval defence at the time), this leads to a very long struggle by a 'White Guard', an irregular corps of bushmen, to dislodge the Japanese and is full of manly and bloody battles, which were part of the heroic tradition of imagined wars in Victorian times. Stanley says that the bushmen dip their fingers in the blood of a dying Tasmanian who had fought alongside them and swore an oath never to spare the life of a Japanese in war or peace. Like most invasion stories the end isn't clear-cut or happy. Such stories of unknown colonies of 'Asiatics' deep in the unexplored regions of the north of Australia, show the nation, Dixon contends, at its most strident and paranoid. But did people at the time have anything in their experience to compare fiction with reality? Were the stories sheer paranoia or explicable as part of the campaigns to establish defence forces and secure borders through immigration provisions? Certainly Stanley tells how one boy in Sydney played games with his friends to fight the invading Japanese before World War One. Was this the acting out of fear or copying of popular yarns and speculation, which Clark said had gone into stories in *Boys Own* magazines, which were a very popular part of daily life?[19]

The use of the ripping yarn to promote defence issues was common in Australia as it was in Britain before World War One. Many of the stories in the *Lone Hand* in 1910–11 were clearly arguing for improved Australian defence forces, a subject which had been firmly on the government's agenda for years. An article 'Wanted at Once! Aerial defence from Aerial invasion' asked: "What will you do? – when the war comes – it will come from the skies." One story by Laurence Zeal 'The command of the air', an exciting fictional story of the first encounter of the Australian aerial corps (which did not exist) with the Japanese air force (which in fact Japan did not have even in 1942), was a ripping yarn arguing the insufficiency of Australia's forces. In the story, an Australian aerial corps plane on patrol in Sydney receives a call to Pine Creek in the NT. They were preparing to leave when an Australian tried to stop them taking off. "Must have cost the Japs some cash to get at a chap like that. But they are pretty thorough, the Japs", said Quelch, one of the heroes. On the flight to Pine Creek, the Japanese jam their wireless. After an air battle between this one plane and a dozen Japanese planes, the Australian plane bombed the Japanese air corps. The story ends in a temporary victory for the Australians but with only 12 planes in Australia's air force and only "one aeroplane with two useless men on it!" that had fought the battle, the General concluded "tomorrow the whole of the enemy's planes will be in the air!" The point of the hypothetical story was that Australia needed a better defence force, one that looked to the future of aviation in warfare.

After the London Imperial Conference's decision in 1911 that the British Empire should exploit the air as a means of warfare, the Australian Minister of Defence, Senator George Pearce, approved the formation of an Australian air arm on 20 September 1912. The Central Flying School and Aviation Corps was officially announced on 7 March 1913 and subsequently established at Point Cook, Victoria. The first mention of the Australian Flying Corps is in 1914. It had two instructors and five flimsy training aircraft.[20] Australia also introduced a form of military training.

One clear example of Australians' ability to distinguish between reality and fiction was the reception of Japanese ships' crews. One of Fox's fictional stories formed part of the *Australian Crisis*. It showed how a minor slight by a Chinese on a ferry in Sydney towards an Australian woman caused a race riot in which the Japanese sailors from the NYK line were stoned and killed by a rampaging mob, after which riots spread and mobs attacked Asians everywhere for days in several Australian cities. Far from rioting when the Japanese Training Squadron actually visited Australian ports, Australians lined the streets in tens of thousands to welcome the Japanese sailors. There were never any reports of NYK sailors being attacked in any city. On the contrary, sailors made life-long friends whom they visited on each trip to Australia.[21]

The ships' visits provide a good picture of how people in Australia reacted to their Japanese allies and give indications of Japan's intentions towards Australia in official speeches and news items. Although coloured by the euphoria of the moment, Japanese statements are remarkably consistent over the decades. Full records of ship visits begin in 1902 when Vice-Admiral Kobayashi first visited Australia. As a visitor over the following three decades, he noted the changes in Australia. He was constantly impressed by Australia's broadness of view and sparse population. He believed that it was important for the cadets to travel to experience different people and broadened their minds.

The continuing visits gained extensive press coverage but drew little Commonwealth interest before World War One. From 1906, because of Hoad's particular relationship with the Japanese navy and armed forces, he organised ever better receptions and onshore entertainment with an extensive official programme. For example, the visit of Japanese

Cruiser *Azuma* under the command of Commander Taro Inazuku and Lieutenant Inouye and the *Soya* under Commander Murakami and Captain Iwamura from 13 January to 3 March 1913 to Fremantle, Hobart, Melbourne, Sydney, Brisbane and Townsville was marked by an official luncheon on 30 January at the Oriental Hotel for two Australian naval and two military officers to entertain the Admiral and principal officers. The State Premier gave the officers free railway passes in recognition that the visit was of some importance but at this time the Prime Minister saw no need for a large garden party of his own with a suggested guest list of 1,000 people.[22]

The ripping yarns with frightening invasion stories were not the only literature to feature Japan at this time. In the 6 June 1903 edition of the women's magazine the *New Idea,* published by the stalwart supporter of White Australia T. Shaw Fitchett of Melbourne, contained reports and stories about the thousands who flocked to the Japanese Training Squadron's ships. These included schools on excursion such as the girls of Methodist Ladies' College, Melbourne, who were photographed on the HIJMS *Hashidate.* The girls met grammar school boys who joked with the crew in English. In an article 'How we visited the Japs by Mollie and me and the kodak', one grammar school boy asked the gunner:

"Shoot-um far, John?" for John Chinaman but was corrected by a friend saying, "Shut up, Curly, he'll get awful waxy if you call him 'John'. These chaps are not Chows y' know."

The girls reported that they had heard that the 'Japs' were taciturn and could not joke but they had nothing but smiles and jokes for the visitors. Another report by 'Chrysanthemum' said it was a rare joy to have the sailors to tea.

> Only those who have moved among this lovable race and learned a little of their delightful ways and customs can realise the pleasure of meeting its representatives under conditions calling for a return of hospitality.[23]

The daily papers printed the schedule for the visits in each port that they entered. Over the usual five-day visits, such as in 1906, people lined the streets to see the sailors and officers arrive. For days the papers were full of pictures of sailors at the zoo and Admirals at official functions and town hall welcomes. Sailors struck up friendships with local people who invited them to their homes. Some friendships lasted for decades.[24]

The *New Idea* was full of the spirit of the Anglo-Japanese Alliance and frequently published items about Japanese culture and curios that accompanied stories of women who had recently spent holidays in Japan especially between 1904 and 1911.[25] One sympathetic article written by the wife of Japanese Admiral Uriu who was serving in the Russo-Japanese War, spoke of situations that many Australian women could relate to because they had recently had some of their men overseas in South Africa in the Boer War of 1899–1902.

We women of Japan feel that we must work, and not sit idle while our brave men are showing such marvellous endurance on the battle-field … The rich and the poor, the high and the low, have one common object, to encourage those who are at the front, to help the distressed families … whose dear ones have died … The Ladies' Patriotic Association of Japan was formed some years back by Madam Joko Okumura, at a time when we enjoyed peace and quiet in Japan. Before the Japan–China war broke out, this lady was much interested in the Koreans. [She] deplored the conditions of the uneducated people of that peninsula. She went there herself, and induced the government to build schools, and also taught the Koreans the Japanese language and literature. The Koreans thought much of her; … After her return, she was collecting a fund to establish a large girls' school, … She was in China at the time of the Boxer rising, and the advance of the Allies on Pekin. Being a devout and religious woman, she made it a practice to attend the funerals of the dead soldiers …[26]

What Australian woman could fail to identify with support for the troops, helping the victims of poverty and ignorance, lobbying the government for schools and grieving with the bereaved? The message was that Japanese women shared similar and, importantly, western values held by Australians. They were not only Allies but like us. But what was Japan doing in the north and what concerned Australia?

Japan and Australia's north

Although news reports and magazines provided information on events involving Japanese in Australia and speculative articles and fiction about defence issues, these bore little relationship to what Japan was actually doing in the region in the 1900s and 1910s. If members of the public took seriously articles such as 'The Pacific a Japanese Pond' published in the *Lone Hand* on 1 December 1910 they would have had reason to be concerned. This article stated that White Australia looked out on a brown pond beyond the breakers of Australia's coasts, which had become Japanese waters. Japan, in two wars (which were in fact on the other side of the world), had in the opinion of the writer "wiped out" Chinese and Russian fleets in the Pacific and "got rid of" the British Navy through the Anglo-Japanese Alliance, which Sissons demonstrated was false. The writer believed that Japan would capture islands all the way to Australia and outclass the USA fleet to land 200,000 men on Australia's coast. There was no evidence for this piece of scaremongering and no evidence that people took it seriously.[27]

Some immigration accompanied trade and shipping expansion into the Pacific. Reports on Japanese activities arrived from Australian and British officials overseas. Within Australia, the first intelligence officers began to collect information and compile reports. By 1913, the navy kept extensive records based on newspaper and other reports of interest concerning Japan and other countries in the region. What did they find and what influence did it have on Australians? Was there a discernable difference between speculative articles of the *Lone Hand* and the reports from official sources?

Japan's shipping expansion included passenger and cargo lines, which did not go unnoticed in Australia, but not for defence reasons. NYK had established shipping services as far south as Australia in 1896. Increasingly more companies and small entrepreneurs sought to develop cargo trade to the south. A.R. Colquhuon noticed the commercial rivalry in 1902 because the new Japanese liners were superior to P&O as tourism to Japan grew at this time. The Australian Navy Office also recognised a threat to Australian trade in Japan's commercial moves. By the 1910s, direct exports of Japanese coal had ousted Australian coal from the Malay peninsular, including Singapore, where the demand for Japanese coal was rapidly increasing. The navy argued that if Japan began a direct export business at lower prices, demand would increase and Japanese ships would capture the existing advantage enjoyed by foreign cargo steamers on the South Pacific route as well.[28]

To some, shipping led not only to trade expansion but also to colonisation. Some Australians saw Japan's growing interest in the Pacific, particularly in New Caledonia as a potential threat to Australian interests. The *Lone Hand* story by A.K. Shearston in May 1911 wrote of a 'colony' of Japanese in New Caledonia who "profess to be miners" in the nickel industry. Many had been in the army and in time the Japanese would have a naval base and coaling station on the island from which they could attack Australia. They already visited Queensland. Shearston called on the Australian Government to buy New Caledonia and to introduce conscription for military service in Australia, which was his real point. Although the Commonwealth government was not terribly interested in the visits of Japanese and their training squadrons, some members of the Commonwealth House of Representatives were concerned that 4,000–5,000 Japanese were living in New Caledonia only 700 miles from Queensland in 1912.[29] On 11 October 1913, an article in the *SMH* came to the attention of the Navy Office in Melbourne. The paper quoted English journals.

> ... the Japanese Government is making preparations to develop trade and emigration in the Pacific. Commander Hosaka, of the Imperial Navy, who recently completed a tour of some of the South Sea Island, has reported to his Government that they are most suitable for settlement, and having great resources still unexploited.[30]

Shearston paid no attention to the facts of Japanese emigration to New Caledonia or that other reports exaggerated the figures. Japanese population of the island was officially 1,900. The Japanese in New Caledonia worked for La Societé Le Nickel and La Societé des Hauts Fourneaux de Noumea, usually on five-year contracts at the end of which they had the opportunity to return to Japan or to stay on, marry local women and even become French citizens. Many started businesses of their own and lived on the island long enough to be shipped to Australia for internment in World War Two, although none of them was found to have engaged in any subversive activity. France had negotiated contracts for Japanese workers for the nickel industry under strict conditions from 1906 after considerable Japanese reluctance about the whole scheme.[31]

A further British report on 8 July 1913 about Commander Hosaka's explorations through Java, Borneo and the Philippines from Conyngham Greene of the British Embassy in Chuzenju confirmed that Hosaka had advised his compatriots who had capital to travel to the South Seas. The Japan Exploration Society planned a two-year exploration cruise through the South Seas, Brazil, Chile and the Pacific shores of North and South America. Fleet Admiral Ito promoted the society. This report on Japan's *planned* exploration shows that Japan was actually a few years behind the *Lone Hand's* estimation of Japan's progress. The exploration, which was mostly conducted by private enterprises, was undertaken because Japanese found themselves increasingly excluded from well-favoured countries under European colonial control. One South Seas Island Company had some Japanese government financial support. Against these Japanese developments, the Netherlands discussed the possibility of a defensive alliance, or understanding, between Netherlands, Australia, USA and Britain. Conyngham Greene further reported that Japan was showing interest in German possessions and had some workers in New Guinea. Four Japanese companies traded in the South Seas of which Nan'yō Bōeki Kaisha was the largest and longest established firm with £15,000 capital and three schooners. It traded in copra, shells and Japanese produce. Nan'yō Kōgyō Kaisha was newly started with only one schooner. It had not succeeded in the Caroline Islands but sailed to the Admiralty Islands where the promoters hoped to gain some property to grow coconut trees. But the German government raised difficulties about leasing land.[32] Peattie's account of Koben Mori illustrates the difficulties and startling differences from the experiences of Japanese businesses in Australia and that Australia really had very little to be concerned about in Japanese South Seas development at this time.

Koben Mori, one of the few Japanese to succeed in Micronesia, joined the Ichiya Co. and went to Micronesia as its representative. In February 1892, it had a store at Panape in the Marianas and at Truk. Mori managed to survive on Moen Island by raising a private army and helping one chief against another. In 1898, he married a chief's daughter and subsequently had 12 children. When Ichiya Co. failed, he went into business for himself but in 1897 the Hiki Co. opened a branch on Moen and Mori became its resident agent. In 1899, he obtained a contract as resident agent for Jaluit Trading Co., a German concern. He attracted 14 other Japanese to Truk, who traded and grew coconuts. This ended in 1900 when the islands came under German rule. The Germans arrested all the Japanese except Mori and expelled them from Micronesia. In 1907, a Japanese merchant ship arrived belonging to the Murayama Co., which obtained permission from the Germans to restart Japanese trade in Truk. A few Japanese followed to trade, fish and farm but there was no real development until the Japanese warships took over in 1914.[33]

The Australian Naval office watched Japanese activities in the islands before World War One in an attempt to see what Japan intended. Officers like Commander J.G. Fearnley had argued in 1909 against Australia's reliance on British intelligence because Australia had a greater interest in Japan than Britain, which was more focused on European developments.[34] On 14 June 1910 he wrote to the Executive Committee of the National Defence League in Sydney that:

> Australia cannot afford to neglect close observation of the developments in Asia, particularly in Japan whose admitted policy is to secure by any means predominance in the Pacific. It would be little less than a National crime to wilfully ignore the disposition of a nation whose expansion has hitherto been characterised by unscrupulous disregard for Treaty obligations, and whose hostile operations have usually been initiated by a surprise attack for which she has made secret but thorough preparations.[35]

Fearnley was playing up the possibility of Japan preparing for a war with the USA to highlight the need for an improved intelligence and security service. There was tension between the USA and Japan at the time and fictional stories of war with the USA had been published in Japan since 1907. In effect, invasion scenarios existed in the literature of many nations at this time, one depicting planes flying into the skyscrapers of New York in 1911, 90 years before such an horrific event actually happened. By 1913, the Royal Navy gave the RAN control of the Intelligence Centre in Sydney. Reports consisted of information gained from overseas newspapers. Little training took place for intelligence officers until after a proper Naval Intelligence Branch was established at the Navy Office in June 1914.[36]

Although Japan's attempts before World War One to expand trade into the Pacific were largely unsuccessful, trade with Australia was a success. This required a considerable investment in research and information gathering of a diverse kind. Shipping companies gathered port information and translated it into Japanese for the use of their vessels throughout the Pacific. Whether Japan had any hostile intentions or would take advantage of the Alliance for its own purposes was a subject of debate. Indeed, Defence estimates of the risk to Australia in 1906 were very similar to those of 1941.

> ... as far as could be reasonably foreseen nothing more than raiding attacks needed to be anticipated on Australian littoral, and that the employment of Armoured cruisers in such attacks was an unlikely contingency.[37]

Only a world war featuring the worst-case scenario with Britain involved in a war in Europe would clarify Japan's intentions through its actions. World War One provided Japan with that opportunity.[38]

Japan and World War One

Japan engaged in two main activities in World War One that affected Australia. The first was the protection of allied shipping in the Pacific and Indian Oceans with the occupation of German colonies in the Asia Pacific region. The second was the expansion of shipping and trade. World War One boosted the Australia–Japan trade, which both sides welcomed given the severe contraction of trade with Europe. Japan's actions took place under the auspices of the Anglo-Japanese Alliance with the active approval of Britain. These activities simultaneously improved relations, increased controversy and caused Australian defence circles some concern when anticipating the peace settlement and the end of the Anglo-Japanese Alliance in 1921. The wartime experience led to closer ties between Australians and Japanese in civilian life.

For the first time the Anglo-Japanese Alliance activated in a war situation. Although in 1919 the Australian navy hotly debated the extent of Japanese naval assistance during the war, Japanese newspapers boasted that they had saved Singapore and other British territory in the east. In 1928, Consul-General Tokugawa wrote in *The Argus*, 23 June 1928, that Japan had patrolled the China Seas in 1914, safeguarded trade routes, joined British ships in Singapore, patrolled from Manila to Aden when Britain had to withdraw to the western campaign, kept Australia from German raids by Admiral Von Spee whom they chased out of the Pacific and safeguarded the passage of the Anzacs to the Mediterranean.[39] Regardless of the later debate on who achieved what, Australians and the government were very grateful for the Japanese naval assistance that had protected the convoy of Australian troops as far as Egypt.

Official Commonwealth attitudes to Japan in 1915 were very different from those of 1913. The preparations for the training squadron visit of 1915 reflected this change. The visits now involved detailed discussions about salutes to flags, military guards of honour, gun salutes for the functions and arrivals in the various ports. This was no quiet personal affair. The five-day programme for Melbourne included dinner at government house, calls on the Prime Minister, State Governor, Lord Mayor, Naval Board, a civic reception, a drive in the country for 40 officers, free passes to several picture theatres and free transport for all men in uniform, not just officers, although they were restricted to 25 at a time on trams and trains in peak hour. Melbourne was host to over 1,500 Japanese sailors.[40]

During the early part of World War One, Japan occupied the German Pacific territory in which it had been interested for two decades but from which it had been largely excluded by the restrictive trade and land lease practices of German authorities, particularly in New Guinea.[41] German territory included the Pelews, Marianas, Carolines and Marshall Islands, Yap, Angaur and German New Guinea north of Australian-controlled

Papua. Britain had suggested in August 1914 that Australia occupy Yap, Angaur and some of the Pelews. Australian forces quickly seized German New Guinea (which surrendered on 17 September 1914). On 15 October, the Germans surrendered all Pacific territory to Australia. But Japan was able to move more quickly than Australia to occupy the territory north of the equator including Angaur. Japan also landed on Yap on 7 October 1914, investigated a German wireless station and occupied the island. Australia intended to dispatch military forces to relieve Japan and secure the islands with Australian troops until the peace talks decided on the disposal of these territories. Lieutenant Commander Hardy of the expeditionary forces of November 1914 was instructed to collect information "which will be of use in considering the future defence of Australasia from attack, particularly from the Northward". During October 1914, Baron Kato had offered to hand these islands to Australia but public demonstrations in Tokyo altered the situation.

Britain's priorities did not support the Australian position.[42] Although the Admiralty in London believed that it was of pressing importance to relieve Japan of Yap, there was difficulty doing so when preparations for effective Australian expeditionary forces that would occupy islands, secure trade routes, police, protect and secure harbours for bases and wireless installations were only in the planning stages. In effect, Britain was more concerned about maximising Japan's ability to keep the sea-lanes open throughout the Pacific and around Australia, and to protect convoys of Australian contingents *en route* to war in Europe.[43] Given these priorities, Britain permitted Japan to remain in occupation of the islands north of the equator and at Yap. Australia was to secure Rabaul and New Guinea. Britain argued that it would be "discourteous" to remove Japan from the other islands especially since they had begun to install infrastructure such as wireless stations. By 24 November, the Australian expedition was cancelled.[44] In a cable on 3 December 1914, the Secretary of State for the Colonies wrote:

As Pelew Marianne Caroline and Marshall Islands are at present in military occupation by Japanese, who are at our request engaged in policing waters Northern Pacific, we consider it most convenient for strategic reasons to allow them to remain in occupation for the present, leaving whole question of future to be settled at the end of the war.[45]

The Japanese Consul-General in Sydney had played some part in this situation by seeking clarification as to whether Australia was proceeding to send military forces to take over the occupation from Japan. The Australian Prime Minister, Andrew Fisher, agreed with Britain that Australia should remain south of the equator. However, on 30 December 1914, the Navy argued that all German islands had been surrendered to Australia. The Rear Admiral of the Australian fleet wanted it on record that Japan's occupation was only temporary and that the Australian expeditionary force had been ready to "give effect to the surrender" but was stopped and ordered to confine the expedition to the south of the equator. A further hand note in the file, unsigned, on 31 December stated in a cable to the secretary for the colonies that the navy had a statement from Japan that it undertook to demand no possessions away from the mainland of China. The Commonwealth took seriously reports of Japanese activities in the occupied territory and particularly hindrances to trade experienced by firms such as Burns Philp. The Commonwealth wanted to place a trade representative at Jaluit to look after Australian interests during the war and sought assurances that Britain had entered no agreements with Japan about the final outcome of German possessions.[46]

Japan quickly moved to set up a central administration at Truk. The governors of the four island groups were commanders in the Japanese navy. In June 1918, Japan announced that a civilian administrator was to be appointed but as a subordinate to the Rear Admiral commanding the fleet. The administration remained military. On all four island groups Japan developed infrastructure, established agricultural and marine industries and improved and centralised trade. Japan also worked the mineral deposits of islands like Angaur, which was rich in phosphates.

The Australian navy gathered intelligence on Japan's intentions and received reports from Connyngham Greene in Tokyo about press reports in Japanese newspapers dealing with the issue of the South Seas. These stated that Japan had taken the islands with their good harbours and destroyed German military installations as an "act of self-preservation" to protect trade. They made the additional point that the occupation of islands was undertaken at Britain's request under the Alliance. In this Japanese views and British views concurred. Greene argued that if Japan had wanted the islands "for herself" she would have taken them in the first week of the war. Reports from the Japanese Diet stated that Japan had made no agreement with Britain for the future of the islands after the war. In regard to Australia, the Japanese papers stated that the Australian people were changing their attitudes to Japan and now recognised that "nobility of principle" had motivated Japan. They hailed the passing of all hostility between Australia and Japan, the expansion of commercial relations and Australia's gratitude for Japan's protection in wartime.

The Japanese occupation of German territory led the Australian Navy to review defence policy in preparation for peace talks. Australia's best defence was to strengthen Rabaul and keep New Guinea because these would make excellent future bases for any enemy. Indeed it was preferable for Australia to retain all German territory north and south of the equator in accordance with the original German surrender. In any event, Australia needed to establish northern bases over the next 10 years, the report argued. Brigadier-General Herbert Foster, Chief of General Staff, wrote in May 1917 that Japan's retention of Islands north of the equator was not a military threat but that if Rabaul was in Japanese hands then that could be. Other contributors to the report felt that if Japan gained control of islands north of the equator they could assemble a large force without Australia knowing before a counter force could be raised. The worst-case scenario was for Japan to obtain New Guinea, which would provide bases for all stores and ships' transports just 750 miles off the Queensland coast. Australia would then need to keep land forces in Queensland for the defence of Papua. "In enemy hands, German New Guinea would form a perpetual and very serious menace to Australia." With Germany no longer a threat the major potential strategic enemy, who was also currently an ally, was Japan.[47]

Japanese shipping companies quickly used the opportunities of World War One to expand. Although NYK had well-established lines into the Pacific including Australia and New Zealand, it almost monopolised the business with Australia for Japanese steamers, sharing it with the Eastern & Australian line, a British company. OSK planned to extend services to New Zealand in 1916. The *Japan Advertiser* 25 August 1916 reported that the war had opened up opportunities. OSK obtained contracts to ship timber to Japan from New Zealand. The first voyage took toys to New Zealand, which Germany had almost entirely provided before the war. It also carried general goods such as silk and cotton goods, matches, porcelain, glassware and lumber. The competition on the route was keen and NYK promptly commissioned eight new ships for the service. It attempted to block OSK from obtaining cargo contracts from Australian firms and was determined to drive them off. The trade with Australia in sulphur, timber, glassware, lacquer ware, cotton goods, wool and other goods was "brisk" and ships were "fairly well filled up" on both routes to and from Japan. In October 1916, Mitsui & Co. began operating a monthly service between Japan, Sydney and Melbourne. The ships were about 4,000 tons and did not call at any ports on the way. After the end of the war, Japanese shipping firms took steps to continue shipping services all over the Pacific and Indian oceans, a fact that did not impress British companies attempting to resume trade on the same runs.[48]

Japanese business expansion thrived and used Australia as a place from which Japanese people could explore the business opportunities to the north in the Islands. Southward expansion followed a definite pattern in the opinion of Australia Naval Intelligence in 1917. The word *nan'yō* had not been clearly defined but intelligence suggested it included all islands between the Straits Settlements (modern day Malaysia) and Australia. Japan had spread over the area encouraged by the material prosperity that the war had brought. The first activity was the acquisition or entry into industries in the area such as rubber at Johore, a sugar refinery at Java and quinine production. In Singapore, Japanese bought property including well-known residential sites. Japanese businessmen bought up land in the Martapura River area of South East Borneo (Dutch territory) from German owners opening up small estates in 1917. The Dutch in NEI were concerned that Britain might lose the war and that Japan might take over NEI or in any event gain control over the development of resources by 1918. The second stage was to establish steamship lanes and banks. Third, teachers, students and professors travelled to ascertain local educational conditions. In Singapore they planned to start Japanese schools for Chinese people. Naval Intelligence cited an extreme article from a Boston newspaper (unnamed) that Japan's economic and trade expansion was part one of a plan for a military empire throughout the Asia Pacific region. But what did Japan actually do after the war? [49]

The peace

With Britain's support at the Peace Conference, Japan took German territory in China and the Pacific north of the equator while Australia retained territory south of the equator. In 1918, the USA was concerned about Japanese business in China but Britain was not. World War One brought increased steel output for the Japanese navy but there was less demand by the 1920s accompanied by dwindling supplies of resources of necessary raw materials. In the 1920s, military theorists in Japan saw the USA and Russia as potential enemies. They believed there was a need to control and mobilise a large, economically-integrated territorial block. By 1922 with the

Washington Conference, naval limitations applied to each of the powers represented in the Pacific. This issued in a period of relative stability.[50]

With peace, large firms such as MBK expanded in China. Mitsui had opened the Shanghai branch to purchase raw cotton and lay the foundation for long-term business relations with China in 1877. China was Japan's first major market for textiles by 1897 when China took 94 per cent of Japan's yarn. By 1919–22, Japan introduced modern textile factories to China. Mitsui invested heavily in China between 1920 and 1924. The great success of Japanese textile mills meant that Japan out-competed and dominated other foreign investors especially from USA and UK. Japanese expatriates who ran the mills and efficient factories relied on Mitsui and other companies which by 1920 had over 40 years' experience of buying cotton and selling exports all over Asia and now the world. Japanese studied local conditions and met them. Their senior management had technical literacy, which could not be said of the British. Japan had also recognised that the key to successful control of trade was foreign language learning.[51]

The China experience developed the philosophy in companies like Okura, which expanded on a huge scale in the 1920s, that it was possible to succeed in the business sector in a country that enjoyed reasonable political stability and opportunity for further commercial expansion and investment. There was no need for the military perspective, which supported obtaining territory through political control or even by force.[52]

In Australia, the Japanese practice of information gathering continued. The Japanese Consulate-General quite frequently requested information from government departments. In 1917, it asked the Navy Office for a copy of 'How to join the Royal Australian Navy' which the department considered just part of the "insatiable thirst" Japanese showed for information.[53] Australian Naval Intelligence remarked that Japanese Officers were "very German" in their methods of collecting information and intelligence. This model involved collecting as much varied and seemingly irrelevant data as possible within a country for possible later use.

The results are generally good, as was seen formerly on the American coast, and the Naval and Military intelligence is supplemented by the commercial, financial, educational and other expert agents, who are constantly travelling.[54]

Articles collected by Australian Naval Intelligence and those sent from the British Embassy in Japan show that some Japanese directly considered what part Australia should play in the region. On 15 June 1918, an article entitled 'The present and future relations of Japan and Australia' by Takeyoshi Takahashi in the *Taiyo Magazine*, argued that Japan was best placed to participate in the exploitation of Australia's resources. Although he welcomed the threefold increase in trade with the war, Japan's proportion of imports was still only four per cent and exports five per cent. It was extremely difficult to develop increased intimacy between the two nations from trade alone. What the writer looked for was an interchange of ideas and participation in the exploitation of Australia's resources to establish the closest economic relations between the two states. Further articles by South Sea businessmen pointed out that Australians understood Japanese people much better because of the war. Japanese goods were welcomed and Japan's part in the war appreciated. The writer lamented the White Australia policy, which prevented the development of Australia's virgin land.

The truth is that if Australia were opened up by cheap labor it would be an easy matter for her to become richer than the United States within 50 years.[55]

To Japan, Australia was an underdeveloped resource and business paradise held back by a limiting immigration policy. To Australia, Japan was an ally that needed watching. Alongside the euphoria of the close relationship between Japan and Australia in wartime, which was still being celebrated in the late 1920s and early 1930s, the Australian Navy retained doubts about some of Japan's wartime assistance to Britain particularly the occupation of former German territories and retained its interest in watching the border area to the north.[56]

Conclusion

The period from federation to the 1920s saw Australia, with the assistance of the restrictive immigration provisions, gain time to develop a defence force while the Anglo-Japanese Alliance still held. Australian newspapers at the time, as Sissons demonstrated, did not show the fear of Japan evident in certain magazines and literary works. In effect, the tone and the experience were friendly and Japan's stated intentions towards Australia remarkably consistent. Although Japan occupied German-mandated territory north of the equator, good relations with Australia increased.

World War One's peace treaties provided opportunities for an expansion of Japanese business within Australia. The 1920s brought *zaibatsu* activity in earnest in Australia. Large firms engaged in co-operative arrangements with Australian firms to develop and export Australia's rich mineral and agricultural wealth. The 1920s also witnessed a boom time for Australian department stores full of Japanese goods. While this explosion of activity was in train, Australian defence forces concerned themselves with watching Japan's development of the mandated territories north of the equator. The White Australia policy was trusted to keep Japanese immigration controlled. The potential threat lay as it always had been argued to the north, not within Australia. This meant that Japan's stated aims of developing Australian resources in partnership were largely ignored. Japan had also hoped for greater international respect and formally recognised racial equality in a clause in the League of Nations Charter. Australian protests had helped defeat this move. What difference was this to make in the relationship in practical terms in the 1920s? How were Japan's expansion plans to play out in Australia? In what ways did the operation of the White Australia policy assist or hinder these aims? What evidence is there, particularly in the way that the Japanese company network developed in Australia from 1920s, for Japan's intentions towards Australia within the context of its policy of developing a Greater East Asian Co-prosperity Sphere?

Chapter 4   **Under the power of the**

zaibatsu, 1920s–40

In 1928, during a two-month visit of His Imperial Japanese Majesty's
Training Squadron to Australian ports, Vice-Admiral Kobayashi laid a
wreath at the new King's Park War Memorial in Perth and praised the
heroism of the Anzacs on the beaches of Gallipoli. Prominent Australian
speakers at the ceremony hailed Japan as the saviour of the nation in
World War One. On 29 June 1928, *The Age* editorial discussed the climate
of widespread mutual friendship after Japan's assistance in wartime and
Australia's aid after Japan's Great Kantoo Earthquake of 1923. Friendship,
it argued, outweighed the suspicion that had been evident during the
World War One peace talks of the early 1920s that had decided the fate
of former German territory and the strength of European, American and
Japanese navies.

> It is impossible to forget that Japan safeguarded our sons on their way to
> the Great War …. In recent years Japan has … suffered terrible natural
> catastrophes. Australia has been swift to render her assistance … which
> has won the gratitude of Japan's citizens. They are eager to cultivate our
> friendship, and in the nature of the Australian people there is nothing

churlish. The latter therefore may be trusted to use the imminent visit of the Japanese Naval Squadron as an occasion, not merely for offering to its officers and men those courtesies which one nation may be expected to offer to another, but to prove to them, by the spirit and the deeds of friendship, that the old evil days of suspicion and disdain have happily and, it is to be hoped, for ever gone.

The 1920s were also a time of frank Japanese statements about Australia's role. On 4 July 1928, *The Argus* quoted the Japanese Consul-General in Sydney, Mr I.M. Tokugawa.

There is no doubt that the Pacific Ocean is more and more becoming the centre of the world's activities …. Australia and Japan, bordering upon that ocean are destined to co-operate with each other and help to maintain the peace and order of that region. I am sure that visits like this, or rather the exchange of visits, will bring about closer relationships between the two nations. At the moment teams from the Japanese Squadron and Victoria are playing baseball. That game is something like our relations in the Pacific. Imagine Love and Peace as the pitcher and the Spirit of the Four-Power pact at Washington as the catcher. Place America at the first base, Australia at the second base, and Japan at the third. I do not think that a better baseball team could be found in the world. These nations … will be able to defend the Pacific Ocean, not necessarily in a warlike manner, but as baseball players would defend their bases.

To *The Age* in 1928, a future war with Japan, a friendly neighbour and a ready helper in emergency, was unthinkable.

We do well to welcome and honor her navy. That Japan would be at war for territory is unthinkable – she needs access to materials in China. Would Japan indulge in war and destroy trade?

Count Yoshu one of the visiting representatives of the Japanese House of Peers in Brisbane in 1923 had shared these views later expressed by *The Age*.

> Japan is anxious to be friendly towards Australia. ... We have plenty of outlets at present. South America is encouraging Japanese immigration. They are affording us special facilities. Then there are vast areas in Manchuria that call for more population, and in Korea there will also be an outlet. Of course, Japanese immigrants would come to Australia if they were invited, but you do not invite them and we say that is a matter for you to decide. We do not interfere with your affairs.

Japan had significant island groups to develop in the Pacific, obtained under mandate from the settlement of World War One. The treaty arrangements limiting naval strength also provided some stability to world affairs. According to Peattie, Japan was content with the naval limitation because it retained sufficient for defence against possible trouble with the USA. Although some lingering doubts had remained about Japanese intentions straight after the 1922 treaty was finalised, these lessened during the 1920s. Even the leftist workers' paper in Brisbane, the *Daily Standard*, commented on 6 August 1923 on the visit of representatives of the Japanese House of Peers and scientists.

> There is no reason at all why Australia should go to war with Japan, or why Japan should ever invade this country to impress its will on our affairs .... When we are told that Japan has designs on this country, what is meant is that Japanese capitalism thinks that commercial aggrandisement lies this way and the argument that we must prepare our defences against these "designs" is the pleas of British and Australian capitalism for advantage over Eastern traders. ... In the light of this, the utterances of members of the Japanese delegations to press interviewers on Saturday are like a refreshing draught. Both scientists and politicians

frankly stated that they were out for the development of friendly relations between Australia and Japan …

Certainly, Japan's Australian trade was substantial enough to protect and expand. With the boom times of the post-war era, new families arrived from 1918 to staff the new companies that opened in Sydney and to expand existing ones. Mr Sawada of Okura Trading, with his Australian wife Thelma, Ken Shimada of Nosawa & Co. with his Japanese wife and children and Sam Hirodo of Kanematsu (Australia), newly returned from Japan with his wife joined the growing population of merchants and company managers with families in Sydney's harbour-side suburbs. In rapid developments, the number of firms in Sydney doubled with large *zaibatsu* entering the existing market and branches and agencies springing up around the country. However, Australia did not notice the size and importance of the *zaibatsu* until Sir Herbert Gepp, the Consultant on Development to the Commonwealth Government in 1932 obtained a Canadian report on the operation of Japan's trade.

What were Japan's intentions for Australia during this time within the consideration of larger policy, even if on the periphery at the southern end of Japan's main operations in the Pacific and Asia? Was there any connection to the sites of the raids? Do the statements by Japan's visiting dignitaries and resident consular staff match what actually happened before 1937 or were they just products of the euphoria of the moment? Were Australians as enthusiastic and friendly as the papers suggest? If we take the statements at their face value, then trade, friendship and mutual understanding would be of paramount importance for the relationship in this era. This chapter examines trade networks and the following explores social networks.

Boom and bust

The 1920s boom in the development of department stores was mutually beneficial to Australian and Japanese concerns. The big stores, Anthony

Hordens, Mark Foys, Grace Bros, G. Myer & Co. and Farmer & Co., for example, played a dominant role in the social life of state capitals in the interwar years. Ladies embraced the experience and the large stores became places to socialise and to inspect first-hand the amazing array of goods available after the war. This growth was sustained in many cases by strong links with country customers through a large mail order service to farmers and housewives in the bush.

The number of Japanese companies increased in the 1920s paralleling the department store sector growth. Although Farmer & Co. bought from Mitsui as early as 1910 and David Jones and Hardy Bros. from 1911, by the 1920s in Sydney for example, Mitsui imported for a startling range of customers from small drapers and corner stores to very large department stores, filling orders for hundreds of Australian concerns throughout urban and rural Australia. The large stores were keen buyers of Japanese goods because they had faced supply difficulties during World War One and opened their own independent factories to produce clothing from Japanese yarn and cloth. This meant they could retail their locally manufactured house brands. Although they advocated buying British, they also bought Japanese goods from the extensive catalogues of silk and rayon materials, toys, crockery, electrical and other household goods.

Australian store managers and representatives maintained personal relations with Japanese firms. Hirokichi Nakamura told his daughters that he worked hard to fill even the smallest order for such valued customers, even ringing the larger companies like Mitsubishi or Nosawa to obtain everything that the customer required. For Mitsui in particular, no order was too small. It would supply local drapery stores with cloth, and grocers with small amounts of canned salmon and matches. In this way, it, like Nakamura, established long-term relations with customers to develop a customer loyalty base and make small profits on extensive transactions. Ken Shimada, Manager of Nosawa, personally took phone messages from small Australian firms for minor orders like tea sets and crockery samples such as that from Mr Arthur of Metropolitan Trading Co. Mr Macdonald of Nathans also rang wishing to see Mr Shimada about jugs on his return form New Zealand. Even through the Great Depression of the 1930s, Japanese provided a good and reliable supply of all types of goods, which was essential in order for big stores to broaden their range of products at affordable prices and help keep Australians in work. Patricia Malloch, my mother, was a clothes' designer and cutter at Foys. Like many Australian families in the Great Depression, her unemployed parents and siblings relied on her relatively secure retail position in Foys' home-brand factory for their survival during the depression.

During the boom time, independent operators like Kuwahata, Nakamura, Ide, Tashima, Muramatsu and others thrived alongside the burgeoning market share of *zaibatsu* firms. Over time small and large firms around the country made their own co-operative connections and carved out niche markets avoiding competition that would damage business. Although 95 per cent of Australia's Japan trade was in the hands of *zaibatsu* companies, small operators like Nakamura made a good living in importing or indenting but were reliant on good relationships with larger firms to survive. It is also clear that some of the larger firms looked to smaller ones for business.

Until 1918–20, small firms and a few *zaibatsu* dominated the Japanese company networks. From 1920 this changed. Table 2 shows that eight firms commenced trading from 1920 to 1922 and ceased trading between 1937 and 1941. Among these were Mitsubishi Trading Co, a branch office of MSK, and Japan Cotton, a branch office of Nihon Menkwa Kabushiki Kaisha, both *zaibatsu* firms. Although the firms had strong personal and business ties with Japanese parent companies, local incorporation gave them more independence than other Japanese-owned firms that were registered as branches of foreign companies. In states such as Queensland, local incorporation was necessary to enable a business owned by a foreign national to purchase land. These differences in state laws influenced the organisation of Japanese firms. Although many firms that established in the boom time survived the Great Depression, 12 firms trading in Sydney in 1922 had wound up by 1930. Of these, 11 traded for two years or less. In the 1930s, *zaibatsu* dominated the Australia–Japan trade but competition between firms did not seek to put small firms out of business but to incorporate them within the network. They had important links into Australian business and were members of the Japanese Chamber of Commerce (JCC) in Sydney. The story of three smaller firms show how important they were.

By the early 1920s, Hirokichi Nakamura was one of the largest independent owner-operators in Sydney. His annual turnover was £200,000. With his extensive contacts, larger firms from outside that city sought his advice and used him as their sole agent to secure orders. When Y. Tashima Co. of Townsville sought to expand to Sydney in 1922, they asked Nakamura's advice. As the sole agent for the firm and its related business C. Tashima & Co. Ltd, Kobe, he advised them to open in Melbourne where the competition was not so fierce. For this purpose, E. Tashima and T. Iwahashi were sent to Melbourne. Nakamura continued to act as Tashima's Sydney agent because his business was so large that it actually prevented Tashima from entering the Sydney market, although it did not prevent them trying.

From 1912 to 1922, Tashima grew with the total wages costs increasing from £243 per annum in 1912 to £678 per annum in 1920. The net profit in 1912 of £1,756 had grown to £5,902 in 1921. This exceeded the operations of Japanese firms in WA. Linked by family ties, Y. Tashima Co. Queensland entered a joint purchasing agreement with C. Tashima & Co. Ltd, Kobe, to act as sole buying agent in Australia for Australian goods with Kobe acting as sole agent for the purchase of goods in Japan. During these years, probably commencing in 1916, Tsurujiro Araki managed the company in Australia. He was reputed to be the nephew of Y. Tashima. The joint purchasing arrangement was renewed in 1924 and 1926.

Table 2: Japanese firms start up and folding dates, Sydney post-1920

Firm	Start	End
Mitsubishi 1920		1941
Osaka 1920		
Murai 1920–21		
Sakakura 1921		
Nippon Kaisha 1920 bought by Kuwahata		
Omiya 1920		
Sowa 1920		
Nosawa 1920		1941
Yano & Joko 1920		1941
Kiku Gumi 1920		1941
Koiso 1920		1940
Japan Cotton 1921		1941
Kiyonaga 1922–24		
Morimura 1922		
Kotoh 1925	1930	
Matsumoto 1926	1928	
Hobokondo 1926		
Iwahashi 1926–29		
Yamashita 1929		1940
Tashima 1899 / Araki 1929		1941
Kobokondo 1929	1936	
Yusen 1937		
Itoh 1930s		1940
Iwai c. 1930		1941

137

However, in 1922, as part of the expansion, Tashima proposed changes to the agency arrangement with Nakamura, which involved accepting a clerk and a certain amount of control by Kobe over his business. On 13 April 1922, Tashima wrote:

> If you want business direct with C. Tashima & Co. Ltd. Kobe, we think they will not object to sending you a clerk to assist you, remuneration to be paid from the Kobe office whether there control of the business be in our hands. We understand it is inconvenient for us to control business in your town as now the market is full of competitors, but if it is under our control it will be convenient for you financially.[9]

Nakamura was incensed at such an offer and replied on 23 April 1922.

> The above seemed to me as if you wished me to surrender my business to you, unconditionally, which I thought most unreasonable, … Certainly for the past six months you were good enough to trust me and let me handle your goods to the extent of several thousand pounds … but my friendly relationships with some customers and my business connections in this city, is not the work of only a few months, but the result of my hard work of a long period of 15 years.[10]

Tashima replied that he would respect Nakamura's position and keep the current arrangement. Nakamura remained a Sydney agent for three years after Tashima was incorporated into Araki & Co. in 1928.

Nakamura's relationship with Nosawa & Co., a *zaibatsu*, gave his business some stability as he regularly placed orders with them for his local Australian customers. He changed his name to Austral-Nippon Indent Co. under new incorporation laws in NSW in 1937. His orders for September and October 1938 amounted to £124-12-10d. Goods included 700 gross yards (91,000 metres) of artificial silk, 93½ dozen georgette handkerchiefs, shoelaces, cultured pearl necklaces, brushes and pyjama cords. In 1939, the largest bulk item that Nakamura imported was elastic totalling 7,459 gross yards (172,864 metres) valued at £1,179-6-4d. Tie material valued at £978, cotton jean material, balloons, galvanised wire netting, caustic potash and dice were among other bulk orders.[11]

In 1939, rising prices, such as a 26 per cent rise in georgette crepe handkerchiefs and steel buttons, caused problems. Nosawa wrote on 30 September 1939 that Australia expected Japanese goods to be cheap but:

> … at present cottons market here is in upheaval reflecting the so unsettled world political situation. We are afraid therefore that we may have difficulty in immediately satisfying you with the prices we quote until your market admits higher prices quoted from Japan.[12]

In 1940, Nakamura's trade volume reduced dramatically by 25 per cent, most noticeably in elastic orders. In 1939, Nakamura placed 42 orders averaging 177 gross yards each but in 1940, he placed only 17 orders averaging 301 gross yards, a significant loss of small orders.[13]

Times had become tough in the early 1930s when the Great Depression started to bite and unemployment rose to over 25 per cent. Just as department stores relied on trying to sell larger ranges of cheaper goods, small and large Japanese firms diversified and Nakamura and Kuwahata & Sons clashed in the effort to survive. Kuwahata died on a health trip to Japan *c.* 1930–31. His Australian-born sons Thomas and Frederick, who spoke no Japanese, inherited the business, which included the Guildford farm, nursery, plant and general importing and indenting arms. By 1930, its business turnover was £12,000 per annum and imports valued at £2,000. The nursery was valued at £4,000 from which the brothers derived an income of £1,000 per annum.[14] Initially in the 1930s, trouble started when Nakamura attempted to increase his importing business.

His daughters reported that at this time they were becoming so poor that they used the silk samples to make their clothes. This increased importing share led Kuwahata's sons to accuse Nakamura of profiting from their father's death. Further trouble ensued with Kuwahata when Nakamura entered providoring.

Nakamura's daughters said that he entered providoring reluctantly. He was ill-suited to the work and felt it was a downward social step. In practice the work involved ringing shipping companies to establish the times that the ships arrived in port then beating the competing providores to meet the ship. The first providore on board generally got the order. Nakamura hired an Australian to assist him and together they boarded a small boat to race to the incoming ships as they entered Sydney harbour. The ships were still moving when they met them and boarding a ship in such circumstances involved risk and a certain amount of skill. Nakamura's assistant James Pratt would first jump on to whatever boarding gear the ship provided and then drag the middle-aged Nakamura after him. When they obtained an order from the Chief Steward they would return to their launch, sail back to shore and rush to the market to buy what the ship required and meet it at its berth. Nakamura also entertained crew off ships at his home in Mosman, a practice Kuwahata had engaged in since the 1890s. However, Kuwahata, having Australian-born owners survived the freeze of Japanese assets in 1941 by diversifying the business into wholesale fish marketing after trade with Japan ceased. The firm continued operations during the war and neither of the brothers was interned. Nakamura's business, however, closed in September 1941 and he was interned in December.[15]

Henry Ide, the other extremely successful merchant who had opened a silk importing business in the 1890s, experienced difficulty in the 1930s. Like Nakamura, business trips to Japan to keep in touch with silk and other manufacturers helped him maintain a share of the Japanese wholesale market. Ide was so well respected that he continued to be invited, along with the principals of *zaibatsu* firms, to regular small intimate dinners with the Japanese Consul-General. He owned a brick house at 18 Dalkeith Road, Northbridge, three acres of land at Wentworth Falls, 80 acres of land at Sussex Inlet and had a rented house at 92 Sailors Bay Road. However the serious trade dispute with Japan in 1936 (when Australia diverted more of its trade to Britain because of the size of trade with Japan) affected Ide. He entered into partnership with Harry Wiltshire to keep the firm operational.[16]

In Queensland, Tashima & Co. of Townsville grew despite its inability to enter the Sydney market in 1922 but merged with Araki & Co., a *zaibatsu* owned by relatives and also managed by Tsurujiro Araki, Tashima's nephew. Araki & Co. was incorporated in NSW in 1922 and purchased the Australian assets of Tashima, incorporating the firm in Queensland as Araki & Co. He became the sole agent in Australia for C. Tashima of Kobe. On 1 July 1929, Araki registered as a foreign company and in 1932 incorporated in NSW as a private limited liability stock company with £50,000 fully subscribed capital, secured by a loan from the Yokohama Specie Bank, which also had branches in Australia, with all the shares held by him and his family. In the financial year of 1931–32, Araki ranked eighth in sales in the Australia–Japan trade with two per cent of the total market. By the financial year of 1940–41, the company ranked fifth with a market share of 6.7 per cent.[17] Its trade was suspended in 1941.

The boom of the 1920s extended beyond NSW and Queensland. Sydney's medium-sized firms like T. Nakano & Co. and *zaibatsu* firms such as Mitsui & Co. had travelled to Melbourne in the 1910s. After World War One, further Sydney *zaibatsu* moved into Melbourne for example, Araki & Co., Z. Horikoshi & Co., Mitsubishi, Okura Trading and F. Kanematsu (Australia) Pty Ltd. Melbourne branches had a steady stream of managers and staff with families through until 1941. Z. Horikoshi & Co. first opened with two staff. Its longest serving

Melbourne manager was T. Yanase with his wife and children from 1922 to 1933. Yanase left to start his own business in Melbourne at the worst part of the Great Depression but did not succeed.[18]

Apart from Tashima, which traded into NT, Nakashiba Bros of Cairns[19] began to move to Darwin after 1924 when Bunsuke returned to Japan. John opened the NAD Co., a store and agency business for pearling interests. Nakashiba joined other Japanese in Darwin including Yasukichi Murakami who owned a photographic shop, Yamamoto, store owner of Cavenagh Street and H. Higashi, a general store keeper and ships' chandler who bought the store when a Chinese merchant died in 1925. Japanese stores sold imported Japanese goods, either obtained through Mitsui and other trading houses in Sydney and Y. Tashima & Co. in Townsville or from concerns in Singapore or NEI. They also sold general supplies, tobacco and medicines. As a child, one interviewee spoke of the wonder of these stores full of toys, kewpie dolls and bright things, which other stores did not have. She loved to browse under the watchful eye of the owner.[20] Certainly the catalogues of Japanese toys sold by the trading companies display a very different range of goods from those generally available in Australian stores.

The NAD store was also an important contact point for Australians and Japanese visitors, including masters of Japanese luggers, to the port. It acted as an Australian commissioning, shipping, customs and forwarding agent for Japanese firms such as the large Kaigai Kōgyō Kaisha (International Development Company in the South Seas) and other companies based in NEI, Dobo, Celebes and Japan. But it also served the local community by selling general drapery and imported fancy goods, tobacco, medicines, ironmongery, tools for agriculture, carpentry, engineering and non-perishable grocery items and toiletries.[21]

Darwin was where west and east coast operations met. Through the 1920s–1930s, Jiro Muramatsu, Master Pearler and businessman of

Cossack, expanded his fleet along the northern sea-lane to Darwin and hired E. McKay as a manager to oversee the Darwin operations. By 1935, his store business orders reached £1,214, placed with Fremantle merchants including Bateman Ltd ships chandlers and general importers and D. & J. Fowler, grocers. In Singapore, he traded with Guthrie & Co. and Otto Gerdau. His banking was not with the Yokohama Specie Bank of Sydney which most Japanese firms used but with the Union Bank of Australia in Broome. He also owned six properties in Cossack. In November 1941, Apart from his pearling fleet of approximately 12 boats, his holdings in Darwin were worth in excess of £11,000. He owned shares in paper mills to the value of about £700. His credit notes in New York exceeded £25,000.[22]

All pearling companies working across Australia's north required provisions and many Japanese businesses from Cossack to Cairns assisted with supplies. Local business benefited from the increased shipping that pearling brought to towns. Businesses in Perth and Sydney benefited from supplying goods needed along the north. The import-export trade to NEI and Singapore (where *zaibatsu* had extensive operations) flourished. Trade with Japan increased the interaction and preserved the health of the trading network for Australians and Japanese. Mergers, agency arrangements and incorporations in Sydney and Queensland resulted from this business growth. However, in WA changes to the administration of the White Australia policy after 1924 increased the size and spread of Japanese business in that state. From 1924, the Department of Home and Territories wished to restrict the number of merchants entering Australia who were importing only small amounts, a decision that was made after the completion of treaties involving Japan after World War One when diplomatic relations normalised. From that time, firms had to achieve an import total of £1,000 or more for each financial year if they wished to extend the stays of Japanese merchants in their employ. If this decision was intended to reduce the number of Japanese merchants in Australia, it was a bad miscalculation.[23] The decision resulted in the formation of the biggest Japanese enterprise in the west, with extensive connections through SEA, Japan and the Pacific, some of which had particular interest in mineral developments and consolidation of Japanese concerns in and beyond the mandated territories.

When the founder of Tokumaru Bros died in WA and his wife in Japan in 1923, Umeda, the manager, was charged with winding up the firm. Its turnover was £4,959, with 40 per cent of its trade in importing and 60 per cent in local goods. Imports from Japan totalled only £382. Umeda's request for extension was granted in December 1924 in recognition of the family circumstances and because he was respected as the Honorary President of the Japanese Society at Broome. But the Secretary of the Department, F.J. Quinlan, warned that "It is desirable that the firm should endeavour to increase its trade between Australia and Japan during the extended period".[24]

Umeda expected to leave Australia on 29 October 1925. However, the possibility of a merger with local firms in similar situations arose. For example, Miki Tsutsumi, who joined the firm of I. Joe & Co. in 1919 as an assistant for the store, was the manager from 1922. By 1924, the firm's turnover was £3,013 with imports valued at only £571. This was a substantial decrease from the 1923 level of £4,000 turnover and £1,050 imports in the first five months of the year alone, an amount which had been sufficient for the Department to permit his wife, Masu, to enter the country. But the extension of stay was in doubt in 1924 for him, his wife and store hand, Hauji Mizutani, because of the decrease in imports. A letter from Quinlan to the Consul-General on 16 December 1924 stated that because of the decreased import trade, Tsutsumi and his assistants could not be granted further extension.

Because of these difficulties with CEDT extensions the firms Tokumaru Bros, I. Joe & Co., Fukumatsu Kitano & Co., Toyosaburo Mise & Co. and Kaichiro Sakai & Co., which had all opened before

federation, decided to merge. Acting Consul-General S. Yamasaki applied
for six months for Umeda to complete the merger. The new firm was
named Tonan Shokai or The Southern Trading Co. and commenced as a
partnership from 1 January 1926 in the name of Buntaro Tokumaru who
was considered by Australian authorities to be a very capable businessman
"of the better class". The merger assisted all involved to remain in
Australia. An increase in business brought permission for another store
hand, Shinichi Nobuichi Shima, who arrived on 26 August 1927 from
Singapore for a two-year stay.[25] Some of the stores of partners were sold
and the business was conducted at the premises of K. Sakai and T. Mise
with a capitalisation of £10,000 mostly consisting of stock. The firm
intended to import and to export to Java. Umeda became its director and
Miki Tsutsumi its manager. Both were granted CEDTs to remain because
"Both are favourably recognised by the European population of the town."
Umeda was believed to have no direct interest in the business, a fact later
revealed as not strictly correct. He left for Japan on 14 May 1926 but
visited Australia each year for a month or two for business purposes, for
example, in November 1927 and again in September 1928 to investigate
iron ore deposits at Yampi Sound as part of Japan's search for mineral
resources needed to fuel its rapid industrial expansion, an episode which
is considered in later chapters. He continued his association and work for
the Tokyo Overseas Industries and Emigration Co. Ltd and the powerful
International Development Co., which had been established in China
early in the twentieth century.[26]

By 1929, the firm's imports were valued at £1,509 with a turnover
of £14,435, which grew by approximately 25 per cent in 1930. Further
expansion in the 1930s led Tsutsumi to apply for assistants to replace two
local Japanese people who had left the firm. At this point the Department
had trouble deciding whether the firm's situation was good enough to
admit an assistant on merchant passport or a substitute worker under
bond. The latter course was chosen. The correspondence arguing for

permission to replace the new workers provides a picture of the firm's operations at that time. Letters from the Consul-General and references from Australian firms such as Streeter & Male Ltd Broome, Burns Philp & Co. of Fremantle, D. & J. Fowler of Fremantle and London, Harris, Scarfe & Sandovers Ltd, Perth, London, Fremantle and Kalgoorlie argued that Tonan Shokai had the two largest stores in Broome and could not carry on with a staff of three where they had previously employed five. The Sub Collector of Customs at Broome supported the applications because his imports were the second largest at Broome. He argued that as manager Tsutsumi had to visit the commercial travellers in their sample rooms for orders, prepare and attend to all customs business in the preparation of entries and examination of goods at the Customs House and Goods Shed.[27]

Tsutsumi, as the manager of an important firm had prominent roles in the town. Like Umeda, he was a leading member of Japanese Society in Broome. He became Honorary President of the Japanese Society in 1926 and its Secretary in 1928. He was also the agent for the Nihon Shinju Co. of Tokyo and the International Development Company in the South Seas, the influential Kaigai Kōgyō Kabushiki Kaisha (KKKK), which looked after indents in the pearling industry. By 1929, he acted as the local agent for the International Development Co. Ltd Singapore.[28]

All of the overseas Japanese firms with which the managers and directors of Tonan Shokai had direct dealings enjoyed wide influence and extensive trade operations in the South Seas. The businesses that merged to form the company were viable before the merger despite the downturn in trade, and the partners in many cases guaranteed residence in Australia as pre-federation arrivals. Changes to the administration of the White Australia legislation in favouring larger firms created a situation that encouraged greater interaction with large overseas development companies and gave Umeda as the new director reason for repeated regular trips to Australia to investigate mineral deposits in Australia. The approval of these businessmen by the department to also act as president or secretary of the Japanese Society in Broome, Western Australia's most influential, also tied Australian pearling arrangements to Japanese business beyond Australia by the 1930s.

Before the 1930s, Australian pearlers had largely obtained their Japanese workforce from Singapore and Hong Kong. Unrest in the industry in the west in the 1920s flared from time to time when workers from Timor accused the Japanese of harsh treatment on boats. The Japanese maintained that the Timorese did not work hard enough. This situation led to a serious riot in 1921, which required 290 armed, special constables to control. Groups of Japanese and Timorese (numbering over 1,000 men) armed with sticks and anything they could find conducted rolling brawls in the town, which led to a call from the locals for a gunboat. As a result the Pearlers Association ruled that no boat should in future contain more than 50 per cent of any one nationality. But despite this limitation, the Japanese Society at Broome exerted great influence on who could work in Australia. In the 1930s, Japan placed greater restrictions on who could work overseas on indenture. In Australia it was sufficient for pearlers to apply to the department for a permit to hire Japanese but it became difficult to obtain them. In effect, the Japanese minister restricted the issuing of permits to six known Australian pearlers including Streeter & Male, and A.C. Gregory, who had to apply through KKKK, the large Japanese firm that dominated in the mandated territories. For a worker to stay on in Australia or return to Australia, the agent of the company inspected the books of the Japanese Society to see if the person was in good standing and had paid his subscription. If anything was amiss, the man was not recommended by the local Society or agent which meant that the Society had the power to exclude individual Japanese from working in Australia if it wished. In the 1930s, the agent of KKKK at that time was Miki Tsutsumi, manager of Tonan Shokai.[29]

The president and secretary of the Japanese Society at Broome were critical to the relations between governments, companies and local pearlers and masters. At any one time such officers were required to keep the immigration and employment documents of hundreds of Japanese people current and in order in close association with the Japanese Consul-General in Sydney and the Department in Canberra. The importance of the choice of President in particular is evident in the correspondence on an appointment in 1928 when Haro Higashi retired. Consul-General Tokugawa requested that a competent person come from Japan to take the position. At first, despite the support of the Sub Collector of Customs at Broome, the Department refused the request arguing that a local person must be available to take the position. Tokugawa wrote unofficially to the department arguing that he needed an educated man capable of handling hundreds of pearlers. A.R. Peters of the department replied to Tokugawa that in view of his personal and unofficial letter, it was reasonable and diplomatic to grant the request. Such unofficial relationships, as we have seen, often cleared impasses in bureaucratic problems presented by immigration law under the white Australia legislation. As a result, Tsuyoshi Kono was suggested and was due to arrive on 20 May 1928. However when he landed, his name was different, Tsuyoshi Shiromoto. This man had an interesting history like many Japanese in Broome. He was employed as a boy in Singapore by Kawano who adopted him and gave him the name Kono. However, the relationship with the family soured when Kawano died and his relatives disputed the will leaving Tsuyoshi with nothing. As a result he changed his name back to his original family name. Shiromoto served in the position until March 1931 when Toshio Fukuda arrived from Singapore to replace him, remaining until June 1941. Fukuda left Derby for Singapore in June 1941 with his Australian wife Rita Mitsue and their two children Kenneth aged three and David aged seven months. He was not replaced owing to the uncertain international situation at the time.

In effect, White Australia regulations were very favourable to *zaibatsu* growth in the 1920s and 1930s which was increasingly linked to worldwide networks. By 1931, the Consul-General in Sydney was only required to provide a list of merchants who were extending stays and of those who were leaving to the Department, placing some of the administration for immigration regulations in the hands of consular staff. The involvement of the Consul-General in administering the entry and travel of merchants showed the degree of trust that was established between Japanese authorities and the Commonwealth government. Such arrangements placed the administration of policies on a case-by-case basis, which made it easier to change policy in response to circumstances. But the size of the company network and its integral relations with Australian business could not have been foreseen in 1904 when the provisions were passed into law. The alterations to qualifications for extension in 1924 that were designed to restrict the numbers of small importers actually led to consolidation of larger firms, which became more influential and better connected overseas. In 1936–37, as later chapters examine, this situation was a factor in the Trade Diversion Dispute with Japan over the size of Australia's trade with that country compared with Britain.

The heart of the company network

The *zaibatsu* constituted the majority of Japanese business activities in Australia from after World War One and was worth millions of pounds per annum. However, small firms benefited from their presence and paved the way for their development and success. Australian firms benefited greatly from the availability of goods and the reliability of supply. Overall the growth in trade with Japan was beneficial. The special provisions of the Immigration Restriction Acts and the nature of their administration recognised this factor. Certainly the ease with which merchants could obtain extensions of stay, which led to decades of residence often with their families, provided a stable management that enabled firms to build good relationships with Australian customers. Knowing the person with whom one was doing business was an important factor in building trust and reliability in any organisation at that time.

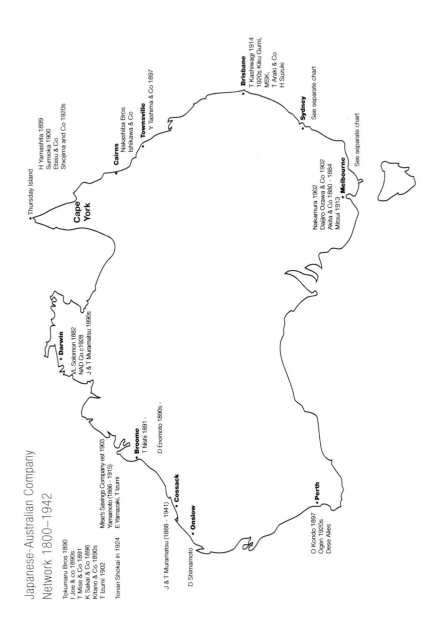

Japanese-Australian Company
Network 1800–1942

Tokumaru Bros 1890
I Joe & co 1890s
T Mise & Co 1891
K Sakai & Co 1896
Kitano & Co 1890s
T Izumi 1902

Tonan Shokai in 1924

Mise's Savings Company est 1903
Yamamoto (1866 - 1915)
E Yamazaki, T Izumi

J & T Muramatsu (1888 - 1941)

D Shimamoto

• Thursday Island

H Yamashita 1899
Sumioka 1900
Ebisu & Co
Shiojima and Co 1920s

Cape
York

• Cairns
Nakashiba Bros
Ishikawa & Co

• Townsville
Y Tashima & Co 1897

• Brisbane
T Kashiwagi 1914
1920s Kiku Gumi,
MSK,
T Araki & Co
H Suzuki

• Sydney
See separate chart

See separate chart

Nakamura 1902
Dajjiro Ozawa & Co 1902
Akita & Co 1880 - 1884
Mitsui 1913

• Melbourne

• Darwin
VL Solomon 1882
NAD Co c1928
J & T Muramatsu 1890s

• Broome
T Nishi 1891 -
D Enomoto 1890s -

• Cossack

• Onslow

• Perth
O Kondo 1897
Ogen 1920s
Dese Alies

The boom of the 1920s led to 95 per cent of Australia's trade with Japan passing one way or another into *zaibatsu* hands by the early 1930s. For example, by the financial year of 1931–32, Kanematsu's share of the trade with Japan was 29.1 per cent of sales, second only to Mitsubishi. Purcell ranked Nosawa eleventh at 0.67 per cent in volume of trade in the late 1930s. Mitsui ranked first with 30.8 per cent, Kanematsu second with 15.3 per cent and Araki with 5.9 per cent. By the financial year of 1940–41, its share had been reduced to 8 per cent and fourth ranking among Japanese firms in Sydney, surpassed by Mitsui and Mitsubishi. These firms' turnover ranged from £1–4 million annually in the early 1930s. Australia showed growing resentment of this success but had failed to take advantage of the opportunities early in the century. As Gepp maintained, the Australian attitude that "anything will do for the East" harmed merchants' chances of success in the trade. In 1932, Gepp called once again on Australians to seize the opportunities. This they failed to do and it is this failure that helped to cement the position of the *zaibatsu* in Australia rather than any plan by the Japanese to infiltrate the country. However, the story of the development of two major *zaibatsu* in Australia, Mitsui and Mitsubishi, their different strategies and rivalry show how integrated they became into the life and business of Australians.

Mitsui was the earliest true *zaibatsu* to open in Australia in 1901. During the 1920s, it changed significantly. Its staff was very stable and comprised a mixture of men who had arrived early in the century and married Australians and men who had arrived from Japan alone or with wives and families. Australians continued to form a large part of the staff. From 1930 to 1939, there were 25 men continuously working for the company in Melbourne most with families, and 36 in Sydney for that period. By 1922, a differential occurred within the staff. Australian salaries were listed separately from Japanese salaries, and although the firm retained some local and Australian character it was becoming a bigger player in a global market. In the 1930s, the accounts are very complex using codes instead of word entry in all departments. It was no longer one player among many but the most aggressive player in Australia. Purcell estimated that in 1932–33 it had 102 employees in Australia of whom 76 were Australians; by 1935–36 this had risen to 110 with a wages bill of £38,000. From 1931 to 1940, when Mitsui had a mean sales turnover of £4 million, Mitsui had 33.7 per cent of the trade in 1931–32 with the lowest point of 23.4 per cent in 1938–39 recovering to 30.8 per cent in 1939–40. Mitsui's basic structure meant that each branch had to make a profit and was responsible for its own decisions. That gave it an advantage in the Australian market.

Mitsui had an active research department. It purchased the *Commonwealth Year Book*, subscribed to most Australian daily papers, which were cut up according to topics and pasted in books, trade related publications such as *Dalgety's Review, Shipmans' Stock Directory* and *The Australian Naval and Military Annual.* Copies of *Australia Today* and many other books were purchased for the Training Squadron. Maps were high on the agenda including those of Newcastle, Maitland, Queensland, the coalfields and the *Marine and Harbour Department Handbook* for Adelaide. This type of research culminated in the 1940s in a boom of book writing about Australia, often authored by trading company managers on their return to Japan.

Mitsui's rival, Mitsubishi was ranked third after Kanematsu with £2.4 million mean sales turnover. Mitsubishi was second in percentage trade but had only 17 per cent of the trade in 1931–32, with its lowest point of 11.7 per cent in 1937–38 recovering only slightly in 1938–39 to 14 per cent. Australian Government Defence contracts in 1940 may have assisted its recovery to 22.6 per cent in 1940–41 before the freezing of Japan's Sterling assets in Australia in July 1941. Mitsubishi entered the Australian market when Mitsui and Kanematsu were already dominant along side a great network of smaller firms. Mitsubishi did not do as well in the Australian field because it gave precedence to a Japanese format of organisation for local and international trade, which actually held it back.

Trading and pearling centres 1930s - 1940s

Mitsui Bussan Kaisha Offices
Hong Kong   Batavia
Singapore   Medan
Surabaya   Bangkok
Davao   Melbourne
Iloilo   Sydney
Cebu   Manila
Semarang

Misubishi Shoji Kaisha Offices
Manila
Hong Kong
Singapore
Surabaya
Melbourne
Sydney

NKK and NKKK Offices
Aru   Geelvink Bay   Manus   Rabaul   Menando   Palau   Davao

The worldwide company operated particularly in Japanese-mandated or occupied territories and was engaged in development in mining, shipbuilding, chemical and electrical engineering and aircraft construction. It built the large passenger and cargo vessels at the Nagasaki shipyards that travelled to Australia on a regular basis after 1896. In 1937, the company had 15 branches in Japan with more in occupied territory, 13 on the Chinese mainland and others at Hong Kong, Manila, Singapore, Bangkok, Calcutta, Bombay, Surabaya, Johannesburg, Alexandria, Beirut, Baghdad, London, New York, San Francisco, Chile, Berlin, Paris, Lyon, Casablanca and Teheran.

Mitsubishi was a highly structured multi-national company. Its Melbourne and Sydney branches were part of Mitsubishi Shoji Kaisha or Mitsubishi Trading Co. Ltd, which operated as part of a worldwide network and cannot be separated readily from that organisation. This particular company formed during a reorganisation of Mitsubishi in 1917 and dates from April 1918 under the MSK name although its operations date back to 1881. The trading company was one of a number of Mitsubishi enterprises, which included Mitsubishi Heavy Industries Ltd, Mitsubishi Warehouse Co. Ltd, Mitsubishi Mining Co. Ltd, The Mitsubishi Bank Ltd, Mitsubishi Electrical Manufacturing Co. Ltd, Mitsubishi Trust Co. Ltd and Mitsubishi Estate Co. Ltd. Sydney branch was the head of the firm in Australia with primary responsibility for Melbourne, Brisbane and New Zealand. Melbourne branch had market responsibility for Tasmania, Adelaide, Perth, Albury and Geelong but needed clearance from Sydney on decisions. Within Australia Mitsubishi's departmental system included metals, machinery, produce (wheat and wool), marine produce (fish canning, salmon and pilchards) and silk and general merchandise. Australian branches imported cotton and yarn through the Bombay branch, jute sacks from Calcutta branch, tea from Shanghai branch, paper, aluminium sheeting and rayon from Osaka branch, timber from Otaru NZ branch, and silk from Tokyo branch. In return they exported wheat to Shanghai, calcium carbonate and zinc to Calcutta, cobalt oxide to Tokyo and wool. It had enormous contracts with BHP Pty Ltd in the late 1930s.

Although the Sydney branch made some decisions within Australia it was required to refer decisions to Tokyo or other Japan based branches that had responsibility for particular products. This was a terminus system, which also determined where products were imported to and exported from. For example, Osaka was the terminus for wool for Australian, South African and Buenos Aires suppliers. Osaka was responsible for aluminium sheeting, rayon and paper. Mitsubishi used its own branches overseas to obtain products. This system of operation meant that unlike Mitsui, Mitsubishi's local branches could not make decisions but needed to refer to Tokyo. One anxious telegram on 14 August 1940 to Tokyo stated.

> you have never replied … your silence may be that you have no requirement at all for Australian cadmium. Nevertheless we greatly regret your lazy and negligent way because unless you reply we cannot tell our supplier anything definite but can only tell them either something vague, or that you have not replied yet. This lack of co-operation on your side will cause some difficulty in our endeavour to maintain the confidence and good will of the supplier. This is especially important … where such an influential firm in Australia is the supplier.'

While Mitsui worked on small profit margins on large ranges of goods, Mitsubishi had trouble convincing Tokyo that it was important to do the same in the Australian market otherwise "all our painstaking efforts will be entirely in vain".

Unlike other Japanese firms such as Nosawa and Mitsui, Mitsubishi was fussy about whom they used as agents or even with whom they did business. They required a full research report in extraordinary detail on an area or firm before agreeing to any business. People like the very successful Hirokichi Nakamura who had only one phone and a couple of staff were quite wrongly deemed people of "scanty means". This was the big difference between Mitsubishi and Mitsui who dealt with anyone who passed a Dunn & Co. credit check. Another major difference between the two companies was that Mitsui was prepared to import and sell anything and find a market for any Australian product. Mitsubishi was fussy about which goods it would handle. That went against the entire culture of Australian business.

Wool and minerals

Wool formed a major part of *zaibatsu* exports from Australia. The wool buyers and managers travelled on a regular basis to the wool auctions in Brisbane, Albury and Geelong. Mitsubishi's V.C. Hemery, G. Munro, R. Lewis and Mr Toi travelled by car to wool stores, markets and sales in 1933. Mitsubishi entered late into the wool trade in Australia, when we consider that Kanematsu had been operating since 1890, Nosawa since 1918, and Mitsui investigating Victorian wool from 1913 after entering the NSW trade shortly after federation. Before 1919, 99 per cent of wool exported to Japan came from NSW. Mitsui was instrumental in substantially increasing Victoria's wool trade and exported 58 per cent of Victorian wool to Japan by 1922. NSW had a predominance of fine merino wool for sale but Mitsui recognised the potential for other wool types and exploited that. By diversifying into different areas of the wool trade, each company was able to grow.

The most interesting wool records among Sydney Japanese firms are those of Nosawa & Co., managed by Ken Shimada, who lived in Rose Bay with his Japanese wife and four Australian-born children. The firm's records contain correspondence with Australian sheep station owners and large firms responsible for organising sheep and wool marketing. They also contain photographs relating to wool buying trips into rural NSW and Victoria in the 1930s. Shimada was involved in organising tours for Japanese officials to view sheep for Hokkaido. His firm was officially appointed by the Japanese government to act as agents to purchase rams and ewes for stud purposes and pioneered the live sheep export trade to Japan from Australia and New Zealand. The volume of the trade was quite substantial, for example, between July and November 1940, 20,400 head were shipped from Australia and a further 1,000 head from New Zealand.

Japanese *zaibatsu* were extremely interested in Australia's mineral resources from the 1910s. Yampi Sound, an area very rich in iron ore, is situated 150 miles north east of Broome, WA. Mining leases had been held in the area since 1900. Nobutaro Umeda, who although Director of Tonan Shokai in Broome and lived mostly in Japan, showed great interest in Yampi Sound, which was reported in the *West Australian*, 3 July 1928. According to the paper, Umeda became interested in NKKK's proposal for Yampi Sound when he returned to Japan in 1926. The Australians holding the concessions to the mineral deposits at the time were approached and Mr John Thompson went as a representative to Japan for further negotiations. Umeda said that he knew that the Australians badly wanted to develop the north and he thought that there would be a good chance for the Japanese to be involved in the Yampi Sound development. Both countries would receive the benefits and the work would help to establish better relations. Japan wanted iron ore badly but, Umeda maintained, Japan did not wish to interfere with or run counter to any of Australia's established policies. Japan would only be buying raw material (not working the mining operation) and was prepared to take 800,000 tons per annum. Japan currently imported 700,000 tons from Malaya and 1.5 million tons from Manchuria but could use all it could get from Australia. The *West Australian* reported on 19 July 1928 that Umeda expected work to commence within 12 months. The issue of Japan's involvement in Australia's mineral development became a national security concern in the late 1930s when Japan increased military output and was at war with China. What this meant for Australia is discussed in Chapter 7.

Importance for and influence on Australian economy of *zaibatsu* firms

How important were Japanese firms to the Australian economy? It is difficult to obtain comparable figures for different firms for the same period but an indication of the size of Mitsui's branch operations in Victoria provide one example in one state for the period of the Great Depression by comparing the variety of sales and profit figures of their Melbourne customers for 1929–30 with the sales tax figures from Mitsui.

Table 3: Amount of sales by month in £000s, Mitsui Melbourne Office

	1931	1932	1933	1934	1935	1936	1937	1938	1939	1940	1941
Jan	–	11.8	–	29.3	46.4	101.0	64.2	63.0	31.6	–	51.6
Feb	19.3	33.2	12.2	33.0	49.0	47.8	9.8	37.3	532.2		42.1
Mar	34.4	18.3	–	40.6	26.2	90.7	16.3	44.7	29.0		46.7
Apr	926.8	18.1		30.7	24.3	44.7	68.0	34.2	22.4		–
May	15.2	82.6		40.9	38.1	47.8	21.0	66.3	44.3		
Jun	144.4	26.4		28.7	24.3	46.0	–	71.0	32.8		35.1
Jul	41.0	37.1		65.9	32.9	65.5	79.8	52.8	56.7		88.3
Aug	31.9	385.2		41.9	51.4	32.8	17.8	31.3	64.9		–
Sep	59.8	63.2		43.8	35.6	37.1	75.8	42.2	61.8		
Oct	119.4	–		49.6	47.6	59.3	48.7	27.8	49.4		
Nov	7.3			50.3	15.4	112.7	112.5	53.8	64.3		
Dec	65.4		57.5	63.5	24.5	44.6	75.3	30.8	–	53.9	
Total	1465	751	–	514	597	573	589	555	1079	–	633

Compiled by the author from analysis of Mitsui's Journals from 1931 to 1941 in NAA: SP1096/6, WOS

The sales results indicate an expected downturn with the onset of the Great Depression. Sales in 1932 are half that of 1931. By 1934 until the outbreak of war in 1939, sales are almost one third of the 1931 levels. Even with the outbreak of war, the recovery is only to two thirds of the 1931 level. There is also a steadying of monthly sales amounts from the mid-1936 onwards with amounts over £50,000 more frequently achieved. This is consistent with the end of the Trade Diversion Dispute and the easing of the depression in some quarters. Nevertheless, the results indicate that Mitsui was able to maintain fairly stable business outcomes and employment throughout the depression.[44]

If we compare companies, Mitsui Melbourne branch's 1931 sales figures were in excess of the profit for Dalgety & Co. The *Wild Cat Monthly* provides some indication of the profit size of Mitsui customers. For example, Farmer & Co.'s profit in 1930 was £64,167 and Mark Foys was £61,359. These firms were large Sydney firms with branches in Melbourne, yet compared with Mitsui's multimillion pound profits, they were earning less than 10 per cent per annum of their Japanese associate when the Sydney branch of Mitsui made a profit of over £2 million. Net sales figures for Mitsui are not available, but it is clear that the Melbourne branch alone was bringing in more per month than sizeable Australian firms managed in a year. The secret of success was that no order was too small, no customer too much trouble and no product impossible to obtain. Business was very hands on. Managers physically went around to other firms to meet and talk about orders. They picked up the phone themselves. They were reliable and kept their word. In times when a particular order was difficult to fill, a Japanese-run firm would ring around other firms to see if they had the particular item required so they could fill the order on time. For these practices large concerns like Dalgety's and the corner draper's shops placed their orders confidently with large and small Japanese trading houses.[45]

How much were Australian firms buying from Japanese companies? Figures are hard to find and usually listed by country only. For example, D. & W. Murray in the 1936–37 financial year purchased £204,237 from Australian manufacturers, £161,000 from USA and £21,424 from Japan. In some months their purchases are listed according to the firms from which they bought. For example, for a two-week period in July 1937, out of total purchases of £847 for cloth, £163 worth was purchased from Mitsui and £657 from Iida, which is over 90 per cent. D. & W. Murray also purchased from Kanematsu and Z. Horikoshi & Co.[46]

Conclusion

A very close working relationship developed between Australian firms and Japanese branches over the 30–40 years of operation before World War Two. The relationship was interdependent and at times symbiotic with Australian firms acting for the Japanese and receiving commission on sales. Japanese firms, like Mitsui for example, relied on Australian firms for wool and metals to export and fill orders in Japan. Australian firms relied on Mitsui for sales in Japan and for goods, especially fabrics, to sell in Australia. This trade interdependence was personal. The same people communicated over decades to organise business. The 1904 amendments and their interpretation materially assisted this growth and began to favour larger firms by the mid-1920s.

The presence of these large and increasingly influential Japanese networks that thoroughly researched Australian conditions led to security questions about what other uses the networks could serve and what information about Australia was being gathered by the research departments of the *zaibatsu*. But even in the mid-1930s, there was no evidence that the companies themselves were engaged in activities that could be interpreted as preparation for war. Although Alfred Deakin had warned in the 1900s against providing Japan with any opportunity of 'interference' in Australian affairs, the commercial power of the trading company network became substantial. By the mid-1930s, Australian security services began to ask whether the companies posed any threat to Australia. Were they being used to cover espionage by the Japanese government? This as we shall see in later chapters was the wrong question to ask. In the late 1930s, security questions intensified when Japan became more militant in its rhetoric and actions in China. At the same time, the

Japanese families living in Australian suburbs were involved in all aspects of ordinary daily life. Was this also of concern? The next chapter concerns Japanese life in white Australia and examines some of the measures taken by concerned security services throughout Australia from 1937.

Chapter 5

Life in suburbia

Bessie Gerard from Jennali in Sydney's south enjoyed holidaying at the beach at Woy Woy where her family owned a house. Nearby, Mr Kuwahata owned the La Palermo Guest House patronised by young Japanese men who lived and worked in Sydney or who were visiting for a time and liked to go fishing. On the beach, Bessie met Hirokichi and they married in 1917 in the Church of England with the blessing of her family. It was 16 years into the operation of the Immigration Restriction Act 1901 and an era that is more usually characterised as one of exclusion, racism, fear of miscegenation and suspicion of 'foreigners'. But the wedding guests were not only white Australian couples and relatives but also Australians with Japanese husbands, single Japanese men and Japanese couples. Hirokichi had been living in Australia for 20 years. He had many friends and business associates among Australians and Japanese. He was well-known and his business was thriving. He built a house in Countess Street, Mosman, where the couple lived and brought up three daughters. Bessie and Hirokichi were not exceptional people, nor of any importance nationally, locally or socially, but ordinary people from 'middle class' roots.[1]

Close by in Mosman, the Nakamuras played tennis with Mr Sawada, who was the manager of Okura Trading, his Australian wife Thelma and other neighbours. At school, the three Nakamura girls were not the only

Australian-Japanese children. At St Luke's Church of England, where the girls sang in the choir, other Australian-born Japanese attended. These children, who could not speak Japanese, played equally with white Australian children. Their home life was the same as any other Australian household. Japanese visitors had to manage Australian food and customs.

Across the harbour, Kenji Hirodo as a small boy also played with his six siblings in the suburban streets of Sydney. His mother was Japanese but he was totally Australian. His father was one of the most powerful men in the Japanese trading company network in Australia but Kenji's life was like that of any other child at the time. He played footy and spoke with an Australian accent. An indication of how Australian the family became lies in their experiences when they went to Japan at the end of 1938 to complete their bi-cultural education. Kenji reported quite a rough time of it particularly as the trip lasted 12 years because they were unable to return to Australia during wartime. He and his siblings were scorned for their poor Japanese. They got into trouble for speaking their native English in public. All they could do in the war was listen to the BBC and watch the bombs fall on Tokyo. Once the Occupation forces arrived, Kenji was quick to meet them through the fence. The Australian soldiers were surprised to hear his Australian accent and even more surprised that he was born in Mosman. He quickly gained acceptance and when Australian immigration policies changed in December 1949, he got an Australian passport and returned to Sydney to work in the trade that his father had helped to build before the war.[2]

In north-west Australia, Jiro Muramatsu joined his father and brother in Cossack. He soon travelled to the Roman Catholic Xavier College in Melbourne for his education. He was the only Japanese boy in the school but the fact that he was Japanese is not mentioned in Xavier's records. Instead he was something of a celebrity as he learned English, won the maths prize and became a valued member of the footy team. The school magazine wrote about his exploits and was sorry to see him leave in 1898 when his father died. Jiro and his family, despite difficulties with the legal provisions of White Australia were well accepted in Cossack, Broome and Darwin. But even his naturalisation and good standing could not save him from internment and death in the camp in 1943.[3]

Such stories exist all over Australia. It was integration before we had coined the term. Indeed, it would have been very difficult in many cities and towns of White Australia not to have had some contact with Japanese people. Much of this was indirect through the ships' visits or through dealings with Japanese merchants, storekeepers, domestic workers, cooks or laundrymen. Sydney had so many Japanese laundrymen in the 1920s that they formed an association, the Dooshikai, to make sure that their shops were not so close together that they impinged on one another's business prospects. Some of the relationships were extremely personal because although the Commonwealth had intended that Japanese should not be permanent settlers, the immigration amendments enabled Japanese people to establish lives and families in Australia. Although the laws were intended to encourage an imbalance in the gender make-up of the Japanese population by permitting fewer women to enter than men, in order to discourage long-term residence, Australian women had no problem marrying respected Japanese gentlemen.

Why did Australians engaged closely with Japanese people when the national policy intended to exclude 'people of colour' from national life?[4] After all, one argument for a White Australia was the desire to prevent relationships like that of Bessie and Hirokichi. Intermarriage produced mixed-race children and the dangers of miscegenation were well publicised. Australian women who had married Japanese did not fear the much-heralded evils depicted in the literature of the times. The lurid stories of Japanese and other 'Asiatics' engaging in unspeakable acts against Australian womanhood in secret settlements deep in the bush were not the reality people experienced as Japanese took part in local community life as schoolteachers, churchgoers and participants in local sporting clubs. The great white walls kept Australia safe and comfortable. Those who were permitted entry had been vetted. The desire to keep Australia white and British was as much a social attitude as a policy. But the fact that Australians were on the whole tolerant and welcoming of the Japanese families in their midst, facilitated the development of family and neighbourhood networks. Examination of the treatment of Japanese in different states reveals that they were not judged on the basis of race as might be assumed, but that social class was more important. Even customs officers distinguished between "a better class" of Japanese represented by merchants, professionals and small businessmen and the "lower types" of maids and labourers. These real stories are closer to those published in the *New Idea* than those of the alarmist *Lone Hand* and challenge the myth of a monolithically racist White Australia terrified of Japanese people before World War Two.[5]

How far did Australians' welcome of Japanese neighbours and Japanese family participation in suburban and rural life, including intermarriage with Australians, extend? Where were the boundaries of acceptance? What influence did Japanese people have in local clubs and societies? Were these activities genuine integration or opportunities for more sinister purposes? What does the role that Japanese people played in Australian society tell us about Japanese intentions?

Entering society

Before the boom in trading houses after World War One, Japanese men mostly married Australian women if they married at all. This was particularly so for laundrymen and workers on stations or in the cane and pearling industries. Merchants had more mobility and money to travel overseas but some of them chose to marry Australian women. Political, bureaucratic and business links of Japanese with the Australian community are understandable but deep social and family links require more explanation.

Japanese men who settled in suburbia often rented rooms in Australian-run boarding houses. They lived in a similar manner to the Australian families around them whether they married Australians or brought out Japanese wives. Documentary and interview records show that Australian girls, like Bessie, met these Japanese men, like Hirokichi, in the same way as they met any other men – through dances, holidays and social occasions. Japanese also frequented ballroom dancing classes in the city where Australian girls attended in groups. Japanese men had money to spend and some of these meetings led to marriage. For example, Violet Umino's sister and their brother married Japanese people and most of the laundrymen of Geelong in Victoria also married Australian women.[6]

Japanese couples and mixed-race couples settled in suburbs like any other couples. An Army map of Japanese living in Sydney in 1940 shows the distribution of 319 Japanese families. Sixty lived in Mosman.

The children of these marriages report that they experienced no prejudice in the 1920s and 1930s and played in mixed groups of Australian, Japanese and mixed-race children. They attended the local churches and even the Japanese men came on special occasions. They also joined the Red Cross and St John's Ambulance. Some men went rabbit shooting with Australian men in Orange and Bathurst. Others went fishing at Woy Woy or hired boats to fish in Sydney Harbour.

How did these people achieve such acceptance in white, British, Australian society? Judith Brett's study of middle-class values shows that the concept of 'a good citizen' was most important before World War Two.

> Citizenship was not primarily a status conferred by the state but a capacity of individuals to subordinate self-interest to the common good. This broader concept of citizenship was expressed through people's participation in the voluntary activities for the social good. Such activity led to acceptance in the community.[7]

Japanese people also exhibited social values, which white families shared, such as hard work, personal initiative and building prosperity. Japanese families lived very well. Those who were employed by Japanese trading companies enjoyed salaries significantly higher than those of their Australian counterparts. The weekly salaries of Australian men and women and Japanese men working at Mitsui & Co. were generally higher than those paid by Australian firms. They also had opportunities for bonuses and overtime work. Mr Pickup, a clerk, received £23 a month in 1917, an amount the average Australian male did not receive until 1928. By 1935, Mr Pickup was receiving £45 a month. In comparison, in 1917 the manager earned £61-12-10d per month, which rose in 1935 to £166 a month. Mitsui's Australian female typists averaged £8 to £9 a month in 1917 and £24 by 1935. In addition to high salaries, Japanese men working in trading companies regardless of their status in the firm received rent and expense allowances. Managers had all expenses paid including clothing for wives, doctors' bills and school fees. The company paid for all memberships to Australian sporting clubs. Even the Nakamura family, with the business achieving a turnover of £200,000 a year in the 1920s, enjoyed the services of an Australian maid and chauffeur similar to that of well-off Australian families. They were economic equals and respected for their achievements.[8]

Laundrymen, who were less affluent but still prosperous, gained the respect of the local community in an era when business was perceived as a service to the community. Denzo Umino and his wife Violet were very highly regarded in Brisbane and later in Chatswood in the 1920s and 1930s. The testimonials of local people assisted them in obtaining the necessary extensions of stay that they were required to seek each year. In 1935, the level of respect for this family was such that the Department of External Affairs informed the Consul-General that Umino need no longer apply for his annual extension. He was granted *de facto* permanent residence.[9]

Apart from ordinary life in suburbia, Japanese-Australian families and Japanese families had opportunities to meet through the business connections of the men. The Nakamuras report that most of the contact with Japanese people took place within their father's business entertaining. Nakamura brought ships' captains, sailors and merchants of other firms home for tea. Further contact took place outside the home but still within a business setting. The Nakamura girls remember family picnic days at the golf club when they played with other Japanese business families. They also recall Japanese men joining their father for fishing trips at their beach house at Woy Woy. One of the highlights of their young lives was the visit of the Training Squadron when they attended the open day by invitation. The crew, who were missing their own families, made a great fuss of the girls. They enjoyed the attention but not all the girls liked the strange food.

Social class hierarchy regulated Japanese social life in the Sydney community. This was something that Australians understood. Consular invitations were extended regularly to merchant families for special events such as New Year's Day and the Emperor's Birthday. It was customary for only the wives and children of the nine most senior Japanese men to accept invitations to the most important days. However, company men of lesser standing generally attended alone. Only one European wife, Thelma Sawada, wife of the manager of Okura Trading, attended such gatherings. Nakamura attended but is placed in the back row for the photograph, reflecting his position in the community but Bessie is not present. Laundry families did not mix socially with merchant families and were not invited to such functions even though merchants might visit the homes of leading laundrymen for business purposes. Many trading company managers visited Denzo Umino who was head of the laundrymen's association or Dooshikai and also acted as the chauffeur to the Consul-General's most important Japanese visitors.

Social class within the Japanese community was also reflected in where people lived. Some, like Nakamura, Yasuda, Kuwahata and many others shared the great Australian dream of home ownership. Ken Hirodo's father aspired to own a sheep station. Although managers mostly rented houses at the company's expense in fashionable suburbs such as Vaucluse, many Japanese bought real estate in NSW where it was legal for foreign nationals to do so. Japanese numbers increased in Sydney at the time of the 1920s real estate boom. The new areas on the north shore with connection to the city by tram, ferry and later the Harbour Bridge made Mosman an attractive suburb.[10]

Japanese families, whether they included an Australian partner or not, lived under two social hierarchies: that of the Australian community and that of the Japanese community. Stratification within the Japanese society awarded higher status to merchant families than to small business owners who were not involved in the import–export trade. However, despite the lower status within the Japanese community of laundry families and people like the photographer Kagiyama, their position as prosperous small business families enabled them to enter the 'middle class' of Australian society where they were often well-known and respected.

Further stratification existed among Japanese-born wives in Australia. Women had their own social lives apart from any involvement in the local Australian community. Senior Japanese wives headed the social life of Japanese women. The hostess's status was determined by two factors: first, whether she was the wife of one of the nine top company directors, and second, whether she was of royal birth through an indirect relationship to the Emperor of Japan. Wives of company directors were also well-educated and cultured to match the status of their husbands. The position in society of their family of birth and the status of the schools that they had attended in Japan determined the social position of wives in the group in Sydney.[11]

The markers of acceptance that the Australian community used in relation to the Japanese are, therefore, very similar to those used by bureaucrats at the turn of the twentieth century to decide questions of domicile. The degree of connection to Australia that the person had was judged by assessing a person's marital status, home ownership and employment situation. It also relied on who would vouch for the person and whether they were in good standing in their local community. There were, however, Japanese who occupied a difficult position under these criteria. Ichiro Kagiyama was one of these.

Kagiyama spanned the social and racial divides and did not find a comfortable niche outside his work. His marriage to an Australian did not last. The couple divorced in 1934. Kagiyama remarried to a Japanese woman who arrived in Australia in *c.* 1938. Just how Kagiyama managed to obtain entry for his new wife is uncertain but his consular and trading connections may have been responsible for the organisation of an exception in this case. Although he enjoyed a close relationship with the trading network as a photographer for official events, he was not afforded the same social standing as the merchants. However, because of his relationship with the Consul and the trading companies, he was not of the same social status as the laundrymen. Neither was he fully accepted into the Australian society he had enjoyed after his change of profession, which moved him out of suburbia and into the commercial area of Kings Cross. His change of marriage partner brought decreased social contact with Australians because his new wife did not speak English. As a commercial photographer and small businessman he was, by Australian standards, middle class but was not accepted into prestigious Australian photographic societies in Sydney because of his commercial as distinct from artistic photography. His pupil, Ishida, however, as a respected merchant employed by Okura Trading and for whom photography was an art, was accepted into the prestigious Sydney Camera Circle of whom Harold Cazneaux and Cecil W. Bostock were members.[12]

Japanese men had their own social life in addition to family life. Mr Iida, manager of Okura, was a wool buyer, and as a result he formed very strong bonds with other Japanese wool buyers. They travelled to the country together and socialised during wool buying seasons. They all enjoyed a drink, so they often had parties at restaurants or at each other's homes. Claims on expenses for liquor bills were very high. Their wives usually became friends as well. Mrs Iida's best friend was Mrs Murase, whose husband was the Manager of Iida-Takashimaya Co.

Ken Shimada spent a lot of time away from his Sydney home travelling to stations on trips organised by Australian Estates and Dalgety & Co. to Albury, Jerilderie, Forbes, Corryong and Parkes. Shimada was often accompanied by his expert wool buyer, Mr Watarai of the Department of Agriculture and Forestry in Tokyo, who brought out his family for his stay in Australia. The Watarai family occasionally travelled with their father.[13] Relations with farmers were longstanding. Ken Shimada developed a good relationship with Mr J.A. Sloane of Neyliona Station at Mulwala. In 1940, Sloane had difficulty with station domestic staff because so many people had been called up for the Army. He asked Shimada's advice on the procedure for applying for a Japanese houseboy through the Consul-General.[14]

As Australian as we are ·

The circumstances behind Japanese residents' experiences of racial prejudice provide further support for the criteria isolated by Brett as appropriate to explaining the acceptance of Japanese families in White Australia. Whether a person experienced racial prejudice often hinged on questions of loyalty and good citizenship in the interwar years. With the possibility of war in the Pacific from 1937, the position of women married to Japanese men was insecure because they had lost their British subject status by marrying non-British men. In 1937, an Act was passed to permit women married to aliens to apply for reinstatement of their rights as British subjects.[15] This provision was advertised in the paper but many women failed to learn about the new provisions. Those who did not apply for reinstatement of British subject status suffered as a result. This is evident in the different experiences of Violet Umino and Bessie Nakamura.

Bessie took advantage of the offer to regain British subject status. This action also secured the rights of her daughters as Australians and British-born. In addition, as a safeguard for the family, Hirokichi transferred all their possessions and funds into Bessie's name. Although he was interned, Bessie and her children were considered loyal. People's treatment of Bessie did not change during the war with one exception. The Red Cross and Volunteer Aid Division of which she was an active committee member and instructor regretfully called for her resignation as they did not wish to have someone so closely connected with an 'enemy alien' on a committee working for the Australian war effort.[16]

Violet Umino was slow to regain her British status, which counted against her. Violet did not hear of the provisions by which she could regain her British status until 1940. She obtained her papers in February of that year. One Military Intelligence officer remarked in 1942: "This woman was sufficiently un-Australian to marry a Japanese in 1918 and to support Japanese nationality until 2-2-1940." She was ordered to move 200 miles inland from the NSW coast until the restriction was lifted in August 1944.[17]

Violet's failure to regain her status within the allotted 12-month period was not the only aspect of her life to count against her in wartime. Her husband's connections to the Consul-General were more direct than those of Bessie's husband, although Hirokichi shared a building with a suspected Australian organisation, The Australia First Movement, which counted against him. Umino acted as laundryman to the Consulate, directors of major trading houses and Japanese ships. This level of contact with important members of the Japanese community brought Umino under suspicion in wartime. However, two other roles were even more crucial. Umino was the head of the Dooshikai, which met at his residence. In addition, he had served as chauffeur to visiting Japanese dignitaries from the Army and Navy, one of whom was a known intelligence agent.

Violet was in a much more vulnerable position than Bessie in 1939. Despite the enormous support the family enjoyed in Chatswood until the outbreak of war, customers did not remain loyal to the laundry once Japan joined the Axis nations. Violet reported that business declined in 1940. It improved after she regained her British subject status and displayed a sign in the window that she was Australian-born and a British subject.

The experiences of prejudice by all-Japanese families are similar to that of Australian-Japanese couples. They report that they were treated very well until September 1940 when Japan signed an alliance with Germany and Italy as Mr Iida reported. He had only recently moved back to Sydney with his family after almost 20 years in Melbourne as manager of Okura Trading when the Axis Pact was signed. The family had settled in well in suburban Sydney after the shock of having to replace Mr Sawada who had died suddenly of a heart attack. It was a terrible experience suddenly to have a stranger in the street call him a 'traitor' and 'a dirty Jap'. The family went to Japan just before the war when the trade situation became impossible in 1941 but some of them returned to Sydney to live after the war.[18]

The approach of war and the experience of war raised questions of loyalty. Australians accepted those who made some commitment to the society and showed loyalty to the nation. Japanese in 1940 and those married to Japanese were assumed to be un-Australian unless they exhibited such a commitment. The internment of all Japanese people regardless of age and gender in December 1941 sharpened the perception of who was Australian and who was not. Criteria for acceptance that were applied to Japanese people before the war remained and were often used by Australians to help to appeal against the internment of Japanese friends. Two Victorian cases show the lengths that people went to. Thomas Nagai and the Takasuka family had no Australian family members to fight for their release from internment. Bessie and Violet, as British subjects fought throughout the war to have their husbands released. In all cases the support of the local community was critical.

Dame Nellie Melba employed Thomas Nagai as a butler at her home in Coldstream in *c.* 1917. After working for Dame Nellie and many other prominent Victorians, Nagai married Muriel, an Australian in Geelong and started his laundry in 1932. The couple had a son. Nagai tried to naturalise in 1915 and again in 1931.[19] When he was interned, the residents of Geelong and the Clarkes of Mildura, where he had worked for some time, wrote persistently to government ministers and to the Prime Minister until he was released. Such persistence could have brought them under suspicion too at a time when Japan was bombing the north of Australia and Sydney had experienced the mini-submarine raid. Clarke complained to the Minister for the Army, Mr Forde, two days after Pearl Harbor:

> ... we know our country laws must be obeyed but it is very hard on some of these people who have lived peacefully in our midst some for over 40 years & who have married & got families here

He pleaded especially for Nagai who had worked for him and whom he had known for 30 years. Nagai was a good Christian citizen, a gentleman of samurai class and trustworthy. He was "Australian in every sense of the word". Unsatisfied with the lack of response, Clarke wrote again on 30 January 1942 and 5 February 1942 arguing that Nagai's internment was "unjust as he has been a very good citizen".

> I would ask the Minister to consider this man as an Australian I know Dame Nellie Melba tried to get him nationalised [sic] over 25 years ago and would if she were still here do her best to have him released as soon as possible on account of his failing health.

Clarke offered to be responsible for him. He argued that Nagai should be able to collect the aged pension the same as anyone else.

When Nagai's appeal against his internment failed, Clarke demanded a review of the decision. "We are 398 [miles] from the sea", he wrote to Prime Minister Curtin. "This trustworthy Christian gentleman was unfortunate enough to be by accident of birth born in a country we are at 'War' with at present." He offered to intern Nagai in Mildura. Again not satisfied with a refusal Clarke wrote to Alex Wilson their Member of Parliament and argued for the need for workers. Wilson wrote to Forde on 15 May 1942 asking that all due consideration be given to the request despite the fact that he understood it had already been refused. Forde agreed to look into the matter but found no new grounds to reconsider the decision. When appeals through Robert Menzies and the Attorney General, failed, Lily Clarke was furious and wrote to the Director General of Security in Canberra, Dr H.V. Evatt:

> I do not know how any Christian gentleman could arrive at such a decision even at a time like this there are always special circumstances this man has lived in our country most of his life and has lived our live [sic]. I asked for his release for special reasons owing to having 3 invalids on my hands in two different homes. It is unjust to keep this man shut up and we are willing to be his guard. We are loyal Australians and sons and daughters of some of its oldest pioneers.

The Clarkes persisted and in July 1943, Mr John Dedman, Minister for War Organisation, wrote to Mrs Clarke that Nagai's health was precarious and he was being released. He was confined to the property at 191 Malop Street because it was felt his presence in the streets of Geelong might affect public morale. His house arrest was not revoked until 28 November 1946.

One example of support for Japanese people in a rural area was that of the Takasuka family of Fosterville. None of them was naturalised. The family arrived in 1905 and extended their CEDTs to continue experimental rice farming. By 1941, Ichiko was a widow as Jo had died in 1940. Her son, Mario who was born in Australia, entered the AIF and served in Crete and New Guinea. Her Japanese-born son, Sho, managed the large tomato farm, which supplied the armed forces. Their daughter, Aiko, was married to an Australian and worked as the local schoolteacher.[20] Correspondence between AMF Southern Command and Forde discussed the Takasukas' situation. Because Sho was of military age, the police were required to intern him, which they were reluctant to do. However the AMF inquired whether Ichiko and Aiko could be exempted from the regulation interning Japanese women. Forde stated that they could not be exempted but indicated that there was no date specified by which the internment must take place. The local police never arrested them.

Sho appealed against his internment. Although the government attorney put up stereotypical racial arguments that Japanese could never develop loyalty to anyone apart from the Emperor and that racial traits were in the blood, local witnesses impressed the Tribunal with strong arguments. Sho, who was thoroughly Australian in orientation, was needed urgently for the efficient tomato production for the army. After long argument, the government attorney was overridden. He had asked for proof of loyalty and proof of what Sho was thinking. How did people know Sho was a loyal citizen? In reply they could not say what he was thinking or whether Japanese people might join community organisations to sabotage the community if Japan invaded, but his actions over many years had convinced them that he was trustworthy and loyal to Australia. He had tried to naturalise several times at the urging of the locals. He was a member of the Volunteer Defence Corps and section leader in the Goornang Platoon. He had helped raise money for the Red Cross. He had played football for 10 years and was a member of the Tennis Association. He was secretary of the I.O.R. Lodge for eight years and elected a governor of the Swan Hill Hospital. All of the witnesses who knew him, his neighbours, business acquaintances and community leaders said he was a loyal citizen and very helpful to people. Some were personal friends and their families socialised with him in his home. One resident was asked again and again about community feeling and gave an exasperated reply.

... you have given a general opinion that he would not cause any unrest in the community [if released]. As far as you are concerned he would not, but what about the other residents of Goornong?
– I could have brought two or three carloads along to testify today.

Because of the high level of community support and the need for his expertise to harvest the tomatoes for the defence forces, Sho was released but restricted to a radius of nine miles from his farm where he was known.

The Tribunal hearings demonstrated that the indicators of loyalty that authorities were prepared to recognise in wartime were very similar to the community standard for acceptance but they also took notice of additional factors. These included length of residence in Australia, the attitude of the community towards the person, the amount of contact with the country of origin or its nationals in Australia, the person's religion and lifestyle, and their 'outlook' whether it was Australian or Japanese. In suburban Australia, Japanese had the opportunity to socialise or to do business with each other. In rural Australia that was less common. But suburban Australia was just as prepared to attend the Tribunal Hearings against internment as their rural counterparts. They also expressed at times an interesting racial twist on who they believed to be "as Australian as we are". The Nakamura case illustrates this. The family said that Bessie received only two refusals from members of the Mosman community when she was gathering witnesses for Hirokichi's appeal. Both were prominent professional citizens of Mosman who regretted that they could not help, as they had known the family a long time but felt they had to remain impartial for business reasons. One was a local doctor. However, Nakamura was seen as Australian to those who knew him to the point that one neighbour called him "The whitest man I ever knew".[21] The well-known facts that Nakamura taught Japanese language at Berlitz School of Languages, acted as Court interpreter, belonged to the Nippon Club in Sydney, ran a trading company and had recently travelled to Japan made no difference to his local support.

Bessie wrote dozens of letters to every government and army official she could think of to have Hirokichi released. She visited their offices without appointments and sat and waited, refusing to move until she was heard. At the Tribunal in NSW, the government solicitor was different from the one that the Takasukas had faced in Victoria. He did not use racial arguments but kept to practical matters and evidence.

The panel inquired into Nakamura's standing within the local Mosman community. They asked if there would be trouble if he were released. The Rev Cameron, Rector of St Luke's, replied that he would be very surprised if any of the parishioners of St Luke's would be concerned by his release. Mrs Crockett, a neighbour, said that she did not know of a man better liked. Brother Michael Eulogious Breen, a Christian Brother, who had helped the family, particularly the youngest daughter, in finding work, also appeared.

> [Counsel for Nakamura:] – Speaking ... to Mr Nakamura's loyalty to Australia, what would you say as to that? ... [Br. Breen] I would not have associated with his case if I had any doubts about his loyalty to Australia, and my firm belief is that he is as loyal as 90% of Australians.
> The Chairman: Can you give us an absolute idea, that is only relative? ... [Br. Breen] I do not understand what you mean ... [Chairman] You say Mr Nakamura was as loyal as a certain percentage of Australians? ... [Br. Breen] His whole interest seemed to be in the progress of Australia.
> [Counsel for Nakamura] And you have no doubts of his loyalty? – [Br. Breen] I am so sure of it I would be prepared to stake my own freedom on it.[22]

Bessie's efforts failed in 1942 but as Hirokichi's health deteriorated in the camp, she redoubled her efforts. He was released in 1944 but was too frail to attend his daughter's wedding and died at his home in Mosman in 1945.

Violet Umino was not in as strong a position as the other families considered above. She and her sister and brother had all married Japanese people. Her husband had been a prominent member of Japanese society as well as an integral part of white society through his business. He spent a lot of time assisting the Consulate-General and trading companies. His home was a meeting place for important Japanese people. It was the biggest Japanese laundry business in Sydney and handled the laundry for Araki & Co., and, at Kuwahata's request, for the Japanese navy when it was in port. Despite this, Violet tried to have Denzo released. She became such a pest to security services by turning up at the internment camp in Hay and travelling to West Wyalong to try to be near her husband that she was placed under a control order herself. She also ran a support club for the wives of Japanese internees, which did not endear her to authorities. Where Bessie had concentrated on obtaining the support of the 'right' people, Violet did not. In fact some Australians who had known the family put in reports to authorities that they felt the family was very pro-Japanese. She was not able to command the respect and assistance from Australians that she had enjoyed when Denzo was threatened with deportation in 1921 in Brisbane. It also counted against her that her husband was so involved in Japanese activities in Sydney. He had contributed to the Japanese Army and Navy funds during the war in China. He had quite a lot of money in the Yokohama Specie Bank in September 1941 where he knew the manager. He withdrew £1,000 to buy a house to give to his son for a birthday present, because of the deteriorating international situation. Denzo was not released from internment until after the war, although his son Douglas who was Australian-born gained early release and took on laundry work. Denzo once again had to fight deportation in the forced repatriation of all interned Japanese in 1946.

Australia–Japan societies and clubs

Very few Australians became members of clubs designed to foster good relations between Australia and Japan. Those who did tended to be involved at some level in their professional life in university education, culture or the media and were all very prominent Australians. Most Australians who knew Japanese people met them through their local clubs or at work. Personal friendships at this level were more numerous than any formal membership of organisations like the Australia–Japan Society, The Pacific Club and the Kokusai Bunka Shinkokai (KBS – The Society for International Relations). In peacetime, members of these clubs had no difficulty in finding acceptance in Australian society. When war broke out attitudes changed and the loyalty of club members was questioned. It became difficult to judge the sentiments of those who had promoted peace between the two countries in the late 1930s at a time when Japan was at war with China and the future was uncertain. One case of a Japanese man who was resident in Australia for 36 years before the war illustrates how membership of societies that crossed the cultural borders could cast suspicion and lead to rejection of him and his Australian associates and family.

Moshi Inagaki[23] arrived in Australia in 1907. At the hearing against his internment on 11 February 1942 his counsel stated that Inagaki had married an Australian woman, Rose Carolyn and had one daughter. He taught a course of Japanese language at the University of Melbourne for 23 years as well as teaching privately at his home. During World War One, he tried to enlist but was refused because he was not naturalised. Instead he worked in translation in the Defence Department. During World War Two until his internment he had worked in the Censor's office. His daughter was married to an Australian soldier who by the time of his interment held the rank of Major in the AIF. These personal facts gave Inagaki a strong connection to Australia and his counsel stated that he had an Australian outlook, was a Christian, and had no interest in politics.

His referees were also impeccable: Sir John Latham, former Australian Minister to Japan and Chief Justice of the High Court; Mr Bainbridge former Registrar of the University of Melbourne; Mr Seitz, Director of Education and Professor Sadler, Professor of Oriental Languages at Sydney University. Such eminent referees generally impressed Australians. This impressive body of evidence should normally have led Australians to declare a man such as Inagaki as "Australian as we are". Although like Nakamura he was married to an Australian and immersed in the community, Nakamura qualified for support but Inagaki did not. Only one of Inagaki's former students spoke for him and the University of Melbourne authorities spoke up because they needed him released to finish examining the Japanese entries for the Mollison Scholarship. Why did Inagaki fail to gain support?

Inagaki believed passionately in promoting intercultural relations. He spent most of his time writing the very first Japanese language textbooks for Australian students. In 1936, he was approached by Peter Russo, a correspondent attached to *The Herald* who had worked in Tokyo for five years and was one of his former students, to act as the Australian correspondent for the KBS. Inagaki's duties were to report to the KBS in Japan on Australian education systems and promote Japanese culture and mutual understanding. For this work he was paid £70 a year for expenses. He was also a member of the Nippon Club in Melbourne, formed in 1939, which met monthly and whose membership mostly consisted of *zaibatsu* managers whom he visited in their offices. Its activities were under surveillance. Even more problematic for Inagaki was a paid trip to Japan to the KBS with his family in 1938. The KBS disseminated books in Australia about Japan's culture and activities in China, some of which were written by Australians who were strong supporters of Japan such as H.V. Millington who had been under surveillance for years. Inagaki was also invited to attend the prestigious welcomes and farewells to Japanese dignitaries like Tatsuo Kawai, the Japanese First Minister in Australia in

1941. Although Inagaki was included in Australian events and helped disseminate KBS material in Australia, he was not well received in Japan. The KBS were, according to Peter Russo, more interested in sending out material than gaining information from people like Inagaki. In addition, Inagaki had not attended a prestigious university or school in Japan and was married to a foreign woman. To the Japanese, he was low status. In Australia, like Denzo Umino, he was too Japanese in his daily activities to qualify locally as an Australian. With the death of his wife, Rose, in 1943, Inagaki had no one to fight for him. He was forced to 'repatriate' to Japan at the end of the war.

Conclusion

Australians genuinely welcomed Japanese neighbours and Japanese family participation in suburban and rural life, including intermarriage with Australians. Sharing common values led to trust and there is no evidence that the integration was false or sinister. On the contrary, lack of integration led to suspicion and lack of support. Violet's lack of involvement in Australian life and lack of support in Australian circles did not help her. Her life and that of her family, who were also married to Japanese, counted against her. Inagaki's immersion in Japanese culture in Australia, which his wife shared, did not help him.

Australian opinions that Japanese people were "as Australian as we are" lasted into wartime. But attitudes to Australians who supported Japanese people could lead to suspicion. In effect, fighting for your man could increase the attention one received from authorities. Bessie and Violet had a running battle with security services during the war. Bessie had trouble over the car, the radio and was subject to surveillance during the war. However, Japanese involved in Australian life were considered less suspicious than Australians involved in societies that promoted mutual understanding. Being a loyal Australian was a deeper issue than skin colour or national origins. It was a matter of a recognisably shared identity with those who supported the Australian way of life and 'outlook'.

The factors that led to acceptance within the community counted for nothing at war's end. While Australians felt a great sense of injustice at the treatment of interned loved ones, friends and neighbours, particularly of elderly men, women and children the youngest of whom was 12 days old in 1941, it was more difficult to assist once the horrors of the war became known and government policies changed. In August 1942, consular staff and merchants like Ken Shimada (and suspected spies like 'Juro' who are discussed in Chapter 7) were shipped to Japan in exchange for allied civilian internees. In many ways these people were the lucky ones. All Japanese who had worked in pearling were reclassified and became prisoners of war regardless of age, health, length of residence and connections to Australia. They were repatriated at the end of the war. Only about five per cent of people who were interned managed to remain in Australia. Yuriko Nagata tells the poignant stories of the remainder of Japanese men, women and children, including babies born in internment who were forcibly shipped to Japan in overcrowded conditions, stripped of all assets and who often had no one to go to in Japan. She calls them "Unwanted Aliens", which was a stark change in status from being "as Australian as we are".

The policy that no Japanese should "pollute our shores" as the new Minister for Immigration, Arthur Calwell stated, stripped Japanese Australians not only of all assets but of all connections to an Australia that had become home. Harmless Australian-Japanese suffered terribly as they bore the brunt of the government's response to the shock of the brutal treatment of Australian prisoners of war by the Japanese. The vast majority had done nothing to harm Australia but because they were of the same national origin as the brutal enemy, they were no longer considered "as Australian as we are" except by a very few people who kept their opinions to themselves for several decades after the war or even kept friendships going through it all as Japanese people kept in touch with them from Japan.

Chapter 6   **Undercurrents: The question**

                             of espionage to 1937

Commander J.G. Fearnley RAN was convinced Japanese people were up to something in Australia from about 1908. It was in his interest to find evidence of suspicious activity no matter how flimsy to support his call for a proper Australian intelligence service, but he never lost his innate suspicion of Japanese people. He wrote: "if there is anything threatening us, ... I cannot too earnestly convey my opinion that an Australian Secret Service is a vital necessity".[1] His location of "suspicious characters" in Queensland was offered in evidence, and included well-respected men like Nakashiba and the Tashima family.

> At ... Cairns Japanese are very well represented. ... it is well known that they have collected all available data as to approaches, sounding etc. of the Harbour, as well as the particulars of the town and back country. Many of the Cairns Japanese were well known to me personally – smart keen intelligent fellows, speaking and reading English fluently, whose presence and work in the district could not be satisfactorily accounted for except of the ground of ulterior motive.

At Townsville again where the Japanese are also pretty numerous, many of them are men of high education and … keen intelligence. Some of them have been frequently observed taking photographs round the district … it is safe to assume that there is little or nothing worth knowing at Townsville that is unknown. One of my personal friends there, has in his employ as cook and housekeeper a naval officer holding two war medals, and who speaks and reads English perfectly.[2]

Fearnley's claim that Japanese were numerous is questionable. Few actually lived in either town. Those who did, assisted Japanese visitors and had legitimate reasons for their activities, which local white people appreciated.

More widespread were reports that Japanese had detailed maps of the coast. Fearnley concluded that some pearl divers and other crew working on Australian-owned boats were not uneducated workers. He had observed one reading Thomas Carlyle's *Sator Rosartus* in English. Further, some of the men wore converted navy issue clothing and had extraordinary skill in handling boats in storms. His claim that men employed on luggers "ostensibly engaged in pearl fishing [were] officers of the Japanese Intelligence Department" charged with supervising the charting of the Queensland coast, had no supporting evidence. Lieutenant R. Bowen in Queensland shared his views. In 1913, Bowen also noted the clothes of the fishermen on Thursday Island and said that they "did not seem to be fisherman class".

The seamanlike manner in which they handle their luggers under full sail in bad weather and the general appearance and cleanliness of the boats denotes these men in the majority of cases have had some service training.

A more convincing report to the Naval Secretary in Melbourne in March 1914 stated that a nurse had found scars on a Japanese in hospital who said that he had served for a long time in the army. However, there was nothing suspicious in the 1900s and 1910s about Japanese who worked along the east coast of Australia, particularly in Queensland, making maps of the areas in which they fished. Japanese gained the same knowledge of the coast as Australian and Kupanger seamen who worked in the area. Even in the late 1930s, precise charts of much of the Australian coastal waters were not available. The Defence Department had ordered a survey in 1911 of what mapping was needed and what maps were on hand. It found that Queensland needed a lot of mapping. It is little wonder Japanese men on pearl luggers, which belonged to Australians and were only permitted to have 50 per cent of a lugger's crew from the same nationality, made maps of the areas in which they worked.[3]

Fearnley and Bowen were in the minority in their interpretation of the significance of Japanese activities at this time. Neither had much knowledge of the training of Japanese naval and army personnel nor of the extent to which Japanese men had to engage in military training at age 20. Some, like Hirokichi Nakamura, left Japan at the age when they were likely to be called up. Former army or navy service by Japanese men living in Australia was to be expected. Japan had fought and won significant naval battles in the 1904–05 Russo-Japanese War. Naval cadets in Japan were required to study a foreign language. Most took English. And when we consider that each training ship that visited Australia had a crew list of up to 500 sailors and officers, it is not surprising that some former naval personnel would return to work in Australia. As the Navy file explained: "It is not usual for Japanese other than sea faring men to come to Australia for the Pearling Industry."[4] In addition, Colonel Hoad had witnessed the tens of thousands of troops involved in the Russo-Japanese War.

WA also had reporters who believed that Japan was spying at this time. In June 1912, when Major Asada visited WA, Major E.J.H. Nicholson of the local Intelligence Corps stated:

That [Asada's] visit was not only premeditated but official and pre-advised was evident by the somewhat elaborate arrangements made to receive him at places where Japanese residents are numerous .... The regrettably absolute ignorance of Japanese [language] by any trustworthy whites makes exact knowledge impossible, but it is almost certain that a complete system of Japanese Agents was disclosed by his visit.[5]

What Nicholson had discovered was that Japanese throughout Australia knew one another and had extensive interconnected networks by this time.

When Asada left, Ichikawa of Mitsui sent him a package of readily available maps and plans, which was intercepted and inspected. Asada telegrammed for further maps of the NT. Defence complained about the state of Australian intelligence provisions on 16 September 1912:

... it would appear that espionage by foreigners is being carried out in Australia. Even after detection suitable legislation does not exist to enable the Commonwealth to protect itself against organised spying ... I am therefore to ask ... for advice as to the further legislative or other steps advisable adequately to protect against espionage generally.

The Attorney-General's Department replied dismissively on 18 October 1912.

I presume that, by espionage, the memorandum intends to refer to the practice of illicitly obtaining or attempting to obtain secret official information in relation to Australia which would be useful to an enemy in the event of war ... The Defence Act 1903–1912 contains provision for the punishment of persons who unlawfully obtain plans, documents or information relating to defence works or unlawfully make sketches or photographs of defence works.[6]

The reply continued that under the Crimes Bill then in preparation, provision was made against taking unlawful soundings and for the arrest of suspected persons. But because espionage was difficult to detect no further legislative provisions could be suggested. The key point established at this time was that no matter how much Japanese research, map purchasing and embellishment and information gathering might worry a small number of Australians, it was not illegal. It could even be argued that because suitable maps were not available, particularly in Queensland, the sounding of waterways by Japanese lugger crews employed on Australian-owned boats was necessary. After all, the Australian Intelligence Corps created in December 1907 and the school of instruction in 1909 with its 80 officers, of whom Captain E.L. Piesse was one, was mostly engaged in mapping the parts of Australia that still required this.[7]

The problems surrounding possible espionage remained into the 1920s and 1930s. What exactly constituted espionage? Could mapping be espionage in areas where no maps were available or where the mapping was inadequate even if Australians employed the people who were making the maps? If information was gained from the public domain through shops or photographs of areas anyone could visit, was this espionage? Although Fearnley envisaged in 1909 that Japan could use the information gained through mapping around Queensland for a surprise landing to capture large stores of cattle and horses, nearly every state had an argument to put that theirs was the most likely point of attraction for an invasion at some point in the future. Fearnley and those who shared his views could think of no other reason why Japan would gather information on Australia to the degree it did. He also failed to acknowledge that Japanese people never failed to research every aspect of potential markets and bought books on Australia that provided statistics on every aspect of Australian trade, commerce and population growth, which was freely available in the State and Commonwealth Year Books and newspapers to which Japanese firms subscribed.[8] Were Australians paranoid or was there real cause for concern about Japanese activities within Australia at this time? What measures did Australia take to watch Japanese activities as the international situation became tenser particularly after 1929? What activities did Japanese people engage in that constituted a threat to national security? What responses did Australia make? What was the role of the Japanese networks in the preparation for war?

Watching Japan

Listening to and watching Japan developed gradually through the 1910s–1920s. It had become a sophisticated art form by 1937. After the Four Power Pact replaced the Anglo-Japanese Alliance as a result of the Washington Conference in 1922, Japan consistently stated that it sought friendship, co-operation and trade with Australia and wanted Australia involved in maintaining peace in the Pacific. It intended to develop its territories and to improve access to the resources it required in the region. In the early 1930s, Japan took over Manchukuo and established a puppet government. In response, Australia improved its intelligence services and attempted to reassess Japan's intentions in the region.

In 1921, Lieutenant Colonel Francis Home Griffiths of the Royal Marines set up the Intelligence Centre in Sydney. By January 1922, Australia had a Director of Naval Intelligence (DNI) and formal reports by Australia Station began. The suggestion, which had circulated since 1919, that each port should have an intelligence officer started to become a reality from 1923. Customs officers reported via a Naval Reporting Officer system. Along the north, missionaries served as coast watchers from 1926. This coast-watching service was extended gradually to New Guinea and other Pacific Islands. Fearnley, now retired and working as a coaling agent, officially became reporting agent at Newcastle in September 1920. He was appointed to obtain information from masters of merchant ships about the Japanese occupied territories; the development of Japanese shipping in the Pacific and the type of cargo carried by Japanese and American vessels in the Pacific trade. Although this was an honorary position, Fearnley agreed because he felt Newcastle was a target. Rupert Long RAN was put in charge of intelligence in Sydney as District Intelligence Officer in 1934 but effectively ran Intelligence before he was formally appointed as DNI. By the mid-1930s, Commander Long ran over 150 agents within Australia and the Pacific Islands. He also had access to information from British and Dutch sources in NEI and other parts of SEA and China.[9]

The Australian Military Forces (AMF) Intelligence Section also watched Japan and produced intelligence summaries. From 1918, reports display some guardedness about Japanese activities in Australia in the years leading up to the peace settlements when Japan was lobbying to retain former German territory and for a racial equality clause to be included in the League of Nations Charter. The Section received information from the British Ambassador's office in Tokyo about all prospective visitors from Japan and an assessment of their intentions. For example, on 29 March 1919, the British advised that Torao Kanbayashi was visiting on visa. He owned mines and the "ostensible object of his journey" was to visit mines and forestry enterprises. He had already visited the Philippines and the South Seas. They advised that there was no reason to doubt his stated purposes. On 1 March 1919, Lieutenant Colonel Kamimura's proposed visit brought the remark:

> Government of Japan wish every facility to be given to the above named officers who have been sent to Australia to study military and economic conditions and wool production.[10]

Australian Naval Intelligence examined Japanese organisations. In 1917, Japan formed a Navy League in Tokyo to which Baron Makata and Vice-Admiral Ijichi were elected Vice Presidents. The League believed that a navy powerful enough to protect the Empire and execute a progressive policy abroad was vital. Further, it maintained that a vigorous naval policy to keep sea routes open assisted the advancement of trade and industry by allowing commerce to flow.

Australia also received information from the Straits Settlements General Staff. For example, in November 1917, it provided information on the aims and objects of the Japanese that now more clearly defined and openly expressed a definite policy of a national mission of *nan'yō* expansion. It defined *nan'yō* as including the Malay states, and archipelago, Sumatra, Java, Celebes, North Borneo, Sarawak and all the islands between the Straits and Australia, but did not include Australia.

> Over all this great expanse of land water the Japanese are now spreading with great rapidity and energy encouraged and assisted by the material prosperity which the war has brought both to the people themselves and to their Government.

The report described the nature of the expansion as trade and investment in rubber, shipping and sugar refining. Commercial agents, teachers and students travelled to study local conditions and systems, particularly in Java. In Singapore, Japanese were acquiring property in well-known residential areas and planning schools. Pan-Asianism was a constant Japanese theme and certainly the Straits Settlements believed that Japan would not stop at peaceful commercial development but were military by nature. Further, on 30 January 1918, the General Staff expressed concern that Japanese in some numbers were opening up small estates in Borneo.

> The Dutch in that part are convinced that the Allies have lost the War; the Dutch are extremely sorry, and look upon the coming of the Japanese as more or less inevitable.[11]

Australia received many reports of ship sightings in the Pacific near Fiji and New Guinea and watched Japan's activities in the mandated islands.

American, British and Dutch sources often assumed that Japan must have been engaging in suspicious clandestine activities in breach of the mandate condition that it not fortify any of the islands. American suspicion and distrust of Japan was greater than anything seen in Australian documents at the time. An American report on the Marianas in 1930s states:

> Nothing is definitely known as to what is going on, but vessels call there frequently, gear of different kinds is landed and it is thought probably that oil storage or seaplane landings are the cause of the activity.

It would be difficult to write a vaguer report or voice suspicions on less information.

A series of detailed Intelligence Reports from 1926 by Captain B.P. Dicker of the 15th Punjab Regiment Indian Army demonstrated much better how far Japan had developed the mandates. Sugar cane and copra production by the Japan South Seas Trading Company or Nan'yō Bōeki Kaisha was extensive with some competition from small firms. The phosphate deposits in Angaur and other mineral operations elsewhere were developed and shipped to Japan. But Nan'yō Bōeki Kaisha still ran at a loss and relied on government subsidy. Shipping throughout the mandates was entirely in Japanese hands. Burns Philp had stopped trading because of the restrictions. NYK ran about 25 steamers a year to the islands.[12]

Reports into the 1930s had certain constant themes. The native population was not treated well and was subjected to a Japanese education when there was any at all. Their land was seized for copra and sugar production and most were forced to work in the sugar industries. Some reported that young boys were made to enrol in military training. The increase in the number of Japanese families sped up the Japanisation of the islands. As to any military or naval activities, reports stated that harbours were improved and reefs blasted to accommodate greater anchorages. It was assumed that this was to accommodate the Japanese 2nd Squadron but there was no evidence. Warships were reported out to sea at times. Islands like Koror in the Pelan Group had a large number of naval personnel who mostly dressed in civilian clothes. There was a belief that a seaplane base and a wireless station existed on Koror. The administrative personnel of the islands were reported as:

> without doubt … naval and Military officers, and the present Governor of the Pelan Group was the Navigating Officer of the Flagship of the 2nd Japanese squadron when it first visited these islands about 1924.

A visitor to the Mandates in 1933 wrote an article for the *Rabaul Times* on 15 September. He was struck that the police watched all foreigners, a display of suspicion, which he claimed dated back three centuries and showed that Japanese attitudes had not changed much. The Japanese population of the islands, the number of large sugar factories, new roads and railways were increasing. This particular article maintained that there had been great fleet manoeuvres involving over 200 vessels at Palau and Saipan in breach of the mandate terms. Japan had chosen this moment, he wrote, to defy the League of Nations and was "a powder-barrel of the whole world" presumably ready to blow up. But in effect there were few reports of mapping activities and sightings of Japanese warships.[13]

Information on Japanese interest in NEI and New Guinea reached Australian intelligence through the Dutch authorities in NEI. These provided indications of Japanese methods of penetration in areas in which they had a definite long-term interest. During World War One, Japanese fishermen, traders and photographers were established at strategic points throughout the NEI archipelago. Intermarriage with locals was also encouraged. Subsequently, an intermittent campaign of stirring up resentment against the Dutch began and by 1930s attempts were made to secure a monopoly of trade and shipping. The Japanese Ministry of Foreign Affairs sponsored propaganda campaigns among the locally born

Chinese and Malays and visits to Japan for Indonesian students and journalists. Agents provocateurs stirred up incidents, which could have provided Japan with a pretext for invasion, but none took place. However, plans for a Japanese administration in the territories were found in the records of the Japanese consul at Manado. This peaceful penetration was conducted in close co-operation with the Army and Navy.[14]

The reports also showed that *nan'yō* boundaries varied in the 1930s. Trading company documents captured and translated into Dutch by NEI officers contain a report written in November 1939 by Misushiro Utamaru, a manager and researcher of the very powerful South Seas company NKKK. It argued that when NKKK began developing from 1921, the areas gained under mandate provided limited scope for Japanese economic activity. Expansion beyond the existing *nan'yō*, especially to New Guinea, was necessary. The report detailed how the company looked for opportunities to take over a firm in New Guinea and succeeded by 1932. It complained about the restrictions that Japanese firms experienced under the Dutch and of unfair competition from Dutch government operations that were attempting to limit Japanese expansion. The writer argued that Japan should define boundaries for *nan'yō* and make its territorial ambitions clearer. It complained that the government had shown little interest to date in the South Sea's problem. The Melbourne *Herald* reported NKKK's move into New Guinea, only 700 miles from Darwin on 20 November 1935. In reality there were only a handful of Japanese in New Guinea, some of whom had previously lived in Australia and who struggled to maintain their small business enterprises.[15]

Formal work by the Japanese Naval Hydrographic Office did not begin until 1933 and was mostly confined to researching published charts. By March 1941, intelligence reports received in Australia contained detailed maps and sketches of many of the islands with a military and naval assessment of capacity for ships at anchor in harbour, and for stores of oil and defences such as guns. But to put this constant watch on Japan in perspective, intelligence reports contained similar information for the activities of other nations in the entire region. The important point is that Australian Naval Intelligence had a constant flow of information on Japan from the mid-1920s. Such information was taken seriously by men like E.L. Piesse, Director of the Pacific Branch in the Prime Minister's Department, who saw no threat from Japan in the 1920s but changed his mind as Meaney points out by 1935 writing under the name of 'Albatross' of the danger of an increasingly militant Japan. Japan had left the League of Nations in 1933 over complaints about its actions in Manchukuo. Australia had less of a quarrel about Manchukuo than other nations, but the all-out war in 1937 in China was different. Because of Japanese activities to the north, especially through trading companies, it was important to establish which Japanese organisations existed in Australia and how many Japanese were resident in each state.[16]

Assessing Japanese activities within Australia

Through the 1920s, as Australian agents began their work for Naval Intelligence, reports were assessed in an attempt to establish whether Japanese were seriously engaged in espionage or not. This endeavour met several problems. First, some reporters were convinced that all Japanese spied, which coloured their decision about what to report. Second, the difficulty remained in defining espionage. Finally, it was often difficult to see what use the information could be to the Japanese. Fearnley's reports illustrate these three problems. Indeed, the DNI, Faquahar Smith commented 21 September 1926 that Fearnley was rather prone to bring anything connected with the Japan into alignment with his set convictions on the Pacific Question. His views were exaggerated.[17]

Fearnley retained his early pre-1910 views in the 1920s. He interpreted all Japanese actions as suspicious and as a probable preparation for invasion. His reports on activities around Newcastle name the Kuwahata family. Over 80 per cent of sailors off Japanese ships at Sydney and

Newcastle gave the farm at Guildford as their shore address. The farm was under observation and the movement of ships' officers to and from it was recorded. Kuwahata's vegetable shop in Newcastle run by Mr Ochi was also under observation. Fearnley reported that:

> Kuwahata is unquestionably in close touch with Japanese affairs in this state, and if there is any organised Japanese Intelligence Corps in Australia, I venture the opinion that Mr Kuwahata ... is a responsible officer in that service.

No evidence was found after Kuwahata senior's death. He had acted as an unofficial immigration agent for the Consul-General, welcoming Japanese to Sydney and attending to the necessary paperwork. The Australian government already knew much of what Fearnley noted and believed it was harmless. Thomas and Frederick, Kuwahata's sons, were not spying and were not interned but assisted Australian security services with information.

Fearnley felt that the number of photos taken around Newcastle had given the Japanese first-class strategic information on the area. As E.L. Piesse said on 31 August 1920, Fearnley's reports presumed espionage but had not established anything.

> In their fondness for Kodaks, Japanese abroad are not behind American tourists, and everywhere they show an alert interest in anything that is new to them. These qualities would have sufficed, without any ulterior purpose to gain for them the reputation for espionage which they now enjoy throughout the East ... Accepting the presumption that espionage is being carried on, what is its significance?
>
> We have been familiar with Japanese espionage in Australia for ten or fifteen years past and most of it has taken place on the coast from Port Stephens to Sydney. It is probable that it still continues. What is its object and what clue does it give to Japanese policy?[18]

Piesse had no answer for his own question and did not specify what espionage Japanese had engaged in for 15 years. Certainly no evidence is extant except Fearnley's suspicions. Piesse argued that the Japanese General Staff was modelled on German lines, which involved collecting information very widely even in countries where it was unlikely to fight in the future, because it was impossible to foresee to which countries a war might spread. Piesse separated information gathering from plans to invade, a position others were not able to adopt. He concluded:

> ... the Japanese collect information about countries without of necessity having a plan to attack them. This, at all events, was the view I found to be held by naval and military attaches in Tokyo ... If they follow this policy, ... there is every reason why ... they should collect information about Newcastle.

Piesse's assessment of espionage reports at this time was governed by his assessment of the danger from Japan. As Meaney argues Piesse was convinced that Japan was a threat before 1914 but adopted a more sophisticated view by the 1920s (when the relationship between Australia and Japan was more relaxed) after gaining more direct knowledge of Japan during World War One.[19]

Naval Intelligence dealt with the problems surrounding the espionage issue by hedging its bets. It instigated a discreet watch on Japanese naval visitors after 1930 in response to Japan's takeover of Manchukuo. The records of the visits of the Training Squadron document the gradual change in attitude. Once Japan was involved in Manchuria, Australian Naval Intelligence both welcomed the fleet, preparing ever more lavish events, but appointed an intelligence officer as liaison officer to the fleet. All DNOs were instructed to report on the activities of sailors and officers on shore. Some reports are extremely detailed with CVs of crew and officers including information on their personalities and their views on international events when they commented at all. Even the representative of Mitsui in Sydney, Mr Ishikawa, did not escape suspicion as he visited the fleet and arranged coal and other provisions, a service Mitsui had provided since 1907. When the Japanese sent letters of thanks to the various dignitaries that they visited or were entertained by in port, including the zoos and automobile clubs, government departments were generally pleased at their positive responses. However, when events in China escalated in the 1930s, a degree of cynicism crept into the interpretation of the kind letters of appreciation from Japanese visitors. Some naval personnel in the department became cynical about the positive sentiments expressed about the Australia–Japan relationship stating that: "The letter appears to be worth nothing one way or the other. The Japanese are ever polite."[20]

The problem for the historian in assessing information on Japanese activities in Australia is not only the definition of espionage but also that most of the reports on espionage date from after Japan entered World War Two. They are written from hindsight. Barnwell's report is one of the most extensive but is it accurate? Some of the people named as suspicious within the Consulate-General in Sydney were Long's agents. What such reports do provide is an overview of Japanese networks in Australia. The recording of these networks by Australians dates from the late 1930s. Some of the clubs were formed late as well, like the Nippon Club in Sydney from September 1938, destined to keep young Japanese men occupied in their spare time and out of trouble with local women.[21] These clubs and their role will be assessed in the next chapter.

Assessing evidence for espionage

There is plenty of evidence for overt information gathering by Japanese throughout the five decades before World War Two. Most of this information was used to write books or to undertake commercial operations. There is very limited evidence for true espionage that could have been used to harm or invade Australia in wartime. One early possible case was the Japanese survey taken from Elcho Island in 1926 when flags and markers were found in May and evidence of soundings activity at other locations such as Cotton Island and Wessel Island. The fact that the Japanese had left signs of their presence suggested to naval officers that the object of the survey was to sound out the anchorage north west of Wessell that would be useful during the pearling season rather than for a later landing in a war that Japan had not yet planned. Fearnley's reports from Newcastle listed all Japanese shipping activities as suspicious, whether a ship strayed a little closer to shore than usual or a visitor drove around the harbour or bought a map, but none were confirmed as linked to any espionage. Yet the information could have been useful later. Doubt about the usefulness of early information for war is most strongly supported by the actual nature of official spying as far as we have evidence for that.[22]

Evidence for true espionage begins when Consul-General Wakamatsu reportedly established an espionage service in Australia probably by 1933–34. On 18 August 1936 an intercept provided evidence of funds allocated by the South Seas Section of the Japanese Foreign Office inaugurated on 9 September of that year to Japanese legations and embassies for secret service work. The purpose was to make active political endeavours behind the scenes on international diplomacy, and to investigate the possibilities of emigration, trade and investment. By 1941, the annual allocation to the Japanese Minister in Australia for intelligence was £30,000. However, because a lot of material was burned by the Consulate-General before Pearl Harbor, it is likely that material relating to espionage was destroyed. But four years of surveillance of all Japanese by Australian police provides information on individuals in the organisation.[23]

There were two types of agents: long-term residents and short-term visitors. Known agents included: a trading company manager of a firm with branches in Sydney and Brisbane and an agency in Melbourne; Denzo Umino, believed to be materially assisting those involved in espionage as part of his work in driving for the Consulate-General and doing laundry for firms and ships; Harry or Henry Suzuki (a.k.a. Ivan Steele) in Brisbane engaged in suspicious activities in Queensland and associated with Umeda in minerals investigation which placed Umeda under suspicion; Professor Seita of Brisbane, suspected because of his associations with the Japanese government, cultural societies and reportedly the notorious international Black Dragon Society.

The company manager, a playboy who did little company work and lost a lot gambling, whom we shall name 'Juro' figured constantly in the network of information and report giving. He arrived in 1916 and when he was repatriated in August 1942, he left debts in Australia totalling £112,000 in federal income tax and £205,000 in personal debt, underwritten by his family in Japan. As far as is known, he became an active agent in 1933. A police informant who befriended him at a popular Sydney golf club shadowed him. He photographed parts of Sydney's road and harbour networks and exported the film in hollow golf clubs. The Brisbane office of his company was a "revolving door" for people under notice and it was through this branch's managerial residence in West End that an elderly Japanese passed on information. In addition, the company was discovered shipping goods that disappeared in transit along the Australian coast. Customs never solved the case of the empty container of goods that they discovered in Brisbane in 1941.

Umino was certainly used by the espionage network. He drove visitors like Major Hashida around Sydney and Newcastle, whose 1941 report on Australia is considered in the next chapter. He was given parcels to deliver within Sydney. His family was also working for various Japanese organisations in Sydney, which brought them under suspicion. His wife's sister-in law, a Japanese woman, worked as a secretary for the Japanese Chamber of Commerce. The head of the JCC was often the manager of Mitsubishi. Another member was a Japanese newspaperman who came under suspicion of espionage after 1937. This paper was a semi-government agency in Japan and part of the F. Kikan espionage network in Malaya in the 1940s. The paper's secretary was the daughter of Adela Pankhust Walsh, Silvia Walsh, of the Australia First Movement that was pro-Japanese. She distributed information to Japanese firms that the newspaper collected. The interconnections between trading networks, the pattern of intermarriage between Australians and Japanese, and the employment and association patterns of Australians who were very interested in Japan before 1937 made it impossible later on for security services to be certain who was loyal and what activities constituted espionage.[24] Reports that detailed Japanese information gathering about waterways, coastlines for shipping purposes, activities of cultural societies and commercial organisations had the same difficulties.

"Summarised reports of Japanese activities", listed by state from 1911–38, included information gathering, soundings, surveying and reconnaissance, interest in minerals and the activities of firms. The report listed inquiries by Japanese about harbours and photographing of harbours, especially by firms such as Mitsui. It noted that 75 per cent of charts purchased in Fremantle in 1931 had been by Japanese. This is in contrast to Tanaka Hiromi's conclusion that the Japanese navy did not have sufficient military intelligence on Australia and that few charts in the Japanese Hydrography Department showed water depths. This fact, Tanaka argues, is testimony to the lack of plans for naval operations directed against Australia. It would be interesting to know the dates of these charts, as the RAN recorded that from 1913 onwards, the mappings and surveying of the north-west coast of Australia was very extensive. Japanese naval officers boasted at Thursday Island in 1920 that the Japanese Navy knew the Torres Strait better than the RAN. By 1935, Japanese charts of the Barrier Reef were better than those of the British Admiralty. Certainly the patrol boat *Larrakia* and mission boats had to rely on Aboriginal pilots across the north of Australia into the late 1930s. Admiralty charts were still inadequate. The purpose of the

Japanese hydrographic surveying was to supplement Admiralty Sailing Directions and the charts were issued to masters of Japanese ships. A similar hydrographic survey of SEA took place from 1933 to 1937. Mitsui had maps of ports throughout the Pacific, which cargo ships used. These sketches and more formal annotations on existing charts were appended to official information from ports about harbour, customs and other regulations. A full set of these documents existed for Australian ports. Mitsui made no effort to conceal this information and did not destroy it prior to World War Two. It remains in the National Archives of Australia today and was examined by Australian intelligence in 1941–42, which found it had no security value. Before 1937, these surveys had an immediate practical purpose but the information after that time was put to a more official purpose with the centralisation of pearling operations in the Pacific.[25]

One Japanese man who acted as a pearling agent in Darwin for many Japanese companies is constantly recorded in history books and stories as being a spy: John Iwamatsu Nakashiba. In addition, the loyalty of his adopted Australian-born and European son, Peter, who spoke fluent Japanese, is often questioned. John's NAD Co. store was a busy meeting place for Japanese off ships. It provisioned ships and acted as the unofficial consul by assisting with paperwork at the port. John and Peter helped the captains of the luggers who were arrested in 1938. They also obtained Australian solicitors in Darwin to assist them to mount the case that cleared the vessels of wrongdoing and led to compensation for the owners. This brought suspicion. Most people in Darwin believed John was a spy. Japanese people also believed he was a spy, but were unsure on which side his loyalties truly lay. The truth is quite remarkable and only emerged in wartime. When John was interned, the Navy protested to the Army. John was not naturalised but he was a commissioned officer in Australian Naval Intelligence. He provided much important information about Japanese pearling in the lead-up to the war. Although the Japanese-born members of his family were interned, the Army tried to find suitable work for them and gradually released them during wartime. John is one example of how a belief can be quite wrong but also quite necessary to protect intelligence operations.[26]

Many organisations existed in Australia to promote good relations and mutual understanding between the two countries. Consul-General Tokugawa founded the Japan–Australia Society in 1929, which eminent Australians joined. One organisation, the Kokusai Bunka Shinkokai (KBS) or Society for International Relations founded in 1934, particularly brought its members under notice. Its aim was to encourage interest in Japanese culture based on the ideal of furthering worldwide exchange of cultural relations in the cause of international peace and better understanding. After World War One, and especially after Japan's withdrawal from the League of Nations, the importance of promoting Japanese culture abroad became recognised. The KBS wrote books on Japanese culture, established Chairs in overseas universities in culture and language and donated and exchanged documents on art and culture. The first issue of the society's journal, *KBS Quarterly*, published mid-1935 revealed how close the organisation was to the Japanese Government. Its president was Prince Fumimaro Konoe, who as Prime Minister would later preside over the foreign policies that brought Japan to the start of the Pacific War. Its advisers included the then Prime Minister, Okada Keisuke and Foreign Minister Hirota Koki. The publications openly recognised the society's official connections, the donations from the Imperial Household, and support from business and government. The KBS was absorbed in 1940 into the Information Bureau within the Japanese cabinet and its purpose openly acknowledged as one of disseminating Japanese propaganda.[27] Within Australia's Japanese community, Professor R. Seita of Brisbane University and Moshi Inagaki who taught Japanese language classes through an arrangement with the University of Melbourne were members. The KBS was suspected of not only disseminating information about Japan in Australia but also using it as a forum for espionage. The Australian evidence for this is slim but suggestive in regard to a few of its members and sufficient to raise official concern.[28]

The trading companies formed the JCC in Sydney by 1933, which became a member of Sydney Chamber of Commerce in 1935. JCC membership included representatives of the Consulate-General, employees of Japanese companies, independent traders like Ide and Nakamura and Japanese newspaper operators. Australian-born Japanese such as the Kuwahata brothers, who did not speak Japanese, were also permitted to join. Members of the JCC comprised the bulk of Japanese working in the Australia–Japan import–export trade before World War Two in Sydney. Before 1937, the JCC had certain roles: to put traders in touch with each other, to liaise with Australian traders, wool buyers and the Sydney Chamber of Commerce, and to fulfil an 'enlightenment' role for the Japanese government. The JCC was responsible for commenting on and replying to any comment about Japan or to any Australian government policy reported in the Australian press or mentioned in parliament. For this purpose the Japanese government funded the JCC £100 in 1936. It was involved in lobbying Australian governments on trade policy.

In 1933, with discussion of sending an Australian trade delegation to Japan, the JCC deplored the lack of understanding in Australia about the favourable balance of trade that Australia enjoyed. International relations, it stated were built on reciprocity of trade, an issue that needed addressing. The 1936 Trade Diversion Dispute provided a major opportunity for the JCC to put Japan's case to the Australian public. In a broadcast on 17 August 1936, Prime Minister Lyons announced that the government had decided to limit the quantity of imports of fabrics from Japan. He stated that Australia depended on Britain to buy its surplus primary produce; that it was necessary to share the Australian market for foreign goods on a fair basis and that there was a need to protect Australian manufacturers and living standards against goods offered at excessively low prices. He argued that Japan had reduced the price of goods three times in one year and blamed the Japanese merchants directly for the dispute, a position that was not totally correct.

If Japanese exporters had abstained from their successive price reductions, which had the effect of flooding this market with goods of a class and value which were dislocating to our whole economic life, the dispute would not have arisen.

In reaction to the extraordinary success of the Japanese in the mutual trade, Australia intended to divert some of its trade from Japan to Britain as the trade from Japan came close to exceeding that of the trade with Britain in some areas.[29] *The Economist* in Britain in 29 August 1936 wrote that Australia was hurting a good customer in Japan.

What are the rights and wrongs of the unfortunate Australo-Japanese controversy? Australia argues that although Japan buys more than she sells, the Australo-Japanese trade is carried out in Japanese ships, financed by Japanese bankers, and organised by Japanese merchants. This comes near to the heart of the matter, which is more political nationalistic than economic.

There was some truth in the statements that the trade was run largely through Japanese firms. But the result was retaliation from Japan and the threat to purchase wool in South Africa. The JCC stated that Japanese branch houses could not exist without making a profit and unless Japan could maintain its exports it could not maintain its imports. The negotiations between the JCC and the government were instrumental in resolving the dispute, particularly with the intervention of Sam Hirodo who worked out a compromise position and Japanese wool buyers returned to Australian auction rooms to standing ovations in January 1937.

Although the JCC role was mostly focused on trade until 1937, its 'enlightenment' role became more central by 1938 as indicated by the following directive.

> Propaganda by the Federation of Jap [*sic*] Exporters' Associations must maintain the nature of a civilian enterprise in all events, subject, however, to secret direction and guidance from our government officials abroad.[30]

This role meant that members of the JCC even though they were not particularly active like Nakamura, Kuwahata and Ide, or who did not attend meetings, came under suspicion.

Vilification of Japanese within Australia

Japan bashing within Australia has obscured the issue of espionage and made it more difficult to assess Japanese actions. This began in the 1930s when pearling interests often reported that Japanese competition could force Europeans out of the trade. They used Japanese information gathering (labelled 'espionage') to strengthen their case and 'national interest' as a catch cry to obtain attention in Canberra. But the missionary lobby did more to give Japanese people a bad name in the 1930s than most other sections of the public who were reported in the press. It is one very clear example of how a local issue grew to enormous proportions and was then interpreted as a national threat.[31] More bad press related to Japanese people originated from wartime intelligence reports, particularly in Queensland where all Japanese were called 'spies', and the subsequent assumption by historians that the claims against Japanese people made in wartime, or afterwards, were accurate.

The 1930s vilification of Japanese people and Japan independent of any actual activity stemmed from the impact that the relationship between

Japanese indentured workers and Aboriginal people had on missionary work. The incident at Caledon Bay NT on 17 September 1932 was one of a number of cases when Aboriginal people attacked those who had entered their land. Ted Egan's book provides a detailed investigation of these killings and concludes that the precise reason for them remains obscure. In short, two luggers owned by Kepert of Darwin were gathering *trepang* from Caledon Bay. The Japanese and Aboriginal crew worked on shore after negotiations with local Aboriginals for use of the beach from 4 September until the killings on 17 September. Six Japanese were attacked and only one escaped alive. This began a police inquiry to find the killers and a media frenzy, which such killings had not attracted before. The articles in the major Australian papers stated that the Japanese had been killed because they had interfered with Aboriginal women and that the government should do more to stop poaching in Australian waters and protect Aboriginal people from invasion. This picture of the Japanese as invading, raping, poaching monsters who even took women into sex slavery, was the view of many missionaries along the north, who in many cases were also official Coast Watchers.

For decades, Darwin-based pearling boats with mixed Japanese and Malay crews had landed on NT shores to collect water, clean boats, hunt and trade with Aboriginal tribes. Some of the Japanese men married Aboriginal women under tribal law. Indeed, Macassans had enjoyed such relations for 200 years before any Japanese arrived in Australia. But the mission stations along the north, which were attempting to Christianise and civilise Aboriginals, wanted this 'immoral' and competing influence stopped. Almost all of the Japanese landings along the north in the 1930s were of this type but interpreted quite differently by the time reports hit the southern press. The stories of Japanese raping and pillaging, indeed invading Australia's coast developed strongly from such reports. One panicky article in the *Herald* in 1937 said that Japan was only three miles off Australia's coast. The Japanese concerned had mostly lived in Darwin or Broome for many years and half of the men involved were local Malays residing legally in Australia. Any mass groupings of pearling boats was usually for safety reasons well out of territorial waters and represented four different nations with between 30–50 per cent of them Australian-owned at any one time. But such feeling was certain to alarm southerners and also give Japanese in Japan the sense that White Australia was indeed a very inhospitable place.

To counter the accusations that the Japanese who were killed at Caledon Bay had provoked the attacks, the Japanese Club in Darwin, headed by Nakashiba asked for a letter from the police stating that there was no evidence to support this position. This request was granted. In contrast, the missionaries and the southern press railed against the government for its failure to deal with the activities of Japanese in the north, (supposedly incursions from Japan, but actually landings by Australian-Japanese residents), and accused the government of fear of Japan and a desire to appease Japan. This vilification of Japanese people and whipping up fear of Japan had no basis at that time in fact but because of the status missionaries enjoyed in the southern community from where they had originated, their interpretation of the events as an invasion, at least in moral terms, carried a great deal of weight. The situation was further exacerbated when the missionaries joined the search for the killers for fear they might be shot on sight. During the months of the search and subsequent trials which received almost daily reports in the southern press, the Aboriginals gradually became viewed as the victims and the murdered Japanese the evil-doers in the Caledon Bay incident. The pressure generated from this time achieved a patrol service along the north by 1936.

The belief that Japan was massing off the Australian coast and planned to invade had its origins in reports in the southern press of events in the NT, particularly after three luggers were arrested for allegedly being in territorial waters in 1937, a charge which was proved false. However, the lurid stories found a prominent place in post-war history writing about the pre-war era that held that Japan planned to invade but was stopped at the Coral Sea and Kokoda. The pearling boats become the agents of giant Japanese combines. Mitsui is often named as the agent preparing to invade and which controlled pearling. There is no evidence that Mitsui fulfilled such roles and these accusations require careful investigation.

One example of strong Australian historical writing that negatively stereotypes the Japanese is Norman Bartlett's book written after World War Two. He represents the Japanese pearlers in the 1930s as 'pirates with slant eyes' who invaded and spied, and against whom Australian pearlers, facing competition, demanded naval action. On the other hand, he also argued, they were businessmen on the right side of the law fishing in international waters, but Bartlett describes them as cunning.

> ... Between 1931 and 1940, Japanese luggers and sampans poached, thieved, raided and pirated along the lonely stretches of the pearling coast from Darwin to the Great Barrier Reef. They left camp sites along the coast of Arnhem Land and Cape York Peninsular, where you can still see piles of 'discards' and broken-down 'smokehouses' ... They left a good many slant-eyed piccaninnies among the coastal natives. And they took back better charts of the Australian coastline than were available to Australia's naval intelligence. The Mitsui Combine was directly interested in the Australian pearling grounds, and the Japanese Navy appreciated the excellent opportunities for charting reefs, atolls, sandbanks and channels from the decks of a pearling lugger.

In this one quote we have every negative charge against the Japanese in Australia for the pre-war era. The interpretation of Japanese-Aboriginal relations, which was largely positive, takes on a sinister tone. The question of maps becomes a preparation for invasion. Mitsui, the positive contributor to the Australian economy in the Great Depression, becomes

a monster combine. The Japanese Navy is poised to strike just out to sea.
These charges receive further investigation in Chapter 7. But as we have
seen, Mitsui Australia had no pearling department nor did Mitsubishi.
Their slim role in worldwide pearling is investigated in the next chapter.
The Japanese navy had undertaken a hydrographic survey but not around
Australia at this early time before 1937.[32] No one was poised to invade at
this time, no matter how much Australians liked to speculate that they
were in imminent danger.

Wartime intelligence reports from Queensland add to the post-war
assumption that all Japanese were engaged in espionage or some furtive
activity as a prelude to invasion. Unlike other states, Queensland records
strongly argue for a sinister web of networks where only a small spy ring
existed. The contrast between these reports and those generated in NSW
for example is stark. NSW had the largest population of merchants and the
highest number of *zaibatsu* in Australia, but only Fearnley accused Japanese
people of spying in that state. Because of the constant surveillance in NSW
and the placement of agents in the Consulate-General's residence, other
members of the security services knew who was spying and who was not.

The Queensland records state that Australia was part of the Japanese
total espionage plan that made a spy of every Japanese wherever he
resided or visited no matter what his normal occupation was. "Every
Japanese in Queensland if not an active espionage agent for his country,
was expected and was willing to assist those who were operating as
Intelligence personnel." The report however does not distinguish between
early information gathering and pre-war organised espionage. It credits
the Tokumu Kikan with organising spying in Queensland. It then links
the mapping and all activity off the Queensland coast in previous decades
with this organisation. The activities of the Kikan need consideration but
it was not initially operational until 1940 in Malaya.

The report names Professor R. Seita, Henry Suzuki and others as
leaders. It names Major Hashida as the chief among visiting espionage

agents before the war. It also claims that Nobutaro Umeda, who was Director of Tonan Shokai in WA was

> one of the highly trained special agents of the Japanese Economic Espionage Section. Acting under instructions form the Japanese Government, he devoted nearly ten years to an intensive study of the mineral and agricultural resources in Australia ... [he] visited Queensland in 1937 and ... closely studied the mineral wealth and the cattle industry in Queensland ... His chief task ... took the form of a blatant attempt to create a Japanese monopoly of the mineral resources of this state. It was hoped that this monopoly would result in Japan receiving an adequate supply of the necessary metals, to enable her to complete her tremendous armament programme.

Although there is some truth in general terms in the report, it requires examination against other more objective evidence.[33]

Conclusion

The stories about spying, which still circulate particularly in areas of Australia that experienced raids, largely result from local rumours and Japanese engaging in amorphous information gathering throughout the decades before the war. Some resulted from post-war arguments that reinterpreted innocent Japanese activities like photography, which even Piesse knew were harmless, or misinformation about the structure and activities of Japanese multinational companies (as we will investigate further in Chapter 7). The Japanese engaged in an extraordinary amount of information gathering around the world. Australia was not special in this regard. What Japanese did before 1937 was minimal in terms of real espionage and those involved were very few. The information gathered by spies at this time was not of immediate use for war. It was gathered mostly around Sydney and Newcastle and it is likely that a small amount of information was gathered in Queensland probably relating to minerals rather than to strategic military information useful for landing or raiding.

In response, Australian security services continued their detailed and careful surveillance and a constant watch on Japan to the north. What part the visiting spies and the *zaibatsu* played after Japan went to war on China in 1937, how this changed espionage in Australia prior to the war and the nature of information gathered provides us with the best views of Japan's plans for Australia. But it is important to note that even in 1937, the information gathered by Japan was not sufficient for any plans to invade Australia or take any other action against Australia in a wartime situation.

THE
AUSTRALIAN HOTEL
J. MORONEY. Proprietor

PHONE CENTRAL 9784 (3 LINES)

106-108 SPENCER STREET (OPP. STATION)

Melbourne, 2 April 1926

Mr H. E. Kennedy:
Customs & Excise Office,
Melbourne.

APR - 8
8 APR 1926

Dear Sir:

I beg to acknowledge your letter of 29th March, with certificate. As my wife is now a British subject by marriage I shall be glad to learn why an exemption certificate is necessary; also why her period of residence is restricted when my right to remain is unquestioned.

We have booked by the "Ormonde" leaving Tuesday evening, April 6th, after a most enjoyable stay. The Australians seem the most cordial people in the world. Faithfully yours

de Havilland

Letter from Mr de Havilland about an exemption certificate for his Japanese wife Yoki, 1926,
(Courtesy of National Archives of Australia, NAA: B13, 1926/6648)

Pearling luggers in the Arafura Sea, 1938. Photograph taken by NT Administrator C.L.A. Abbott.
(Courtesy National Archives of Australia, NAA: M10, 2/87)

Unknown. From the private collection of C.E.W. Bean.
The Royal Australian Navy Squadron and the Japanese Training Squadron in Sydney Harbour during a visit by the Japanese Navy in May 1906. The protected cruisers HMS Powerful and HMS Challenger and the Japanese training cruisers Matsushima, Hashidate and Itsukushima can be seen in the middle. A crowd of people have gathered in the foreground to watch the cruisers in the harbour. Caption on the reverse of photograph "The Royal Navy and Australia' The Australian Squadron and the Japanese Training Squadron in Sydney Harbour"
Black and white photograph cMay 1906 Australian War Memorial (P02751.053)

h Other's Poin

By Vice-Admiral Seizo Kobayashi

It is rarely that a newspaper has the good-fortune to obtain from so eminent a visitor as Vice-Admiral Kobayashi a special article which frankly discusses national aims and contrasts. The Admiral believes that in the thorough understanding of points of view lies friendship. In this article he dwells, not only on Japan's attitude at the Geneva Conference and the reasons therefor, but on such everyday matters as differing national customs, and the effect they have on the viewpoint from which one country regards another

Opposite Page: Japanese warships, Melbourne 6 July 1928
(Courtesy of National Archives of Australia NAA: MP124/6, 603/203/347)

Above: Vice Admiral Kobayashi, *The Saturday Herald*, May 1928
(Courtesy of National Archives of Australia NAA: MP124/6, 603/203/347)

Officers of Japanese Training Squadron, June 1932. *The Age* (Courtesy of National Archives of Australia NAA: MP124/6, 603/203/347)

Opposite Page: 'Our Japanese visitors as Wells sees them', from the Melbourne *Herald*, 4 July 1928 (Courtesy of National Archives of Australia, NAA: MP124/6, 603/203/347)

VICE ADMIRAL SEIZO KOBAYASHI

HIS IMPERIAL HIGHNESS PRINCE TAKAMATSU

COMDR. F. IWAIHARA

CAPT. M. IDEMITSU

COMDR. H. WAKI

MR. I. M. TOKUGAWA CONSUL-GENL FOR JAPAN

SKETCHED AT MENZIES YESTERDAY

WELLS

A series of caricatures made by Wells at yesterday's official luncheon given by the Japanese Consul-General (Mr. Tokugawa) and the Honorary Japanese Consul (Sir William McBeath) to the Japanese officers at Menzies' Hotel.

EIGHTY-SIX ACRES OF THE N.S.W. COASTLINE OWNED BY JAPANESE

STARTLING PURCHASES

AT MIDDLE HEAD, JERVIS BAY, BARRENJOEY

At Jervis Bay.

foreign syndicate in a country where they are permitted to hold the fee simple of land. BUT THE NAME OR YOKOHAMA-ROAD LACKS AUSTRALIAN COLOR.

BIG ESTATES BOUGHT NEAR ST. MARYS

The purchase has been effected by a representative of a Japanese

SUBDIVIDED IN JAPANESE NAMES

PLANS OFFICIALLY SANCTIONED

Going West.

syndicate whose name is given as Kinjira Outehe.

Australia is possibly the only civilised country which permits

E IGHTY-SIX ACRES of the coastline of New South Wales are in the hands of Japanese owners.

This remarkable fact has just been brought to light—the purchases having been effected during this year.

Here are the facts:—

SIXTY-FIVE ACRES OF LAND PURCHASED BY A JAPANESE SYNDICATE AT JERVIS BAY.

TWENTY ACRES OF LAND PURCHASED BY A JAPANESE SYNDICATE AT BARRENJOEY, NEAR ETTALONG BEACH, BROKEN BAY.

ONE ACRE OF LAND PURCHASED BY A JAPANESE SYNDICATE AT MIDDLE HEAD, SYDNEY HARBOR.

That completes the Japanese ownership of our coastline, but not the purchases by Japanese syndicates.

HALF AN ACRE HAS BEEN BOUGHT AT FAULCONBRIDGE 51 MILES FROM SYDNEY, AND ONE OF THE POINTS ON THE MOUNTAINS WHICH OVERLOOKS SYDNEY DIRECT.

Another Japanese syndicate has purchased a big estate near St. Marys, on the Penrith line, and the subdivision of roads and streets bears Japanese names.

THE PLANS HAVE RECEIVED THE OFFICIAL SANCTION OF THE FEDERAL AUTHORITIES.

At Middle Head.

foreigners to hold the fee simple of land.

IT IS SAFE TO SAY THAT AUSTRALIA DOES NOT DESIRE SO COMPLETE A TRANSFORMATION OF HER NOMENCLATURE TO PROVIDE FOR YOKOHAMA ROAD OR TOKYO STREET IN THE MOTHER STATE.

IN JAPAN

No Purchase Allowed

To me the interesting point of the above story is that I know very well that no Australian and no foreigner of any nationality may own a foot of the "sacred soil of Nippon."

If foreigners have for business or other reasons to own land in Japan it has to be done through Japanese nominees, an extremely risky business. It can be had in the name of a company provided the shareholding and directorate of the company is predominantly Japanese.

The main cause of dispute between Japan and the United States has arisen from the claim of Japanese subjects to own land in California. In 1913 in reply to protests by Tokyo against the Webb Law, the Federal authorities at Washington drew attention to the Japanese law on the subject. The Tokyo authorities drafted an ameliorator law, which was recently promulgated, but which does not substantially improve the conditions of land ownership by foreigners.

The possibility of a foreigner being

WHY DO JAPANESE want land in the areas mentioned?

JERVIS BAY is practically the headquarters of the Australian Navy, and our principal naval base. BROKEN BAY is the one sheltered inlet between Sydney and Newcastle, capable of accommodating big ships.

MIDDLE HEAD commands an uninterrupted view of Sydney Heads. Portion is a military reserve, carrying Australian fortifications.

FAULCONBRIDGE is 51 miles from Sydney, 1465 feet above sea level, and by its situation overlooks the city of Sydney and its immediate coastline.

THE ESTATE near St. Marys seems a more suitable purchase for a

Broken Bay.

Opposite Page: 'Eighty-six acres of the N.S.W. coastline owned by Japanese' *Evening News*, 12 December 1922

Mitsui Bussan Kaisha balance of selling contracts at 31/10/28, (Courtesy of National Archives of Australia, NAA: SP1096/5, Box 43)

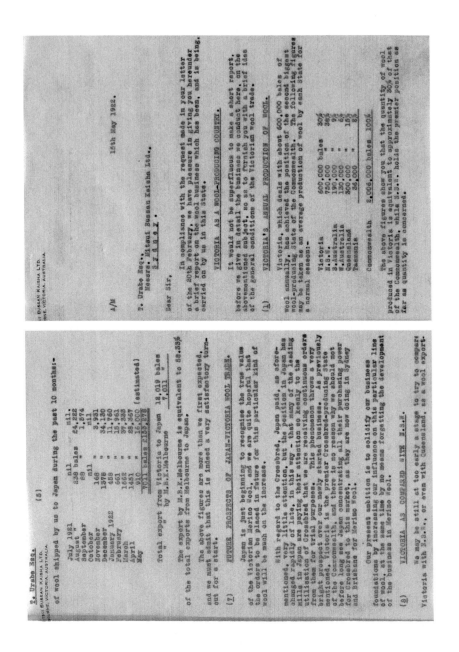

MITSUI BUSSAN KAISHA LTD.
...BOURNE, VICTORIA, AUSTRALIA.

15th May 1922.

A/M

T. Urabe Esq.,
　Messrs. Mitsui Bussan Kaisha Ltd.,
　　　　S y d n e y .

Dear Sir,

In compliance with the request made in your letter of the 20th February, we have pleasure in giving you hereunder a brief report on the wool business which has been, and is being, carried on by us in this State.

VICTORIA AS A WOOL-PRODUCING COUNTRY.

It would not be superfluous to make a short report, before we dive in detail the business we conduct here, on the abovementioned subject, so as to furnish you with a brief idea of the general conditions of the Victorian wool trade.

(1) VICTORIA'S ANNUAL PRODUCTION OF WOOL.

Victoria, which deals with about 600,000 bales of wool annually, has achieved the position of the second biggest wool-producing State of the Commonwealth. The following figures may be taken as an average production of wool by each State for a normal season:-

Victoria	600,000 bales	30%
N.S.W.	750,000 "	38%
S.Australia	190,000 "	9%
W.Australia	130,000 "	6%
Queensland	300,000 "	15%
Tasmania	36,000 "	2%
Commonwealth	2,006,000 bales	100%

The above figures show you that the quantity of wool produced in Victoria is equivalent to approximately 30% of that of the Commonwealth, while N.S.W. holds the premier position as far as quantity is concerned.

T. Urabe Esq.　　(5)

of wool shipped by us to Japan during the past 10 months:-

July 1921	nil.	
August "	230 bales	
September	88 "	
October	nil	
November	166 "	
December	1376 "	
January 1922	458 "	
February	661 "	
March	1662 "	
April	1451 "	
May	910 "	16,000 (estimated)
	Total bales	£133,278

Total export from Victoria to Japan 18,019 bales
　　　" by M.B.K.Melbourne　　　　7,011 "

The export from Victoria to Japan is equivalent to 58.23% of the total exports from Melbourne to Japan.

The above figures are more than we first expected, and we must admit that this is indeed a very satisfactory turn-out for a start.

(7) FUTURE PROSPECTS OF JAPAN-VICTORIA WOOL TRADE.

Japan is just beginning to recognise the true value of the Victorian Merino wool, and we are quite hopeful that the orders to be placed in future for this particular kind of wool will be much on the increase.

With regard to the Crossbred, Japan paid, as afore-mentioned, very little attention, but the position in Japan has changed rapidly of late. In this way - that many of the leading mills in Japan are paying their attention so keenly to the utilisation of Crossbred that we are receiving continuous orders from them for trial purposes. This phenomenon throws a very bright prospect over our newly started business. As previously mentioned, Victoria is the premier Crossbred-producing State of the Commonwealth, and there is no reason why we should not before long see Japan concentrating all their purchasing power for Crossbred to this market, as they are now doing in Sydney and Brisbane for Merino Wool.

Our present ambition is to solidify our business line foundations by increasing our influence on this particular line of wool, at the same time by no means forgetting the development of the business in Merino wool.

(8) VICTORIA AS COMPARED WITH N.S.W.

We may be still at too early a stage to try to compare Victoria with N.S.W., or even with Queensland, as a wool export-

Mitsui Bussan Kaisha report on the wool industry in Victoria 15 May 1922

Patricia Malloch, designer and cutter at Foy & Gibson Melbourne,
in the 1930s with hand made clothes. (Padgham family photographs)

Tonan Shokai partners, Broome, WA, formed January 1926, L–R Back row: J Imata, F. Kitano; Front row: K. Sakai, T. Mise, S. Umeda (Courtesy of Noreen Jones and the Mise Collection)

海上雲遠

Mitsubishi Shoki Kaisha advertising for the Datson Car 1934 (Courtesy of National Archives of Australia, NAA: SP1096/1, Box 43, Eastern Distributors Correspondence Folder)

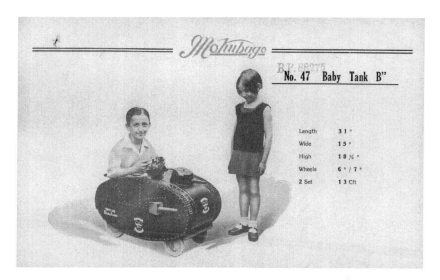

No. 47   Baby   Tank   B"

Length	31"
Wide	15"
High	18 ½"
Wheels	6"/7"
2 Set	13 Cft

Japanese imports before World War 2 included toys such as this 'Baby Tank', listed in Nosawa & Co Catalogue c 1932, (Courtesy of National Archives of Australia, NAA: SP1098/12 Box 13.)

An invitation to Mr Keiji [Ken] Shimada to attend a celebration of the birthday of the Japanese Emperor (29 April, 1937) (Courtesy of National Archives of Australia, NAA: SP1098/12, Box 12).

St.Kilda   Caulfield.S.2

Dear Mr Wakamatsu,

      The Victorian teachers will soon be leaving Melbourne
for their trip to Japan,and are very excited about it. I am hoping
that they will receive a good impression of Japan,and on their return
to Australia have good and impressive reports to make.
      If you do not think me too presumptious to ask such
a favour, could you give them a letter,stating that they are invited
teachers from Australia,so as to help them at the various ports of c●
in Japan,for as you know there are very many questions asked,and it i●
all very bewildering to innocent visitors,and they become rather
distressed about it. I am anxious that all their impressions be good,
and wish them to sense and feel our progressiveness and greatness as a
Nation.   As you know, they will be a good advertisement for us on thei
return to Australia, especially as many people here, have peculiar ideas
about the East. Sometimes they make me feel very vexed. I have again
mentioned to them to ask advice from you,when they call at the Consulate.
      Now I wish to tell you ,how grateful I am to you for
taking an interest in me in general. The other day,Mr Shirani, from the
Mitsubishi,mentioned to me that you had asked him and the Japanese
Society in Melbourne, to co-operate with me.   For that reason
Mr.Shirani asked me to re-join the Japanese Society as one of their member
and further stressed the point that membership fees would not be required
from me.
      I gladly accepted their offer ,and was made a member.
I told Mr.Shirani,that the reason that I had been so long away from them,
was, not because I did not desire to work with them, but finance blocked
membership for me.   Now,on your recommendation, and the goodwill o●
the members of the Society,I shall do my best,to work with them in ●
furthering the spreading of our language and culture,and in all ways to
help.
      I am sending you a copy of Book.I., the first of my
series of text books. This book is for sub-intermediate,and for very
young beginners. This publication just came to hand. I have to thank
the K.B.S. for help in publishing it. I am hoping that Books 2 and 3
will soon be ready for sale here. The chief aim of this book,is that
it can be bought by the poorer student, as many text books of the
Japanese Language are heavily priced, except our own Education Department
Readers. These the students find difficult for use,without help,as
they are entirely in the Japanese print.
      I am presenting one of my first books to all the
Schools and Institutions in Victoria (at present) who are,or might be
interested in the study of the Japanese Language,and also to important
people.

Letter of Moshi Inagaki to Consul General Wakamatsu in 1938.
(Courtesy of National Archives of Australia, NAA: C443, J53)

Father Gsell's Heroic War With the Jap Slavers

For 23 Years He Has Fought Against the Wicked Traffic, Buying the Helpless Native Girls to Protect Them and Sheltering Them on His Unique Island Sanctuary—But Now His Enemies Have Learned a New Trick

BOYS AND GIRLS!

Don't Buy Japanese Toys—

Because the cruel Japanese Generals and Admirals are killing thousands of poor, harmless Chinese children with bullets and bombs. They are doing this on the orders of the greedy, rich men of Japan who want to rob the Chinese people of their land and goods, and are sending soldiers, aeroplanes, tanks and warships to China to do so.

You must not blame the millions of Japanese people who are poor—they have no wish to harm the Chinese people, who are their brothers and sisters—it is the few rich men of Japan who are to blame. These are very greedy and cruel (just as most rich men are in ALL countries), and rob their own countrymen just as they intend to rob the Chinese.

If you stop buying Japanese goods then the rich men of Japan will soon run short of money and will not be able to buy more bullets and bombs with which to kill the Chinese children; but if you keep on buying them, then the Japanese warmakers will be able to buy enough arms and ammunition to capture China and will then come to Australia to try and capture our country and will kill Australian children (perhaps your own brother or sister) in order to do so. The Japanese Generals and Admirals have said that this is what they intend to do, after they have captured China.

So, for the sake of the Chinese children! For the sake of your own country! For the sake of your brothers and sisters!

Don't Buy Japanese Toys!

Take this home and show it to mother and dad and ask them to boycott ALL Japanese goods.

If you want to know how to help, ring telephone number MA 7857 or get your mother or dad to call at:

727 GEORGE STREET, SYDNEY
(Issued by the N.S.W. District Committee, Communist Party of Australia.)

The Forward Press Pty. Ltd. (40-Hour Week), 395-7 Campbell St., Sydney.

Above: Father Gsell's heroic War 1938 (Courtesy of the National Archives of Australia NAAACT: A659/1, 1939/1/7919)

Left: Communist Party Pamphlet, c1937 (Courtesy of the SEARCH Foundation)

Form N.

COMMONWEALTH OF AUSTRALIA.

Nationality Act 1920-1936.

DECLARATION BY A BRITISH WOMAN, WHO HAS MARRIED AN ALIEN, THAT SHE DESIRES TO RETAIN, WHILE IN AUSTRALIA OR ANY TERRITORY, THE RIGHTS OF A BRITISH SUBJECT.

(1) Full name.

(2) Full address.

(3) Husband's full name.

I,[1] *Elizabeth Frances Nakamura*

of [2] *8 Countess Street Mosman*

the wife of:[3] *Hirokichi Nakamura*

who is of *Japanese* nationality, having acquired his nationality by reason of my marriage to him at *At Thomas's Balmain West* on the *22nd* day of *September* 191*7*.

hereby declare that I desire, while in Australia or any Territory to which the *Nationality Act* 1920-1936 extends, to retain the rights of a British subject.

(Declarant's Signature) *Elizabeth F Nakamura*

Made and subscribed at *Sydney*

this *16th* day of *November* 19*37*

before me—

(Signed) *John Try_____*

(4) Judge, Police Magistrate, Commissioner for Declarations, or Justice of the Peace.

(Title).[4] *Justice of the Peace for NSW*

Registered in the Department of the Interior, Canberra, F.C.T., in Register No. *1*, page *53*, this *Seventh* day of *January*, 19*38*.

(SEE OTHER SIDE.)

J.R. Pun_____

By authority of the MINISTER FOR THE INTERIOR

By Authority: L. F. Johnston, Commonwealth Government Printer.

Declaration by a British Woman, who has married an alien 1938 (Courtesy of Nakamura family)

JOINT STATE COUNCIL
VOLUNTARY AID DETACHMENTS
FOR NEW SOUTH WALES

CHAIRMAN:
THE LADY WAKEHURST

MEMBERS OF COUNCIL:
COL. A. M. McINTOSH, C.C.M.G., BASE H.Q., E.C.
DEPUTY CHAIRMAN.

ACT. STATE CONTROLLER:
DR FRANCES C. B. McKAY

HON. SECRETARY:
MRS. R. L. SNELLING

TELEPHONE: BW 6997

SURGEON LIEUT.-COMMANDER E. SUSMAN (NAVY)
WING COMMANDER H. J. MELVILLE (AIR FORCE)
GROUP CAPTAIN H. R. G. POATE } ORDER OF ST. JOHN
DR. FRANCES C. B. McKAY
MR. WILFRID E. JOHNSON } AUSTRALIAN RED CROSS
MRS. JOHN MOORE, O.B.E. } SOCIETY

"WYOMING,"

175 MACQUARIE ST.,

SYDNEY.

JS/SC   26th May, 1942.

Mrs. Nakamura,
Countess Street,
M o s m a n.   N.S.W.

Dear Mrs. Nakamura,

              We are wondering if you have ever heard from
the Joint State Council how very much they have appreciated your
work in the past.   At the first meeting to which I was present
the value of your work was discussed and Lady Wakehurst herself
said then that a letter expressing same should be sent to you.
May I add to this my own personal gratitude for all you have done
for the Scottish 218 Detachment, instructing them, so that they
passed through many exams with such high efficiency.

              The Council wishes you to know that it is a
national not a personal matter that terminated this happy relationship with you as an Instructor.

                          Faithfully yours,

                          Joyce Snelling

                          ――――――――――――――――――――
                          Deputy Assistant Controller

Letter from Voluntary Aid Detachments for NSW to Bessie Nakamura (Courtesy of Nakamura family)

Kindly address all communications
to the Hon. Secretary:-
~~Mrs. P. LEAHY, M.B.E.~~
~~MILITARY ROAD~~
~~MOSMAN~~

AUSTRALIAN RED CROSS SOCIETY
N.S.W. DIVISION
(INCORPORATED)

Mosman BRANCH

5 Moruben Road
Mosman
March 21st 1942

Dear Mrs Nakamura,

At the class on Friday, a hearty vote of thanks was passed by acclaimation to you, for the great interest & wonderful instruction you gave the members. This I was asked to convey to you, as many expected you to continue, otherwise would have expressed their thanks personally.

Yours faithfully
F. M. Northcott
Hon. Sec.

Personal handwritten letter of thanks to Bessie Nakamura from Australian Red Cross
(Courtesy of Nakamura family)

My Dear wife　　　Thursday 9th Sept 1943.

Yesterday I received your letter for my Birthday greeting dated 28th, It was contained Young Naidao with it and please to know all are happy & well at home, This morning I was very happy in receiving a big parcel containing loving thoughts of my family and find every thing listed (2 Parcels together) in perfect condition, I have to thank yourself & Girls for their kind thoughts, I have already spent two birth days away from my good wife & family and how long more they going to keep me away from home I do not know, but one thing we must all thankful for our good health, I also very please to hear that some good friend took you for a drive etc also all neighbour are very kind to you all, my advise is to keep your mind free from pessimistic idea, try and form happiness that our turn of luck are within sight, by the way, I am fail to place who Mrs Tolease is, do I know her? however glad to know you have such kind friends, recently I was reading a Book of noted old Japanese priest and wonderful psychologist who says that both Heaven & Hell is within your palms, The greed, anger, and worries, these 3 poisons create Hell and when you remove these 3 poisons from your mind you will realize yourself in the Heaven, we feel we are in mid summer here, I peeled all warm clothing & soon be wearing athletic singlets & shorts with love Yours, Hut Nakamura.

Letter to Bessie from Hirokichi Nakamura sent from internment camp, Barmera, SA 1943
(Courtesy of Nakamura family)

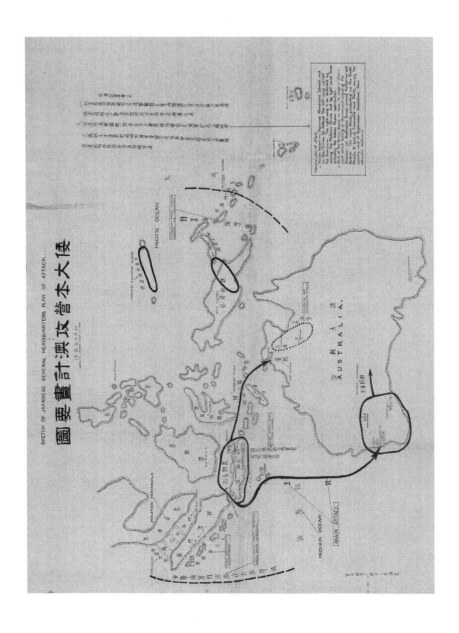

Sketch of Japanese Central Headquarters plan of attack, known as the 'Chinese Map',
(Courtesy of National Archives of Australia, NAA: A7941, 46).

Chapter 7

Dangerous years, 1937–42

Japan's war in China in 1937 caused alarm. In the months after the Rape of Nanking in December 1937, Japan's aggression became real and invasion literature resurged in Australia. Stories like 'The Awakening' by George Mitchell brought tales of an unnamed Asian enemy invading and taking all but Melbourne and Adelaide. Erle Cox's *Fool's Harvest* serialised in November 1938 in the *Argus* was an invasion story of ongoing warfare to free Australia and seemed to predict that war might last decades. Willard Price's factual book *Japan Reaches Out*, published in 1938 declared that "Australia is one of the direct objectives of the southward advance" and pointed to Japan's interest in wool and minerals. Piesse had written in 1935 that Japan presented a danger but he expected raids on shipping and blockades but felt that invasion was "remote".[1] Whether any of this was so or not, Australian authorities took security precautions.

If Australian writers and authorities were nervous and cautious, then Ichiro Kagiyama, the photographer of Kings Cross in Sydney, was terrified. In 1938, he left Australia with his wife and returned to Japan in a panic. He was worried that he had been spying and thought that he might be arrested. The NSW security services watched Kagiyama but were not worried about his activities. Kagiyama had constant contact with Japanese firms and the Consulate-General because he photographed so many events. He had been asked in the 1930s to record broadcasts from Radio Tokyo on wax cylinders and leave these with the tobacco kiosk near his home for collection by a person who worked in a Japanese shipping company. The kiosk owner had reported this activity to the police who followed the parcels. Because there was sufficient gap between Kagiyama leaving the parcel and the collection of the parcel, the security personnel were able to listen to the recordings to discover their content. They later found that the harmless content of the broadcasts were typed up and distributed to companies. No action was taken. However, it identified a means to disseminate messages from Japan, if such a convoluted means was needed, and the watch continued.[2]

Between 1933 and 1936, Japan had a period of relative peace, which provides some insight into its intentions. It had occupied Manchukuo, set up a puppet government in 1931 and achieved a ceasefire with China by May 1933. But in 1937 Japan was at war again and invaded China. Although we tend to see Japan's actions as internally united, the objectives of this war often saw the interests of business, politics and military forces in open conflict. Okura for example had opposed military violence as most businessmen did. Okura wanted what Howe calls 'business imperialism' where reasonable political stability provided the opportunity for further commercial expansion and investment, which became known as the Okura principle of government that enabled development with direct Japanese investment. This set the army and the *zaibatsu* at odds because the army did not believe it could achieve control without force and wanted China as a population outlet. This difference led the army to develop five-year plans for Manchuria from 1936, which discouraged the older *zaibatsu* and encouraged new firms to develop. State planning of this kind was not conducive to the principle of combining trade with private foreign direct investment supported by some *zaibatsu*. This principle is important for Australia because it meant that some of the older businesses represented in Australia were not necessarily supportive of war as a means of expansion in the late 1930s and that not all *zaibatsu* agreed among themselves. However, by 1936, the initial reluctance of business to be involved in Manchuria eased as Mitsubishi and Mitsui set up munitions manufacturing in Manchuria and China and big business donated in appeals for air defence. As Wilson says there is little evidence that the *zaibatsu* actively opposed extremists at this time, and then later co-operated reluctantly, because the ties between business and the military were close at officer level. Their main concern was to engage in stable profitable enterprises, while avoiding the impression that they supported military conquest, in order to preserve their overseas reputations. Japanese Chambers of Commerce played a role in many countries in explaining Japan's actions in China, including the JCC in Sydney, which disseminated pamphlets even to the Chinese community. They were returned quite badly defaced.[3]

It is also important to realise as Wilson points out, that it was during the time of relative peace, 1933–37, that the environment developed in Japan in which military and bureaucratic interests became interwoven. We often think of this as a sudden upsurge in militarism but

> … it was not spectacular events like the invasion of Manchuria which performed an integrating function among the different institutions and factions that made up the Japanese state; indeed, significant sections of officialdom remained unmoved by such external events. Rather, a comparative quieting of the external situation after 1933, a heightened emphasis on incorporationist campaigns required gradualist means and significant bureaucratic input from 1935.[4]

This means that the centralisation necessary for the development of complex war plans involving the most important sections of Japanese society post dates 1935 and the extensively held pre-war fear of Japan theory asserted by some Australian historians. The period from 1937 is the critical period we need to examine for Japan's intentions towards Australia. It is this period that witnesses the consolidation of pearling interests in the Pacific and the increase in visitors to Australia who were more obviously engaging in research that could be used for military purposes. But what were Japan's plans for Australia? Was the emphasis in Australia that of the Okura principle or of the army as evident in China? Would Australians be pulling rickshaws up Bourke Street for rich Japanese business magnates, or more likely chauffeuring them about in the Rolls, the De Large or the latest Ford sedan as some Australians already had in the 1920s and 1930s?

Australia had its own idea about what constituted preparations for war on the part of Japan. High on the agenda were any signs that Japan was consolidating operations that might move south and threaten Australia's north. A further consideration was any attempt at economic penetration or attempt to buy up or control Australia's resources. A third was any espionage on the part of visitors. In some respects Australian authorities were correct that these activities indicated preparation for war but when compared with Japanese sources on actual preparations there are significant differences. What is important is that, contrary to Bob Wurth's charge that Dr Evatt jeopardised Australia's security as Attorney-General, Australia was very alert and took significant steps to defend against a variety of eventualities.

Japan's centralisation and consolidation to the north

The centralisation of pearling and other economic activities in the South Seas was an extremely complex affair and is still subject to research.[5] Longfield Lloyd, the Australian Commissioner in Japan sent a basic summary of the advent of centralisation to External Affairs after its announcement in a Japanese paper on 23 April 1937. Before this time, there was no umbrella organisation for pearling in the seas to Australia's north. In this announcement, the Overseas Ministry stated the size of the pearling fleet to the north of Australia at 160 boats with about 2,000 men. This is consistent with sightings by Australians at the time. The Ministry invited the general pearl fishery enterprises of Japan to join the Japanese Pearling Company (NSKK) organised by the Ocean Colonisation Company (whose daughter company was NKKK) and the Pacific Pearling Company. The independent pearlers would participate through a share distribution arrangement in return for "purchase, control or financial accommodation of their ... boats". The Company would supply all necessities for fishing operations, transport and sales of catches. The pearl fishing, the debts and credits of the two companies would be transferred to the new company over time.[6] It was this organisation that had taken over the Japanese-run firms owned by Japanese men in NEI and Pacific Islands to the north, including the Japanese mandates, some of whom fished in territorial waters to Australia's north and visited Darwin to provision.

Lloyd argued that as a result of the consolidation, he expected the Japanese fleet to increase. In effect the pearl fleet shrank. On 22 June 1938, fishers in Dobo were experiencing financial difficulties related to the share float for the centralisation of the pearling interests. By August 1938, the tendency was to concentrate fishing at certain key points such as Davao, Menado and Momi in New Guinea, Dobo in Aru Island and Dili in Timor.[7] However Dobo was having other problems by 1939. *The Northern Standard*, an NT paper, reported the fleet movements and expectations of numbers fishing in the Arafura Sea, as John Nakashiba informed it each year about the next pearling season. On 21 and 25 April 1939 Nakashiba reported that they were experiencing a bad season. The Celebes Trading Co. (in Dobo and owned by Germans) closed down early in the year because of the unsatisfactory price of shell. Only 60 boats arrived at Dobo from Palau to commence the season. With low prices for shell some were extending fishing to other products in the seas near Fiji. Beds at Aru Island had become infected. Further, Germany's annexation of Czechoslovakia, Nakashiba said, had closed the large market pearlers had previously enjoyed in Czechoslovakia, reducing the demand for shell. Nakashiba reported that some pearlers were in Darwin to try to sell their shell in order to buy stores but had not found buyers. They intended to attempt to sell in Broome. Initially, therefore, even by mid-1939, the centralisation of pearling had not increased the industry or the number of vessels to Australia's north. Further, reports that luggers were looking to other fish products were verified by a telegram on 1 September 1940 from the British Ambassador in Tokyo. He reported that Captain Okashima, one of the men arrested and cleared in the lugger cases, was in charge of the operations of the *Kokoku Maru* mother ship and 10 luggers that were now permanently based near Bathurst Island in international waters to catch turtle. They planned to double the fleet because of the success of the catch.[8]

Many studies credit Japanese fishing along the north in the years before the arrests of three luggers in 1937 with being part of the strategic thrust south of the Japanese navy. What credible evidence exists for this view? At what stage do the centralised pearling interests impact significantly on the space along Australia's north and what relevance does this have in the preparation for war? External Affairs obtained reports on the activities of Japanese firms in NEI and the South Seas from 1921 onwards. The structure and interrelatedness of firms was as complicated as tracing today's multinationals and their related enterprises and public private partnerships with government. Firms tended to co-operate for certain commercial activities that might only form one part of their total business as we saw in small Japanese firms in WA. There were over 100 different operations of Mitsubishi alone in the area but pearling is not mentioned as one of their businesses.[9]

The expansion and diversity of the trading companies was due to their operating procedures. They grew by adding new items to merchandise and opening new branches where they could trade in a new product. They charged commissions on foreign trade transactions. As the number of products handled grew the overseas network improved and enlarged via the *bu* system. This was the establishment of separate departments to handle specific commodities that were important and traded in large volumes such as rice, raw cotton and coal. The point is that branches were set up to handle particular products. The different *zaibatsu* as we saw in the comparison of Mitsui and Mitsubishi in Australia varied in organisation and the means of central control. The local branch's concern for its own profit could make it focus on that rather than on a co-operative strategy with other branches. Branches competed with each other at times. This also means that identifying the activities in which a branch was involved can be achieved through an examination of the accounts in the ledgers for the various departments of any given branch. Thus it is certain that Mitsui Sydney had no department for pearling.

Given that the development of companies was based on the acquisition of products, many firms large and small opened in the South Seas and NEI. Mitsui was spread from the Middle East to San Francisco. In some cases firms would form an association to assist in the organisation of trade. For example, in February 1921, the British Embassy in Tokyo reported that trade in the South Seas was under the patronage of an association called Nan'yō Kyōkai whose head office was in Osaka. Most of the leading firms in Osaka belonged to it but none were involved in pearling or fishing. "Note. Well known firms like Mitsui & Co., Mitsubishi & Co., Ito & Co. all of which have branches in Singapore, Manila, Batavia do not appear to be members of the Nan'yō Kyōkai [*sic*]."[10]

Later reports provide details of the development of companies in NEI and New Guinea that either supported the Japanese expansion or were directly backed by the government. One report states that the first official Japanese colonisation company in NEI was the Oriental Development Company substantially backed by the government and founded in 1908 to instil Japanese ideas in agriculture and trade and industry with a view to exploiting the islands gained after the war. The company had originated in China. It had no success in NEI because of the competition from independent companies that were already successful in Dutch territory.[11]

The South Seas Development Company or Nan'yō Takushoku Kabushiki Kaisha bought up a Japanese company at Menando and a stream of naval officers travelled back and forth from Palau to NEI. It was interested in founding fishing industries to help the navy. Even the NKKK, the principal subsidiary of the Oriental Development Company, failed in NEI and moved to New Guinea to cultivate cotton. A report said that the company set up the Tokyo Palau air route and operated seaplanes with naval command officers on active list. Harbour facilities were organised near Palau in May 1939 with oil reserves. A close relationship existed between the navy and the NKKK in New Guinea.[12]

The NKKK internal report of November 1939, 'Japanese enterprises in Dutch New Guinea' written by Utamaru Mitsushirō[13] head of the office and researcher of NKKK, emphasised the undeveloped state of New Guinea particularly on the Dutch side. It states that very few Japanese lived there which only include three individuals who lacked the finance needed to continue their endeavours. On Aru Island, Japanese were eight per cent of the population of 110 people with some large businesses in Japanese hands such as a coconut enterprise, which belonged to an unnamed Japanese bank and the Nagano Timbermill and Shipyard. The pearling industry comprised six boats and 49 crew members. The report particularly complained of the *lack* of Japanese government support and interest in New Guinea (except for one visit by the Minister for Business abroad Mr Nomura in October 1939) although the company felt that it could play an important part in the *nan'yō*. In 1939 the company offices were in Monakwari with 48 Japanese and their families. They employed 2,800 'natives'.[14]

NKKK was of concern in NEI by 1937 and the Australian government departments received regular reports from the British Consul General Fitzmaurice in Batavia on its activities. NKKK operated in what was known as the 'outer nan'yō' the area outside the Japanese-mandated territories. It targeted potentially profitable industries or undeveloped areas where small concerns operated and bought up independently-owned businesses. By February 1938, reports suggest that it had merged Nan'yō Kohatsu Kaisha into its operations. This was the largest firm in New Guinea, which had already caused concern in Australia (prematurely) in 1935.[15] *The Herald* on 20 November 1935 reported a new NKK concession in New Guinea as:[16] 'Japan our next door neighbour. Big lease in New Guinea', a title that made New Guinea sound like a threatening outpost of the Japanese empire. The map showed the 214-square mile lease at Geelvink Bay to the north west.[17]

Reports on NKK intensify in 1937. The 30 October report from Batavia stated that NKK was expanding its daughter industries in sugar, alcohol production, cotton and shipping in Palau, New Guinea, the Celebes and Timor. It was also involved in marine products especially around Menando. Further reports of its relationship with NKKK in the outer *nan'yō* continued in 1938. All Australian government departments involved in the interdepartmental conference of 1939 had received these reports during the previous decade.[18]

Although NKKK and NKK both supported the southern thrust of the Japanese government, they did not always do well against the existing private concerns, especially when competing against large multinational firms like Mitsui, Mitsubishi and other *zaibatsu* that were well respected and long established. Although these new companies failed to compete with existing businesses, which were supporters of the Japanese government's *nan'yō* push,[19] they became more worrying in 1940 when Japan joined the Axis powers. In particular in November 1939, there was already some fear that Japan might invade NEI when Germany invaded Holland. Australia became alarmed when NKKK was interested in extending its air service into Timor.[20]

Was Mitsui involved in the southern advance as some historians have maintained? Mitsui had been in the Pacific, SEA and NEI from the nineteenth and early twentieth centuries. However, it was not involved in pearling as such but in selling shell. A search of the sources on Mitsui and Japanese writing about Mitsui makes no mention of Mitsui having any pearling fleets or subsidiary pearling companies anywhere. Maeda discusses Mitsui's global investments in the 1930s.[21] He lists China and SEA where Mitsui was involved in natural resources such as cotton, machinery, textiles and pig-iron. In addition, the policy governing trade changed in Japan in 1937 with the emphasis placed on export promotion especially from overseas branches to third countries or foreign-to-foreign trade. This thrust was intended to earn foreign exchange reserves and linked the foreign exchange allowance to export performance to trade financing schemes. Mitsui's own history written in 1937 lists all its branches and associated companies. In 1937, Mitsui Bussan Kaisha branches were in Palembang, Batavia, Semarang, Sourabaya, Sydney and Melbourne. There was no agency with a pearling company listed in 1937.[22] The records of Mitsui & Co. confirm this. None of the letterhead for the times lists Palau as having a branch. Further, no ledgers have pearl shell sales entered. The structure of companies confirms further that any involvement Mitsui had in selling pearl shell was not significant enough to warrant a separated department.[23] Further, the attraction of Australia to firms like Mitsui was always wool and minerals.

Back in Australian waters, Japanese made a more a concerted effort to keep luggers away from the Australian coast after 1938. The arrests of luggers in 1937 for entering territorial waters off an Aboriginal reserve, stopped "all serious cases of trespass on Arnhem Land Reserve. The Japanese pearling luggers … kept outside the territorial limits". They were not permitted to do what they liked along Australia's north coast in the years before the war but were watched carefully.

In December 1938, a secret Defence Department report assessed the repercussions of the arrests of the luggers in 1937 and subsequent NT lugger cases in which they were cleared of all accusations. This revealed the existence of various confusing sets of provisions in law for entering Australian waters at NT, Commonwealth and state levels. The Departments of Interior, Trade and Customs, Health and External Affairs were concerned to establish a means of unified control. The Commonwealth was also in two minds about continuing the patrol boat service along the north as it consisted of only two boats and could only operate in territorial waters when most fishing took place in international waters. However, well-organised patrols they argued "let Japanese see that we do control the north coast". There had been no reports of disorderly conduct by the Japanese owned vessels since the central organisation of the Japanese fleets.[24] In this way the problem of Japanese luggers off Australia's north appeared under control.

But naval files demonstrate that there was serious concern about Japanese naval activity north of New Guinea by 1939, unrelated to the boats fishing in the Arafura Sea. From 1936, every little diplomatic incident involving Britain and Japan caused Australia to review its response to requests from Japan for visits by training merchant ships. However, the Navy with its wider view of the issue than the Commonwealth departments, issued its own minute paper on 3 January 1939 stating that pearling and island trade were aspects of Japanese expansion. Japan's navy advocated increased expansion as Japan became concentrated in the hands of a few men engaged in "economic aggression supported where necessary by military action". Southward expansion had not taken on the military character of the westward expansion into China, which was "fortuitous" but the Navy felt that might soon change. The Navy argued that Australia could not compete with Japan on equal terms but remained in a defensive position economically and militarily. The Defence paper and the Navy minute paper named the Nan'yō Kohatsu Kaisha as associated with the Nippon Shinju Kabushiki Kaisha in the organisation of the pearling fleet.[25]

After the interdepartmental conference on 4–5 July 1939, the report urged investigation into measures that could be developed to prevent the possibility of economic penetration of Australia by Japan through the pearling industry, recognising that the industry was now too big for any measures to have any impact. This argument demonstrated that the Commonwealth was rather late in attempting to stop Japanese economic penetration of Australia given the multimillion pound *zaibatsu* operations in the country over the previous decades. It was also concentrating on the wrong industry. However, the report continued, ambitiously, that it was necessary to exercise control over the southern expansion, which it saw incorrectly as mostly related to pearling operations moving further south. It also argued that although the Australian pearling industry was languishing, they could not afford to let the towns become deserted. From a defence point of view some assistance to the industry was essential. It advised negotiation with Japan on limits to the taking of shell, the need for vessels to report at a port for medical examination and provisions for them to land for wood and water. It recommended the extension of the patrol boat system in Queensland along the NT and WA coastlines and Papua New Guinea. A standing advisory committee was also recommended.

It was not until 1941 that consolidation of other areas such as Japanese commerce and cultural associations affected Australia. For example, in September 1941, the Overseas Compatriots' Association formed as a result of a meeting of representatives in Tokyo from 27 countries with the purpose of maintaining close associations between Japan and Japanese residing overseas with the headquarters in Tokyo. The association acted as agent for overseas Japanese and aimed to educate the rising generation in matters of overseas significance and to develop overseas trade. It sent forms to Japanese in Australia via consulates to collect information on Japanese in the country, their clubs, organisations, schools, their legal status in Australia, their occupations, financial position and the reception of Japanese radio. The visit of Major Hashida from January to March 1941 had gathered a large amount of information on Australia that demonstrated a desire to consolidate trade.[26]

Resources and economic expansion

Japanese exploration for new mineral sources was interpreted as preparation for war. Extensive studies of what Australia had to offer in terms of resources and economic expansion increased after 1939. Japan's southward advance in the 1930s was in part concerned with the need for iron ore. This was viewed with great suspicion in Australia. Longfield Lloyd, the Australian Trade Commissioner in Japan, wrote on 6 October 1937 that "the use of Japanese capital for economic development is a feature of Japanese penetration and 'special interests'". Before the 1930s, Japan had imported small quantities of iron-ore from the South Seas and from Australia since the beginning of World War One. By 1931–32 exports from Australia only amounted to 13,000 tons per annum but Japan's increase in heavy industry led to imports from Australia reaching nearly 300,000 tons by 1935–36. In 1936, mines in Malaya became operational with Japanese capital and in that year 931,000 tons were mined in this way. In other southward areas Japan carried out development by providing the capital and agreeing to take the entire output of the mine. In this way a dummy company was set up. This was the proposal in Australia. Purcell estimated that Mitsui, Mitsubishi, Nippon Mining Co., Nippon Sangyo, Ishihara Sangyo and Japan Electric Yamashita from 1936 onwards proposed over £2.3 million in investment in mineral development in Australia in Tasmania, Cape York Peninsula and Yampi Sound. He estimates that by 1940 Australia would have provided 42 per cent of Japan's iron ore if the proposals had gone ahead. These projects were stopped through a unilateral embargo on exports of Australian ore from 1 July 1938 and spelled the doom of other contemplated projects. Longfield Lloyd felt that the Yampi Sound endeavour was unquestionably part of the whole scheme and could only result in the occupancy and exclusive right over a portion of Australian territory by Japanese interests perhaps for 50 years. "A hold from which these people will not be either then or in the interim readily loosened once the agreement is allowed to become operative". The story of mineral exploration in Australia shows part of what Japan was after.[27]

Early in 1938, the Lyons government, concerned about the investment of Japanese companies in Yampi Sound, announced an embargo on the export of iron ore from Australia. The stated reason was the shock discovery of the shortage of iron ore for Australia's needs. However concerns about iron ore shipments to Japan had arisen earlier in 1937 after Japan went to war in China. The *Queensland Government Mining Journal* reports a suggestion in Parliament that the state should make sure no iron ore deposits were supplying foreign nations with the raw materials for war machines. The Minister for Mines (Hon T.A. Foley) replied that no leases of iron ore were being granted at present. A committee was investigating the accessible deposits of ore in Queensland and that the Commonwealth was establishing whether Australian deposits were sufficient to meet Australian needs. New leases would be available to Australians.

The *Journal* also reported:

> Mr Umeda [Director of Tonan Shokai in WA but resident in Japan] had recently interviewed him and the Under Secretary for the Mines Department, and had pointed out that his main objective was to interest Australian capital in the exploitation of Australian iron ore deposits, and that his interests were prepared to guarantee a market for that product. Mr Umeda even went further, and said that the interests he represented would guarantee Australian capital engaged in mining operations for Japanese requirements against losses. However nothing definite was arranged. Mr Umeda thoroughly understood that under Queensland laws no person other than a British subject could obtain a title for mining leases in Queensland.[28]

The *Journal* recognised that Japan was a "pauper" when it came to basic metals.

After Dr Woolnough delivered his report on Australia's mineral resources to the Commonwealth Government, Prime Minister Lyons announced that Australia was placing an embargo on the export of iron ore to preserve existing resources. The report, Lyons maintained had revealed that Australia's resources were not as extensive as first thought.

On 25 May 1938, the Consul-General requested the government to review its position on the export of iron ore. It detailed the development costs that Japan had already incurred in the Yampi Sound project with the support of the WA government. Its development of the area was first explored in the late 1920s when Umeda, also a Director of Nichigo Mining Co., brought out experts from Japan and attempted in 1928 to raise capital with the involvement of local Australian investors. A report in the *West Australian* on 3 July 1928 alleged that Umino began to interest NKKK in the proposition. The intention was for NKKK to buy the ore and ship it to Japan. After initial problems, the project commenced in 1936 under the Yampi Sound Mining Co. Ltd whose managing director was V.F. Walsh of Perth. Nichinan Mining Co. of Osaka held sole rights to export the ore. Nippon Mining Co. had purchased blast furnaces that were already in Singapore awaiting transhipment to Australia. This company was actively developing iron ore in Manchukuo. H.A. Brasserts & Co. Ltd, an English concern, was to develop the mine with a loan from Nippon Mining Co. because WA law forbade the use of Asiatic labour in mineral development. The estimated amount of compensation that could be claimed was over £90,000.[29]

The Consul-General's office had copies of a report containing the full history of the discovery of minerals at Yampi Sound from the time when the first leases were granted in 1907 and the first survey conducted in 1908. It knew the types of ore available in the deposits and the projected amounts. Mitsubishi provided up-to-date information on Australian exports of iron ore. They also had information that enabled a comparison between SA ore deposits and those of Yampi Sound, which led them to conclude that there was no fear of Australia exhausting its deposits any time soon. Given Umeda's involvement in Queensland, the Consulate-General may also have been aware of the reports in the *Queensland Government Mining Journal* of 15 September that stated that the preliminary survey results indicated that Australia had sufficient iron ore for many years. The Yampi Sound Mining Co. Ltd believed that the competitors in other states, who did not want the mine developed, had put pressure on government. The most recent survey by Dr Woolnough was, Walsh argued, not conclusive because it did not include details of the deposits in WA.[30]

The Japanese believed that the embargo could not be justified on the basis of a projected future shortage of iron ore for Australian use. Indeed such a position was a sharp change in policy and no Commonwealth emergency could be identified to explain this. The Consul-General believed that this measure was aimed at Japan and pointed out the need for equity in access to world mineral resources in order to maintain "cordial relations".

A letter 24 May 1938 from T. Wakamatsu to Prime Minister Lyons stated:

> ... the Imperial Government cannot understand why the Commonwealth Government, despite their former assurances, have decided to adopt such a drastic measure without any domestic emergency having arisen to justify the subversion of the development of work at Yampi Sound, in ... which a huge amount of Japanese capital has been invested ... in the hope of contributing to the mutual prosperity of the two nations.
>
> It is the most earnest desire of my Government, ... that , in the interests of the maintenance of friendly relations between our two countries, and also in the light of the significance of freedom of trade, especially of free access to resources, the necessity for which has not only been recognised by most of the countries in the world, but which has also been earnestly urged by certain Powers as a practical means of achieving appeasement in the world,

the Commonwealth Government will reconsider their decision, particularly as it does not appear that any thorough and practical investigation has yet been made which furnishes the people of both Australia and Japan with concrete evidence of the realities of the situation.

Extensive correspondence and visits between Lyons and Wakamatsu resolved nothing. Lyons asked for understanding and assured the Japanese that the embargo also affected the USA. It was not aimed at Japan. Given the information that the Japanese had on Australian mineral resources, this was not convincing. A British Government telegram from Tokyo expressed the opinion that while Britain understood the reasons why the Commonwealth had taken this step, it had an unfortunate effect on Japanese official opinion.[31]

There is at the best of times a tendency amongst some sections of Japanese public opinion to align themselves with those in Germany and Italy who consider that the only means by which the "have-not" State can ensure themselves adequate supplies of raw materials is to the strengthen their armaments that they can eventually "take" what they require; this tendency is likely to be increased by what has occurred and the faith of those who have placed reliance in public declarations relating to freedom of access to raw materials may well be shaken.

Australia had taken this step at a time when Britain was attempting to secure adequate protection for British interests in China. The telegram asked that Australia consider exporting small supplies from SA to Japan.

The Japanese Consul-General and the Australian companies involved sought legal advice about the embargo, in particular whether it was constitutional. Supporters such as A.C.V. Melbourne and Nobutaro Umeda also attempted to have the embargo lifted without success. The mine closed its operations in November 1940.

Japanese companies were also very interested in Queensland minerals at Mount Morgan and Iron Island. Hisatoshi Okoamoto, Shinzaburo Noda and Sadamu Matsemoto visited the Queensland Mines Department in October 1940 with a proposal to develop ore at Iron Island. During this time, Harry Suzuki assisted Umeda in his tour of Western Queensland. Also known as Ivan Steele, this motor mechanic knew the outback well. A security service report of 26 September 1942 noted the number of Japanese missions to Mount Isa before the war. In addition, Yampi Sound was not the only area in WA under exploration by Japanese concerns. In February1940, Masunori Omori reported to Danzai Kaisha of Tokyo about the extensive undeveloped mineral deposits in the Darling Ranges east of Perth. Omori returned to Japan without managing to form a local company to realise his hope of trading with Japan in bauxite.[32]

To complicate matters between Australia and Japan at this time waterside workers at Port Kembla decided in November 1938 to refuse to load the SS *Dalfram* with pig-iron destined for Japan. The intricacies of the dispute cannot be detailed here but basically, Union Secretary Tom Roach put it that the pig-iron should not be exported because success to the "Japanese Fascist militarists in China will according to their own statements inspire them to further attacks on peaceful people which will include Australia". Further, he argued, it was difficult to understand why the government was at pains to ban the supply of iron ore to Japan in developments like Yampi Sound yet permit the export of pig-iron which could directly be used for military purposes. Over the following weeks, Federal Cabinet and particularly Robert Menzies tried to end the deadlock, which continued into mid-January. Menzies, perhaps echoing British sentiments, declared it would be extremely provocative and dangerous of Australia to impose sanctions on its own against Japan. The dispute ended after arrangements for proper talks between the trade unions and the government and the ore was loaded for Japan.[33]

In accounts of the pig-iron dispute, such as those of Martin, the part played by the Japanese Consul-General is not included. Mitsui files contain correspondence on the issue and cables back and forward to Japan. In these we learn much more about the Japanese side of the issue. The pig-iron concerned was 24,000 tons contracted for between Mitsui, Mitsubishi and BHP. The shipping company agent was the Australian McIlwraith McEachern. Both it and BHP had very long associations with Japanese firms in Australia. Initial cables to Japan from Melbourne stated that the loading had been suspended because stevedores were boycotting war material. There is no suggestion in the cable that the pig-iron was not war material. A 12 December cable said that 200 tons of BHP cargo bound for Shanghai had also been refused by Sydney labour and it was suggested that the shipment be postponed. Wakamatsu wrote to Lyons that the shipment was part of Japan's promotion of trade relations with Australia. He reminded Prime Minister Lyons that Japanese manufacturers could turn elsewhere for resources if need be. The JCC telegraphed Lyons that its members were losing large sums daily because the goods were delayed. They were discouraged that a small section of the Australian community "repeatedly interfered" with their efforts at reciprocal trade. If the matter were not resolved it would affect general trade and penalise those who were doing their utmost to foster reciprocal trade. Lyons issued a statement that the government had no intention of discontinuing pig-iron exports because the amount was small compared with iron ore and did not prejudice Australian supplies. It would not permit elements outside the government to determine policy, in this case Australia's attitude to the conflict in China. The JCC, Mitsui and Mitsubishi also put pressure on the Australian firms involved to find workers who would load the ship. Certainly cables to Japan on 9 December stated that BHP was preparing to load it themselves if necessary, although this still had not happened by mid-January.[34] Indeed, the Japanese in Sydney put considerable pressure on the government over the issues, with the threat of diverting trade away from Australia. Public feeling in Australia was high. On 8 February 1939, *The Herald* reported threats against the Consul-General, Mr Wakamatsu, who was receiving police protection.[35]

Espionage within Australia

The visit of Major Sie Hashida raised great concern in government and defence circles. Newspapers asked if his activities were a prelude to war. *The Sun* wrote on 29 January 1941 in 'Japanese Visit':

> ... when a Japanese army officer lands on our soil with a self-confessed desire to 'get some ideas of our military methods,' uneasiness must surge through the minds of all clear-thinking Australians on the assumption, of course, that our present Administration intends to comply with his wishes. Anxious as we may be for peaceful negotiations and political understanding in regard to Pacific problems, it cannot be denied that Japan is an Axis partner, and that we are at war with the Axis.

The *Daily Telegraph* on 18 January 1941 announced 'Japanese officer can't see forts' but told its readers that Major Hashida was here to see all he could of military training and industrial methods. The Minister for the Army, Percy Spender denied that Hashida had asked to see defence installations.

Hashida travelled throughout Australia from mid-January until mid-March 1941. He was assisted by Mr Miura of Kanematsu and Harry Suzuki (a.k.a. Ivan Steele) in Brisbane, and Denzo Umino, Mitsubishi and Domei News in Sydney. He also met Mr Iida of Okura Trading. In Melbourne, he had dinner with of Mr Matsuura of Mitsubishi and three of his acquaintances on 20 February. Most of his work was done through the Consulate-General in Sydney with Mr Nomura of Kanematsu and Mr Yanase of the Consular staff assisting him. He also visited the Chinese Consulate.

Hashida had expected to be watched but was surprised and annoyed at the level of surveillance. Police escorted him around Sydney Harbour and the Army and police kept all of his movements within strict bounds. He wrote on 23 February in Melbourne that: "the net for the spying on Japanese is very strict." He visited Percy Spender, Minister for Defence, on 17 January, whom Hashida maintained did not understand Japan's standpoint with the Tripartite Pact nor its policy of southward advance and was determined to assist England. By 25 February, Hashida appealed to Consul-General Akiyama to see if he could have the surveillance reduced. Akiyama told him to remember that, according to External Affairs, he was to be treated as a military man of a friendly power.

The information that Hashida collected was of three types. Most extensively he observed the topography as he travelled by road through NSW to Melbourne, via the coast to the hills around Adelaide and along the beaches of WA. Driving to Melbourne he noticed the telegraph lines and road conditions. On 25 February, when he was refused a visit to the coast and military installations, Major Machin agreed instead to take him to Mt Lofty ranges to a winery. Hashida saw from this high point that the beaches were wide and the sea shallow and wrote: "landings everywhere possible". But around Adelaide the low mountains hindered military activity. He concluded that Major Machin was a typical Australian, honest but "his stupidity was amusing". Hashida's interests were also in coal transportation and the areas around military training places like Duntroon, which he flew over.

The military information that he collected concentrated on troop numbers, how many people were called up as this was announced and where armed forces were stationed and trained. He concluded that Australia was concentrating all its defence against Japan and relied on the USA. American Information Officers arrived in Darwin during his stay.

Hashida worked at the Consulate on other information gathered and sent this to Japan via ships like the *Canberra Maru* on 28 January.

Whatever its exact nature, it was extensive. Hashida wrote that Nomura of Kanematsu brought material (unspecified) and although it was "gathered with so much difficulty" they could not sort it all. He decided to send it to General Staff. Such extensive information gathered by companies would have had a commercial basis because this was their specialty. A further clue to the nature of this information lies in his remarks about the policy statements that managers of the firms made to him. Most of these discussions were with Mitsubishi and Okura Trading. Both companies realised the need for better methods of communication between officials and private persons but they differed in their perspectives on general policy. Mr Iida of Okura supported the position that Japan should negotiate a peace with Australia. This is consistent with the Okura principle that originally operated in China. Mitsubishi, however, advocated that the government should centralise Japan's worldwide foreign commerce, which included Australia, reflecting its own international organisation. This would have been an enormous undertaking, but only an extension of the rapid consolidation of firms in Japan that was already taking place at the time.

Mitsubishi particularly operated in Japanese-mandated or occupied territories and was engaged in the development of mining, shipbuilding, chemical and electrical engineering, and aircraft construction.[36] By 1939, Mitsubishi's branches in Australia moved minerals on a global scale. In May 1939, Sydney branch was importing graphite from Fusan. Chile was advising Tokyo head office about ore for smelters in Korea an arrangement that dated back to 1935. Melbourne branch was trading in zinc from the Electrolyte Zinc Co. in Tasmania to Calcutta branch. Small Australian mines wrote to MSK asking for business, for example, W.H.T. Riding of Coffs Harbour, NSW, and B.G. Nicholl in May 1937 from Iron Island in Queensland. Mitsubishi had a long-term contract with Broken Hill Association Smelters Ltd for 1,000–2,000 tons of lead concentrate monthly. However, in 1940, when Sears of BHAS Ltd informed them that the British Government was taking all the supplies, they asked him to lobby the Australian government to permit some pig-iron to be exported to Japan because, they argued, it was important to promote international friendship and confidence in the current world situation. By 12 March 1941, J.F. Murphy, Secretary of the Department of Commerce notified Sears that a monthly quota had been set for Japan. MSK mining started to refine nickel from New Caledonia, which Seattle branch bought. MSK was also attempting to obtain copper in rock form from New Caledonia but by January 1941, that colony had placed a ban on all export of metals to Japan except iron ore.

Major Hashida himself viewed Japanese expansion in both military and non-military terms. He wrote on 10 March that the Japanese who had died in the pearling industry in Broome in the previous 50 years were "victims of our overseas expansion". Of major concern to him during his visit was the fact that Australia was far too aware of threat at this time. He was anxious that Australians should not gain too much insight into Japan's policies. He observed that there was a fair amount of talk about Japanese families returning to Japan, which was true and reported frequently to intelligence. Many were leaving early in 1941, in fact a large number of wives and children left on 21 February on the *Suwa Maru*.

More worrying to him were press reports on a possible pact between Japan and Russia, which had big headlines in the papers.

They directly link the Southward Advance with it …. Mc Ewen, Minister for Air, has said that Australia should not rely on England alone but should take her own measures. Both facts stated together show too much nervousness … The general situation becomes more and more serious according to my opinion. The papers have been at the Consulate General for information of the evacuation of families.[37]

Such a pact would mean that Japan had no potential enemy in its region and it was obvious that it could move troops south. The day before, he had written that if Minister Kawai did not come very soon to open the Japanese Legation in Australia, "we shall lose our chance for diplomatic actions". Clearly Japan was working on plans that could be negotiated with Australia at the right time and that plan was under construction in 1941. It is clear that it involved control of commerce and minerals but had nothing to do with pearling. It is also clear that Hashida was concerned to see what kind of opposition Australia would mount to Japan's plans for a diplomatic arrangement and also what defences it had. The fact that he inspected all coastlines, major roadways and terrain meant that no particular plan existed at that stage for a military operation but that all information might later be useful in keeping with Japan's normal espionage strategy. It may also have meant that the information that Japan had at the time on Australia's coastline and road systems was inadequate. Those who had supposedly spied for decades either did a very poor job or had not spied for military purposes at all. It is also interesting that Mitsui is absent from serious policy discussions, when historians in Australia most often mentioned Mitsui as the 'combine' ready to support an invasion.

Hashida also worried about the heavy surveillance that Japanese experienced in metropolitan and rural Australia at the time. The interrogation of Denzo Umino at his hearing against his internment on 18 May 1942[38] reveals that the examining members of the Tribunal had good security reports on Hashida's movements and of the people whom he had contacted. Umino admitted that he took Major Hashida to the Blue Mountains with Mr Otabi the Vice-Consul to show him "the best views". They also knew that the Consul had written to Umino in December 1941 just before war was declared to find out how many Dooshikai people, wives and children remained in the city. They also knew the results of the search of Denzo's house. The members of the Dooshikai had been asked to collect money for Japanese soldiers in China and had collected wool to knit socks. They also knew that Umino was in touch with Harry Suzuki (a.k.a. Ivan Steele) of Brisbane and members of the Brisbane

Japanese Society who were under surveillance. Umino had also listened to radio broadcasts from Tokyo. They listed most of the important consular officials in Sydney as Umino's regular contacts including the spy, 'Juro'. Umino also had links to the shipping company to which Kagiyama took his radio broadcasts. In effect they challenged him on every aspect of the surveillance reports that they had gathered on him and his contacts since 1939. Most importantly, Umino also knew Mr Yanase with whom Hashida had worked at the Consulate.

Japanese travelling in country NSW were under the surveillance of local police. Their Australian drivers were questioned about Japanese activities on the trips and local police made a report to the security services. On return to Sydney, security service officers visited photographic shops to view the processed prints before they were collected. Although no real suspicion fell on the wool buyers through these trips, local people reported that some farmers were in sympathy with the Japanese. These accusations were always investigated. The reports indicate that while police and local firms that dealt with Japanese understood the purpose and nature of the trips, some local people initially had second thoughts in 1940 about relationships they had taken for granted over the years. Innocent photographs of a local hotel were interpreted as strategic information by a few rural people with vivid imaginations who were worried about a Japanese takeover of unlikely places like Parkes. However, those who had known the Japanese wool buyers for many years had no change of heart in relation to the innocent nature of their rural visits.[39]

Japan and immediate preparations for war

Regardless of how prepared for war Australia thought Japan was from 1937, Lieutenant-General Fujiwara states boldly that Japan was not prepared for war in 1940. It had no intelligence on the Dutch, British and USA colonial areas. Major Hashida's diary supports this. Hashida made the statement on 3 February:

Although I studied with Yanase at the Consulate General the whole afternoon, we made no progress. We have gained the impression that Army and Navy have always been too late in this kind of investigation.

Information on how Japanese espionage prepared for war in SEA provides a means of assessing the activities of Japanese in Australia to that point. F. Kikan and organisations like it were separate from the Army but they prepared the way for military operations.[40]

Fujiwara's account of F. Kikan in SEA demonstrates that when operations began in 1940 they were completely unprepared to undertake espionage in Malaya and Thailand. The method was to place agents in trading companies and hotels. They used Mitsubishi, Mitsui and the Consulate in Bangkok and Domei wireless in Singapore. The main aim of their operation was to gain the support of the local people for the Japanese against the British, particularly in India. At this time the reason for entering a war was given as national survival and the establishment of a Greater East Asian Co-prosperity Sphere. Once the army took an area, local Japanese would be useful to the military administration. Many had lived in the area for 10–30 years, including small businessmen like shopkeepers, and photographers who, having suffered constant surveillance under the British and endured a "life of humiliation", would be willing to cooperate.[41]

Fujiwara expected war to break out at first in October but was later told it would be 28 November 1941. They had final notification of the date of war and smuggled arms and hand grenades into the Bangkok embassy in case the British found the invaders and attacked the embassy. They also worked ahead of the Army in December 1941 in Malaya and in NEI especially in Sumatra and areas like Ache which wanted freedom from the Dutch. The plan was to use Sumatran youth to safeguard infrastructure against Dutch destruction when Japanese troops landed. However, the British began to collect a lot of material on F. Kikan and took counter measures. F. Kikan believed that the war was intended to free subject peoples and to establish a co-prosperity sphere but found that the army's treatment of the local people was arrogant, often brutal and created conflict. In effect it failed to deliver the promised co-prosperity sphere and the freedom it had preached.[42]

This evidence of Japanese methods just before war broke out is useful in examining what happened in Australia. Overwhelmingly the Japanese gathered commercial information and general information about Australia, although requests for maps increased after 1940, including a British Admiralty Chart for Singapore and a detailed map of the wool districts of Australia's east coast. Trading companies played a major role in this research, which was worldwide. For example, Mitsubishi produced major reports on areas such as California and Argentina but not one comprehensive report on Australia. Instead, companies like Mitsubishi subscribed to organisations and periodicals that provided statistics and current information. This was sent from 1940 to the Economic and Research Bureau in Tokyo.[43] Australian intelligence reports throughout the decades before the war rightly note that Japan not only requested information from government departments on everything imaginable but also bought books and collected newspaper cuttings. The tradition of writing books and reports continued from the time that Watanabe visited in 1893. However, Hashida needed to collect the correct information for the Army and Navy.

Comparing what Japan actually did to prepare ahead of military action with what happened in Australia, there are significant differences. First, the detailed information gathering for war purposes, which Hashida appears to have engaged in, was very late. F. Kikan was in Malaya in 1940 and a tentative date for war had already been set. Further, in SEA, Japan proposed to use local people. In Australia there was still support for Britain and Hashida notes throughout that people regretted the end of the Anglo-Japanese Alliance. Australia was strengthening defences against

Japan and relying on the USA. Local Japanese were divided in opinion about Japan's role in Australia. This meant there was no chance of stirring up Australians against Britain. The best hope of influence in Australian affairs was by means of a pact or normal diplomatic measures. This was Kawai's role, but he had not yet arrived.

Given that the White Australia policy was originally planned to prevent as Deakin put it "undue influence" in Australian affairs, it is hard to see that Japan could reasonably have expected to succeed. However, in the years before the war, Japanese companies intervened in trade matters. The 1936 resolution of the Trade Diversion Dispute was largely due to the intervention of Sam Hirodo. Intervention in the iron ore dispute in 1938 had little effect on the outcome of the resumption of trade with Japan in that product but pig-iron certainly continued to assist Japan's war effort in China. Unions had mounted a virulent anti-Japanese campaign, even among children, not to buy Japanese goods including Japanese toys. The argument was that Australian minerals sold to Japan were made into bombs that were dropped on Chinese children. They might one day soon be dropped on Australian children. Although Robert Menzies broke the blockade on shipping pig-iron to Japan, the government became much more unco-operative towards Japan after 1939. However, one of the most ironic partnerships that was undertaken with the outbreak of war in 1939 illustrates the extraordinary boundaries crossed by trade. Mitsui and Mitsubishi gained Australian government defence contracts to import cloth from Japan, which was needed for parachutes and Australian defence force uniforms. Foy & Gibson, for example, converted its dress design and production section, according to Patricia Malloch, to make underwear for Australian troops from Japanese cloth. Even in September 1940 just as Japan was about to sign the Axis Pact and invade Indochina, the Commonwealth accepted Mitsubishi's quote for 500,000 yards of cloth for Army Ordnance stores.[44] But after Japan signed the Axis pact and invaded Indochina, Australia joined Allied measures to freeze Japan's assets in July 1941 in an attempt to curb its expansion. These measures had the opposite effect and partly hastened moves towards war against the USA and Britain.

Far from appeasing Japan, the archival files for 1940 and 1941 show an Australia increasingly resistant to pressure from Japan even on the commercial front. The military preparations were sufficient to give Japan the impression that Australia was not undefended and certainly more aware than Japan liked, regardless of historians' arguments about the actual adequacy of our intelligence or defences. Japanese trading companies had less and less influence the closer the war came.

During 1939–41, Mitsubishi in particular mounted a constant campaign to barter goods to overcome wartime restrictions on certain classes of goods that Japan particularly required. In December 1939, Mitsubishi's Osaka branch asked the Melbourne branch to lobby the government to allow the bartering of cotton and other piece goods for Australian wheat. In January 1940, the JCC engaged in a heated exchange with J.N. Lawson, the Minister for Trade and Customs, on the issue of permitting Japanese importers to have import licences and to enter barter arrangements. In 1940 and 1941, Mitsubishi made several further unsuccessful attempts to lobby A.G. Cameron, Minister for Commerce, to permit Japan to exchange goods for those required for Australian defence use. On this occasion Mitsubishi suggested that Australia buy cotton in exchange for zinc and lead concentrate to the value of approximately £107,000. They made the point that Mt Isa and Broken Hill had a "fair supply" and that such an exchange would not use any Sterling funds. The government did not reply. Undaunted, Mitsubishi offered on 2 August 1940 to supply 250 aircraft to the Aircraft Production Committee of the Commonwealth Government over a period of 18 months, which came to nothing. On 1 June 1941, they put forward a proposal to Senator George McLeay again to barter wheat but this time in exchange for Japanese tinned crab and salmon but received no reply. Mitsubishi also explored ways to import yarn into Australia through its office in Bombay and attempted to buy from New Zealand via the London office. Trading within the British Empire through its network of offices was one avenue it tried to circumvent wartime trade restrictions.[45]

The schemes to barter for pig-iron and steel were more aggressive and began in November 1939. Although the government shunned these attempts, Australian companies continued to explore options with Japanese companies. Correspondence with Paterson & Co. Ltd in Perth began in 1940 and continued until as late as 16 September 1941 after Japanese assets had been frozen in all Sterling currency countries. Mitsubishi was interested in alumite deposits in WA and bauxite ore. The aim was to ship it through Yamashita Co. for manufacture in Japan. In addition, Mitsubishi's contracts with Mt Isa Mines Ltd continued. It enjoyed a £100,000 line of credit with the mine from 1938 to 1940.

Conclusion

Major Sie Hashida hurriedly sent unprocessed information to Japan on ships during his visit from January to March 1941. He had a clear brief from the Japanese Navy and Army to gather information on Australia. This was several months after Japan had signed the Tripartite Pact in 1940 and Japanese preparations for war in Malaya and NEI had begun. The information he gathered personally was related to strategic matters. He specifically records information on terrain and coastlines that were or were not suitable for landings or that could form good harbours or should be ruled out. These are not where Japan raided but were concentrated in NSW, SA and WA's harbours near areas rich in mineral resources. He noted the processes for producing and moving coal. Trading companies provided so much information that he could not process it. He stated that his work with consular staff on the particular issues he had been sent to investigate made little progress. Obviously he was either faced with too much information from which to distil a plan or the information did not fit the suggested lines of investigation that the Japanese armed forces wanted to follow. We do not know the exact nature of the information that he sent back to Japan or if it was ever processed.

Hashida's visit also showed that Japanese companies in Sydney had different views. Hashida was not impressed with Okura's peace plans. He was concerned that Australian suspicion and military defences were growing and that if Kawai did not arrive soon, all diplomatic advantage would slip away. Hashida did not want a worried Australia. His diary strongly suggests that the information was for policy consideration in regard to Australia for a coming conflict whose approximate commencement date had been set and involved Malaya.

Far from lax security, Hashida was worried that Australian security was tight. Certainly, Australian intelligence kept a constant watch on Japan in the Pacific, in pearling and trade but the consolidation of pearling interests in the South Seas was not part of a move on Australia's coast and pearling in the Arafura Sea actually decreased. Despite the security, Hashida and other Japanese had no trouble in investigating mineral developments or in attempting to negotiate with Australians to establish companies to export ore to Japan but Australian policy blocked the export of raw materials while continuing to export readily usable pig-iron. In these measures, Australian missed the point. The Japanese showed far more interest in the resources that Australia could potentially supply in the future and in working out ways to obtain them through trade, rather than in investigating ways to invade the country and take what it needed by force.

From 1937, Japanese in Australia were shadowed and warrants were prepared in 1940 to arrest them all. From the Australian records at this time, we can say that Australia made every attempt to determine what plans Japan had for Australia in the event of war but although some conflict looked certain, its timing and nature was not obvious. Australians also concentrated on identifying a military plan for an invasion rather than on something more akin to a diplomatic stranglehold over policy as a means to obtain resources. In this Australia was blinkered. It is unfortunate that the majority of Japanese who had nothing to do with any preparations for war became suspect and even labelled spies after the war.

When the bombs fell on Pearl Harbor, Hirokichi Nakamura's reaction was very different from that of Denzo Umino. Nakamura knew it meant war probably on Australian soil as all Australians feared and particular trouble for him as a Japanese national. He headed home from his holiday with his family and was arrested in the dead of night with all other Japanese in Australia, the youngest of whom was 12 days old.[1]

Australians began to worry about an invasion not just with the reports of the bombing of Pearl Harbor but also of Malaya. Although all Japanese were interned, the public began to report seeing Japanese everywhere: on ferries, in parks, in the local street. These reports were investigated and in every case the people concerned were Chinese who had been born in Australia. There were no Japanese in the country or in pearling areas ready to pounce as the invasion literature had predicted.

Going against the general trend, Denzo Umino, who was trusted with driving spies around Sydney and presumably had heard a good number of conversations, had no belief in a Japanese invasion. He went off to work as usual, thinking it was a Japanese propaganda stunt, not the start of a war. His wife, Violet, was asked by the Aliens Appeal Tribunal at the hearing against her restriction in 1942:

> Did he ever discuss with you the possibility of war breaking out
> with Japan and Australia? – He has always said there would
> be no war.
>
> Did he say why? – He said he thought they would get trade. In
> fact, on the morning the war did break out he would not
> believe it and he went on with his business. That is why,
> when the Military Police came they could not find him.
>
> Mr. Bradley [attorney]: Do you mean to say he said that after
> Pearl Harbour [*sic*]? – I said after breakfast, "There is
> bombing at Pearl Harbour". I said, "I am sure it is war,"
> and he said, "Oh, it will be propaganda". He would not
> believe it.[2]

With such divergent beliefs and reactions to the start of the war expressed by two people intimately involved in the Australian-Japanese networks what did Japan plan for Australia? Why did it not invade? What did our troops save us from?

Examining the myths

One of the strongest beliefs about the war is that the Japanese in Australia helped to prepare for the raids on Australia and an invasion that failed. This book has examined the records in Australia for Japanese activities including all the intelligence gathered by the various security and intelligence services before World War Two. As we saw in Chapter Six, apart from the small spy ring centred on Sydney from about 1933, there was little active spying in Australia. The major evidence for spying of a military nature is in the diary of Major Hashida, which was confiscated by Dutch authorities after his visit to Australia in March 1941. This evidence shows that Japan was not ready for war at this stage. Further, that it did not have sufficient information on Australia for any plans. To that point, some Japanese authorities had only vague ideas about where Australia might fit in the establishment of a Greater East Asia Co-prosperity Sphere, if it was included at all.

The allegations that some historians have made that 'combines', supposedly in control of pearling to Australia's north, gathered information for action against Australia and knew enough to do so are based on faulty post-war statements.[3] The statement by Mary Albertus Bain in her book about pearling in Australia, unfortunately, does not provide any source for her information on Mitsui. It has been repeated by many historians since and taken as correct. But when we examine the structure and activities of Mitsui and Mitsubishi from the hundreds of boxes of pre-war accounts and correspondence seized by the Australian Army in 1941, it is clear that they were not involved in organising pearling fleets to Australia's north. In effect, the fleets were organised by a separate company established in 1937–38. The luggers behaved themselves and stayed away from Australian waters after the lugger cases of 1938. However, the *zaibatsu* were involved in gathering enormous amounts of information about Australia from the 1900s.

The nature of the information gained by *zaibatsu* in Australia was overwhelmingly commercial but included detailed general information about Australian government, commerce, society and way of life. As a post-war report on Japanese activities in Australia also found, major firms were:

> ... legitimate trading concerns whose sole function was commerce ... there is no information available that would indicate that any of them were established only as covers for espionage.[4]

However the report acknowledged, as we found in Chapter Six, that some minor branches did little business. This certainly applied to the suspect branch of 'Juro's' firm in Brisbane.

Information of a general type and commercial information was readily available in bookshops and through government departments. Mitsubishi in particular made it a habit of producing detailed reports on areas in which it wished to trade. This obsession with information was a practice that Australians found hard to understand and often interpreted as having a sinister purpose. Captain Fearnley was one officer who believed that every piece of information and every photo must have some military use. He was in the minority. However, as Lindsay writes, after the war, many other Australians remembered seeing Japanese with Kodaks buying up postcards and maps and understandably wondered if it had been innocent tourist activity or not.

The charge that Australian security was lax before the war, as Bob Wurth concludes, is extraordinary. The surveillance records of security services in the 1930s take up hundreds of shelf metres in the National Archives of Australia. For example, one series of files of the Investigation Branch for 1919–46 runs to 66.6 metres and includes surveillance all over Australia. Case files in SA run to 29 metres and there are 4.5 metres of extant files for the Sydney Japanese alone. This does not include investigations undertaken by the departments that administered the White Australia policy (which are even more extensive and include surveillance material) and are still held in every state and territory of this nation. Nor does it include the 3,114 boxes of Japanese company records held by the National Archives of Australia in Sydney. Neither can it be substantiated that Australian intelligence services lacked information about what Japan was doing in the South Seas, NEI or SEA.[5] The stories of Japanese people in this book (with three exceptions: Hirokichi Nakamura, Sam Hirodo and Mr Iida), which are totally reconstructed from information collected by security and police officers, testify to the detail and quality of the information that Australian security services gathered.

What security surveillance tells us is that only a handful of Japanese were engaged in espionage or information gathering that could be used in wartime. Major Hashida is the most important example. The surveillance reports also highlight the tendency in parts of Australia to suspect foreigners who were seen to compete with Australians in some business endeavour, missionary activity or who threatened jobs. This was particularly so in WA and Queensland which depended on agricultural and mineral development. The great interest that Japanese showed in Australian mineral development heightened suspicions. Queensland workers and the NSW Communist Party certainly believed that Japan was after some kind of commercial imperialism in Australia that would threaten jobs and that also could be used to gain material suitable for the manufacture of armaments. These beliefs had basis but much of the suspicion was racially based particularly in Queensland as the colourful language of its surveillance reports demonstrate. This fed into the stories of spying after the war.

A recent argument put by Peter Stanley is that Australians were so fearful of Japan for 50 years before the war that the fear affected how they saw the real crisis in 1942 and that this led to the belief today that an invasion was to happen in World War Two when none was planned. We will examine the question of a plan for an invasion below, but it is not true that Australians feared Japan for 50 years before the war. The evidence points in favour of good relations and friendship until the period 1937–40 when people became suspicious and hostile from September 1940. Australians in their thousands welcomed Japanese ship visits at a time when Stanley and others maintain that they feared an attack or invasion from Japan soon after federation. Australian businessmen even after war broke out hoped the war would end soon and that it would bring only a temporary interruption to the lucrative trade. Australians married Japanese people, welcomed them into their homes as friends, worked with them in community organisations and clubs and even in the armed forces and Volunteer Defence Corps. Mario Takasuka of Swan Hill fought in the AIF in New Guinea after serving in Crete. The Japanese whom Australians had befriended were declared "as Australian as we are", even in wartime as friends and neighbours fought to have them released from internment or saved from forcible 'repatriation' in 1946.

Even newspapers exhibited few fears of Japan in the first two decades of the century, as Sissons demonstrated. After the period of good relations in the 1920s, when Vice-Admiral Kobayashi was invited to lay a wreath in memory of the Anzacs at Kings Park, Perth, Australians still continued to live alongside Japanese people as they had always done when Japan took Manchukuo. Even the Commonwealth government was quite happy to continue to export sheep to Manchukuo for a breeding program after Japan was at war with China in 1937.[6] Only after the Rape of Nanking in 1937 did Australians begin to see a brutal, unjustified side to the Japanese army but this view was not transferred to the Japanese that they knew or met in daily life in Australia until *after* 1944 when reports of the treatment of Australian Prisoners of War came to light. If anything, the feelings of friendship went underground and have only resurfaced in the last decade. To express feelings of friendship experienced in the 1930s and 1940s perhaps seemed a betrayal of those Australians who died. It was certain to be misunderstood if expressed. This made it easier for *all* Japanese who had ever lived in Australia to be made the villains in exaggerated post-war stories of plots and spying against Australia in preparation for an invasion that never happened, just as they had been portrayed in the fictional stories early in the century.

Who did fear Japan before World War Two? Certainly lurid tales entertained the public but this was part of a genre of literature, which had been popular since the 1870s and which is still with us. Only the villains in the story change with time. The resurgence of stories that include the Japanese as invaders or raiders in 1937 is the only one that relates directly to actual events at the time. Japan was at war with China and the question was, rightly, where else might it go because the definition of the *nan'yō* was not fixed. This problem of Japan's intentions caused concern but not fear and alarm in Australian defence circles, a concern that was sufficient to prompt intelligence gathering from the 1910s. A lot of this activity came from Australia's desire to be independent from British intelligence, which focused primarily on the need to defend Britain rather than parts of the Empire such as Australia. British defence plans for the region did not satisfy Australian defence needs regardless of the potential enemy. The arguments for an independent navy and intelligence service were well founded and based on objective military assessments of potential future risk. The argument consistently was that Australia might face raids and disruption to supplies and commerce. Japan was not the only prospective enemy in the decades before the war, but by the mid-1930s it was seen as the most likely. In the 1910s, Australian authorities felt that Australia had about 10 years or so to strengthen defences to the north. The safety of New Guinea was paramount in strategic thinking. Because of these defence concerns, Australia had good intelligence on Japanese activities to its north right up to the outbreak of war.

The supposedly lax administration of the White Australia policy is one reason given by Bob Wurth for Japanese spying in Australia. As this book has shown, the policy was very carefully administered throughout the period. It was designed to vet who entered rather than exclude any group absolutely. In this it succeeded. The policy did cause ire in Japan at times when Japan was lobbying internationally for concessions in peace treaties or for commercial arrangements. However, the Consul-General was given a very strong role in vetting Japanese who entered and in recommending them to the Commonwealth. This did not mean that entry was totally automatic or that Australian officers did not conduct their own exhaustive investigations into all Japanese individuals who applied for extensions of stay. However, the changes to criteria for extensions of stay had an ironic effect from the 1920s when the department sought to limit the number of small merchants and only permit those who imported more than £1,000 worth of goods to remain, thus strengthening larger firms.[7]

Until late 1940, the information gained by *zaibatsu*, and largely collated by their Australian employees, was for innocent immediate business use, but the companies gained a powerful place in Australian life.

Most notable was the development of the wool industry, the relationship with Australian stores and the exploration and exporting of Australian mineral deposits in conjunction with Australia's biggest companies. This development was mutually beneficial to Australians in peacetime but the role of the *zaibatsu* in Australian life was not even noticed, and then only in passing, until 1932. By this time, the *zaibatsu* and the Consul-General formed the essential centre for all Japanese networks in Australia. This overall network included innocent local integration, intermarriage and small business. But the structure, centred in Sydney, was in place throughout the country. Before the war there was nothing sinister in this and the existence of such a network was required by the provisions of Australian immigration regulations and by the necessities of keeping in touch in a *diaspora* situation that involved a vibrant international commercial base.

After the war, the *zaibatsu* assumed monstrous proportions in the reports collated by French, British and Americans involved in surveying Japan during the occupation. This has also had an effect on the way historians view the *zaibatsu*, who often use the word 'cartel' or 'combine' to describe them as sinister organisations with an aggressive commercial agenda. Little investigation of their actual activities in Australia appears in any scholarly work. In 1947, the Inter Allied Trade Board for Japan, consisting of representatives from occupying forces, described Japan's trading company network and its associations as the "most pernicious instruments of trade discrimination".[8] The Board was concerned to ensure that Japan's trade could no longer be monopolised by this network. The Board's minutes of 8 April 1947 stated that the trade organisations in Japan were so well organised before the war that they excluded other countries as much as possible from taking part in Japan's export trade and to a certain extent the import trade and transport of products from Japan. This was a reversal of the situation, which had existed in the early decades of the Meiji era when foreigners controlled Japan's trade and coastal shipping, leading to the bankrupting of Japan's merchants.[9] This post-war view of the *zaibatsu* dominates references to pre-war *zaibatsu* activities.

A further objection against the *zaibatsu* was the belief that they bore substantial responsibility for Japanese aggression in the 1930s leading to World War Two. The antecedents for this were traced back into the nineteenth century. These views often appeared in papers in the 1950s, which reported the perceived threat from the regrouping of Japanese companies particularly after the Peace Treaty of 1952. However, although the *zaibatsu* and their apparent resurgence received a lot of attention after the war, it is not clear as to what the actual pre-war reality was, particularly in Australia in regard to any plans to support aggression. Further, the papers that reported the regrouping of firms in the 1950s did so with fear. Reports linked the increasing size of Japanese trading firms with the possibility of a return to aggressive policies, which might once again threaten Australian security. Clearly in the 1950s, the *zaibatsu* were named as the major suspect in identifying who was responsible for the war. On the surface, *zaibatsu* operations in Australia appeared peaceful but did the commercial penetration have a different side? Was it a threat and can the commercial activity be separated from Japan's military agenda?

Japan's plans for Australia

What plans did Japan have for Australia? Japan had no plan to invade despite the fact that some historians rely on an alleged invasion map known as the 'Chinese map' to support that view. Peter Stanley argues that this is a fake. The evidence he gave for that from Australian documents is inconclusive but statements in other Defence and External Affairs files from 1943 and 1947 clearly show that the information came from Chinese General Staff. W.R. Hodgson of External Affairs stated categorically that information from Chinese Military Intelligence had been shown to contain "a small quantity of facts drawn from reliable sources while the remainder is surmise". The fact that the information came from Japanese-occupied territory also aroused suspicion. The information on Australia contained in the reports from the Chinese is in some instances incorrect, suggesting that it was not gathered in Australia as Japanese intelligence information was.[10]

The importance of New Guinea[11] for Australia has never been in question but according to recent research of Japanese sources, it was never on Japan's planning table for World War Two and is rarely mentioned even though 220,000 Japanese troops died in the campaign out of the 350,000 Japanese troops that Australian and other Allied troops pinned down for three years as MacArthur moved towards Tokyo. Henry Frei's research into why the Japanese were in New Guinea states that a Foreign Ministry position paper submitted to the Japanese army on 24 July 1940 in preparation for the conclusion of the Axis pact in September has one paragraph that reflects on India, Australia and New Zealand as belonging to the Greater East Asia new order "in the near future" but says nothing of New Guinea in particular. The "future" was estimated at 20 years *after* SEA was incorporated, placing it somewhere about 1960, and which would entail recurring war with Britain and her allies according to the Total War Institute's elaborate 'Draft of basic plans for the establishment of the Greater East Asia Co-Prosperity Sphere' dated 27 January 1942. New Guinea simply was not on the list of war objectives in stage one of Japan's basic war plan but Rabaul was. This stage of the war, which was to be wrapped up by April or May 1942, included the Malayan Peninsular to Pearl Harbor. Its aim was to eliminate Dutch, British and US navies to secure the raw materials from SEA.

Australia's administrative centre for PNG was a threat to Japan's main naval base at Truk 1,500 miles north of Rabaul. Therefore Japan took Rabaul. The navy had asked the army already in August 1941 for troops to secure Rabaul. Admiral Yamamoto saw it as an important move against the US navy in any attempt to defeat it in mandated waters. Until after 23 January 1942 when Rabaul was taken, New Guinea did not come into the picture. But the next night Rabaul was attacked by planes from Salamaua and Lae so something had to be done about the bases on PNG, which were occupied on 7 March. But on 10 March Lae was bombed from Port Moresby so it had to be occupied.

Frei argued that: "The more successful Japanese troops were in southeast Asia, the bolder their imaginations and the greater their appetites grew". This sparked several plans, one of which was an advance towards Australia. However, Admiral Yamamoto was against invading Australia. He preferred to take Midway or try again in Hawaii. The next best option was to cut Australia off from US supplies, Fiji, New Caledonia and Samoa, which became known as Operation FS. The attack on Port Moresby became a preliminary move.

This view of the place of New Guinea in Japanese planning is supported by the work of Hiromi Tanaka. He argues that the campaign was outside initial expectations and planning. Initially Japan entered China and headed south to cut off the British and US supply line to the Chinese. When the US cut off trade relations in July 1941, the lifeline of the Japanese economy was severed leaving the supply of iron and oil and importation of raw material in turmoil. The direct motive for war in December 1941 against the USA, Britain and Holland was to procure essential raw materials. The Malay Peninsular and Indonesia were rich in oil and minerals and were termed the southern resource belt. The initial policy was to seek peace and plan a cessation of war to secure these regions as colonies.

Strategic planning from about 1930 believed that in any war with the US the US navy would retreat to Hawaii and then regroup and re-engage in the Philippines. The Japanese then expected to defeat the US navy in that area. But in the actual war, the US did not retreat but General MacArthur moved to Brisbane and used the region as a base for the counter-offensive. Japan had not anticipated this. It lacked information on the region.

The army, on the other hand, had hastily conducted surveys just prior to the outbreak of war on the ability of the southern resource belt to provide resources for military materiel. It was necessary to occupy New Guinea and the Solomons in order to enforce a blockade of military supply routes from the US to Australia and to prevent an expected Allied counter-attack from the south. The occupation of Rabaul was pushed through by the navy in opposition from the army. The strategy to invade Port Moresby was also prompted by the navy to enhance the defense of Rabaul. But the army used to massive land campaigns adopted a passive stance concerning operations promoted by the navy in the southern region.

The navy had two offensives in the region: to capture Port Moresby and to occupy Samoa, Fiji and New Caledonia in order to enforce the blockade between the US and Australia. But Allied forces advanced north along the MacArthur axis from Bouganville, the north of New Guinea and the Philippines towards Japan. The second offensive was against the US navy along the Nimitz axis from Gilberts through the Marshal and Mariana Islands.

In Japanese terms there were three fronts: China; the southern resources belt opposed by the British, Australian and Dutch and the Western Pacific War against the Americans. The plan to take Port Moresby was to protect Rabaul and prevent Allied offensives operating from Australia. Port Moresby could also be used as a possible advance on Australia "in the future". The failure of the overland and seaborne campaigns to capture Port Moresby signalled the end of these operations and the end of the first stage of the war.

The second stage in New Guinea, according to Tanaka's evidence, was political to hide the defeat at Guadal Canal from the Japanese people and hail it as a change of direction rather than a defeat. But the realisation came slowly that the Allies wanted the Philippines not Rabaul. The purpose of establishing a line of defence through New Guinea was to keep in check the Allied advance and to buy time to strengthen vital positions in the Pacific. In effect, Tanaka argues, the war in New Guinea was prosecuted from necessities that arose out of the course of the first months of conflict. Japanese strategic planning lacked clear policy and proceeded by reacting to Allied movements. What this research into Japan's plans tells us is that Japan was not united on war plans in World War Two just as it had not been united in Manchuria in 1931–33.

Although New Guinea was not on Japan's drawing board for the first stage of the war, the navy and army recognised the importance of preventing the USA from consolidating in a position from which it could counter-attack. Unexpectedly, this position was Australia and New Guinea. Hashida knew that Australia was increasingly leaning on the USA. If Tanaka is right and Japan expected General MacArthur to retreat to US territory, then Hashida's information was ignored. Australia should have been expected to afford the USA every facility in a time of war, including providing MacArthur with a base. Despite this miscalculation, had Japan not needed to fight in New Guinea, or had it won in New Guinea, Australia would have been isolated behind a very aggressive military-controlled area in striking distance from its shores. The raids on Australia proved Japan was within reach. They had the effect of making shipping and commerce, not to mention the peace of Australians, just that much more difficult and dangerous.

Saving Australia

When Australians suffered attacks by Japanese planes they understandably thought an invasion was imminent, but this was incorrect. When Australian troops fought and died in New Guinea and other parts of the Pacific, they too believed it was a fight to defend Australia from invasion. However, they also participated in a wider war than any action designed to defend Australia. As Peter Stanley argues, Australian-centric views can interpret World War Two almost entirely in terms of saving Australia or a battle for Australia without reference to wider issues. Checking the aggressive military advance that Japan had made into the Pacific and SEA was just as vital in itself as ridding the world of Hitler. In this Australians fought and died heroically. But we can go further. The diggers also saved Australia from a nasty fate, but not from a military invasion.

Were the Japanese in Australia responsible for the raids that did not bring invasion? The evidence is that intelligence material collected in Australia for the possible distant future and, although unplanned, military purposes, does not match the areas that Japan raided. The areas raided related to two of the three different fronts of Japan's war effort. Air operations in NT, Queensland and WA and raids down the east coast including Sydney had the effect of unsettling supply lines, unnerving, injuring and killing the population and attacks on 22 ships in Australian waters that killed 621 seamen and wounded many more in a period of 18 months in 1942–43.[12] The New Guinea campaign was quite separate with no connection to the raids, but it was important. The raids were not, as we now know, a prelude to invasion, nor was an invasion planned. What then did Japan want in Australia?

Japan planned to develop over time a Greater East Asian Co-prosperity Sphere, possibly over two to three decades. Speculation abounded in the 1930s about the boundaries of the sphere and whether it included Australia or not. The achievement of the sphere is usually assumed to be by military means. There is some evidence that Australia did figure in Japan's future plans. Those plans were aided by the nature of the administration of the White Australia policy, which had encouraged *zaibatsu* growth. This is its single most important contribution to Japanese activities in Australia before the war. Without the huge impact of the *zaibatsu* on Australian economic life, Japan's plans for Australia could have been very different.

Consistently, reports state and actions confirm that Japan wanted resources: easy access to resources through trade with nations that were friendly and politically stable. Australia fitted this description. Australia and Japan had enjoyed increasing mutual trade for four decades by the late 1930s. Even the trade dispute of 1936 had dented and reduced but not ultimately damaged the trade. Japanese companies continued to seek arrangements to discover, develop and export Australian minerals. They had spent decades researching the potential for the Australia trade and had up-to-date information. Endeavours at Yampi Sound and in parts of Queensland aimed at long-term reciprocal benefits with mines in Australian hands, assisted in some cases by Japanese finance, and Japan buying up most if not all of the minerals. In the late 1930s, minerals were used to feed the factories engaged increasingly in manufacturing armaments, aircraft and shipping. The Brisbane workers were right that Australian minerals contributed to Japan's war effort. This industrial and military colossus was owned and operated by *zaibatsu* with involvement from the Japanese government, which was increasingly concentrating industry and other areas of Japan's economy into fewer hands. When Major Hashida arrived in Australia, the firms he spoke to suggested that the government take over commerce. This provides a key to something of Japan's intentions for Australia.

Two factors indicate that the network would have been important in Japan's plans for Australia if its side of the war had gone differently: first, the fact that the firms were not liquidated in 1941 and second, the commercial plans devised by *zaibatsu* before 1941. The *zaibatsu* were raided on 8–9 December 1941 and records seized but they were not totally closed down. These large firms still had business on the books and assets to assess. They had kept on some of the Australian staff after assets were frozen in July 1941. The Commonwealth appointed administrators for all of the companies but Kanematsu was able to continue trading by changing its name to J. Gunton & Co. Because of its peculiar employee share arrangement and listing, it qualified as an Australian company not as a foreign company. The work of administrators continued long after the war. The Australian government placed all Japanese assets in the hands of the Controller of Enemy Property until the terms of the Peace Treaty were clear. Only at that point could the assets of enemy firms be dispersed, a process that took the administrators of Japanese assets in Australia until the 1960s. The fact that companies remained in existence meant that trade could have been easily resumed once hostilities ended. This was a hope often expressed by Australian and Japanese traders in 1941. In Mitsubishi's Australian records there are detailed diagrams of how the firm could gain control of all stages of trade from the actual point of production to the final sale, including shipment and finance. Several complex diagrams display for example how wheat from a primary producer that passed through a country store would be handled by a Mitsubishi broker through either the Wheat Board or by bypassing the Wheat Board to a Mitsubishi importer in partnership with an Australian primary produce firm then exported in Japanese ships to a third country. Other examples involved importing, for example, jute from Calcutta to Melbourne financed via London branch with Mitsubishi handling all the stages of the transaction.[13] The centralisation of commerce was no pipe dream suggested to Hashida but something to which the *zaibatsu* had given a great deal of thought. It was not a new idea but one that had been progressing steadily in Japan from the early 1930s.

Reports written in 1947 detail the concentration of business and banking in *zaibatsu* hands. By the end of 1938 in Japan, 75 per cent of bank deposits were in *zaibatsu* hands and 77 per cent of advances in industry and commerce were *zaibatsu* initiated. Mitsui in particular controlled 112 of the top 687 Japanese companies. A USA report stated that the companies had power over the economy that was unparalleled in any other industrialised country. Seventeen *zaibatsu* controlled one quarter of all paid up capital of joint stock companies in Japan. In addition, they were responsible for 51 per cent of coal production, 69 per cent of aluminium production, 99 per cent of bank savings assets, 88 per cent of steam engine production, 74 per cent of fire insurance and 40 per cent of real estate.[14] It would have been easy to use diplomatic pressure to add Australian business into this centralisation.

Bob Wurth maintains that minerals played a part in an Australian policy of appeasement towards Japan, which had been the general approach under White Australia in an attempt to avoid war or invasion. In this book, particularly in consideration of the years from 1937–41, the evidence suggests that *resistance* to Japan's attempts to negotiate for minerals is more the order of the day rather than appeasement.[15] Hashida was worried that Australia was suspicious and watchful. He noted the degree of troop training and movement. He wanted Kawai to hurry up because Japan was in danger of losing any diplomatic edge. Although Wurth paints Kawai in a genuinely friendly light, and no matter how genuine or otherwise his friendship may have been with the Curtin family, he had a definite mission in Australia, which from what Hashida wrote included calming Australia's fears. None of this suggests appeasement by Curtin or anyone else, but rather a doggedness on Australia's part not to give in to anything that might be against the national interest in terms of supplying war materials to another nation and an awareness that Japan was on the move. In view of the scale of Japan's war preparations over so many months it is a startling idea that Kawai would have had any power to change any decisions being made in Japan or that Curtin could have had any real influence whatsoever that would have altered the objectives of Kawai's mission. Australian security services were sharply aware of Japanese activities on a daily basis. Australia had a long history of genuinely entertaining Japanese guests while keeping a wary eye out for any untoward activity and even kept spies in the Consul-General's residence. The problem was that as Australia was not sure what Japan would actually do, it took every opportunity to learn more and had to be ready to react if necessary.

In any event, over previous decades, Australia had provided much of what Japan required in primary produce. As Purcell estimated, if Yampi Sound had gone ahead in 1938, Australia would have supplied Japan with 42 per cent of its mineral needs. This potential cannot be ignored. With a

Japanese victory, Australia would not have been in a bargaining position. It would have been easy to reinstitute the networks of companies and people throughout the country that had existed before the war. Instead of blocking developments like Yampi Sound, refusing to budge on tariff levels, export and import quotas, leases and purchases of land, licences for all manner of prohibited areas under the White Australia legislation and the very restrictions build into the administration of the Immigration Restriction Acts themselves, Australia would have had little option but to agree to Japanese proposals. Australian commerce would have come under Japanese centralisation in some form. In effect, the concept of pushing rickshaws up Bourke Street has a fair measure of truth in it.

Japan did not need to invade Australia. It already had most of what it wanted and knew the precise potential for what it might obtain but had not yet managed to secure under negotiations with the Australian government. Japan considered Australia a friendly power and an ally in keeping peace in the Pacific. Australia was Japan's second base, as Consul-General Tokugawa had said in 1928. Unfortunately, its first base, the USA, had blocked Japan's access to resources and made its trade untenable, a factor that contributed to war. In the first instance, isolating Australia and negotiating for resources made most sense. The interviews that Hashida had with companies suggest trade was critical.

The campaign in New Guinea, so fiercely fought by Australian troops, saved Australia from an insidious fate of control by Japan. Our diggers believed they were saving us from possible invasion but can we imagine a life of control over Australian policy by a Japanese government that could at any time decide to back up its needs by force as it had elsewhere? The military invasion may never have come, but the possibility of it would have been a real and constant presence in daily life with little means of relief. It would have been a far cry from today's situation where, as a result of Japan's defeat in the war, Australia enjoys a mutually beneficial relationship with a democratic Japan. To say there was no Japanese plan to invade Australia in 1942–43 does no dishonour to the sacrifice of our troops but rather makes much clearer what they saved us from and what we can be grateful for. Since the Peace Treaty of 1952 and a democratic Japan, both countries have been able to enjoy the resumption of trade hoped for by those who built the trade to mutual advantage before the war. Both countries have enjoyed a relationship built on treaty arrangements, such as the Treaty of Commerce (1957), and a firm basis of mutual friendship rather than enduring an uncomfortable relationship built on fear.

Notes

Introduction – Raiding Australia

1   (Ed) Gabrielle Chan, *War on our Doorstep —Diaries of Australians in the Frontline in 1942*, 2003, pp. 42–43.
2   *Ibid.*, p.70.
3   *Ibid.*, pp. ix, xiii, 75, 91,110, 112.
4   Peter Stanley, *Invading Australia: Japan and the Battle for Australia, 1942*, 2008, pp. 87–201. Henry Frei, *Japan's Southward Advance and Australia from the Sixteenth Century to World War II*, 1991. p. 56. D.C.S. Sissons, 'Australian fears of Japan as a defence threat', Senate Standing Committee on Foreign Affairs and Defence - Reference: Japan, 1972. Bob Wurth, 1942: *Australia's Greatest Peril*, 2008, p. 370.
5   Stanley, 2008, pp. 21–86. Neville Meaney, *Towards a New Vision: Australia and Japan across Time*, 2007, pp. 2–3. Robert Dixon, *Writing the Colonial Adventure: Race, Gender and Nation in Anglo-Australian Popular Fiction, 1875–1914*, 1995, pp.135–154.
6   Bob Wurth, *Saving Australia: Curtin's Secret Peace with Japan*, 2006, pp. 25, 39, 182–186. Craig Wilcox, 'The Battle of Boucaut Bay.' *Wartime*, No. 28, 2004, pp. 6–8. C.L.A. Abbott papers, NLA: MS4744, Box 15, Commonwealth of Australia Commission of Inquiry under the National Security (Inquiries) Regulations in the matter of an inquiry concerning the circumstances connected with the attack made by enemy aircraft at Darwin on 19th February 1942 before his Honour Mr Justice Law, Commissioner, First Report. p.13.
7   David Horner, *Inside the War Cabinet: Directing Australia's War Effort, 1939–1945*, 1996, pp.146–149.
8   Pam Oliver, *Allies Enemies Trading Partners: Records on Australia and the Japanese*, 2004, records listed on pp. 62–71, 126–51.

Notes

9   Pam Oliver, 'Interpreting "Japanese Activities" in Australia, 1888–1945', *Journal of the Australian War Memorial*, May, 2002. Pam Oliver, 'In Peace and War: The Japanese Role in the Defence and Security of Australia to 1943.' Public Lecture, 30 October 2007 at 'Speakers' Corner', National Archives of Australia, Canberra, pod cast at <www.naa.gov.au>.

10   Stanley, 2008, p.13.

11   Interview with Mrs. Iida on 7 February 2004, conducted by Toshio Swift of the Museum of Sydney and used with the permission of Mrs Iida and Ms Swift.

12   NAA: ST1233/1, N19133, Hirokichi Nakamura, Security Services dossier, first folio, Report of 19 October 1941. See also Security Service dossiers in NAA: C123/1, NAA: BP424/1 and NAA: A367/1.

13   Horner, p. 63.

14   NAA: SP1098/12, Box 9, Correspondence between J.F. Guthrie of Geelong, November 1941, and Ken Shimada of Nosawa & Co.

15   NAA: A367 /1, C72449.

16   Interviews: Naida and Joan, daughters of Hirokichi Nakamura, January 1997, held by the author in Sydney and used with the permission of the Nakamura family.

17   Miscellaneous Records of Japanese trading companies, NAA: SP1098. See extended descriptions in Oliver, 2004, pp. 62–71.

18   Horner, pp. 34, 85. Alan Powell, *The Shadow's Edge: Australia's Northern War*, 2007, pp. 99–101. Henry Daly, "Americal" 1942-46, Les Américains en Nouvelle-Calédonie, nd, p. 7. See also Australian War Memorial <www.awm.gov.au/units> '2/3 Independent Company'.

19   Stanley, pp. 13, 108. Pam Oliver, 'Japanese immigrant merchants and the Japanese trading company network in Sydney, 1880s to 1941', Paul Jones and Pam Oliver (eds), *Changing Histories: Australia and Japan*, 2001, pp. 1–18.

20   Michael McKernan, *All In! Fighting the War at Home*, 1995, pp. 96-131. Chan, pp. xi, 6, 9.

21   McKernan, pp. 130, 133. <'Battle for Australia' @ www.anzacday.org.au/history/ww2bfa>. 'Australia's war 1939-1945' @ <www.ww2australia.gov.au> Steven L. Carruthers, Japanese Submarine Raiders 1942: A Maritime Mystery, 2006.

22   AWM 124, 4/339, 'Naval Intelligence Report for 20–27 Feb 1942'.

23   Horner, pp. 77, 80,81, 84, 143. My italics in the quote.

24   AWM 124, 4/339, 'Naval Intelligence Report 30 Jan – 6 Feb 1942'.

25   Wurth, 2006, p. 177. *The Argus*, 4 September 1942, pp. 1,3. Horner, p. 149.

26   Wurth, 2006, pp. 97–98.

27   Patrick Lindsay, *The Spirit of Kokoda: Then and Now*, 2002, p.19.

28   Pam Oliver, *Empty North: The Japanese Presence and Australian Reactions, 1860s–1942*, 2006, pp.176–178.

29   Stanley, pp. 54–58,126–129. Wurth, 2006, p. 211. Regina Ganter, *Mixed Relations: Asian-Aboriginal Contact in North Australia*, 2006, pp. 215, 224–225.

30 Wurth, 2006, pp. 61–2, 211, 241, 258, 277. The 305 cases of documents Wurth mentions are in the National Archives of Australia Series C123/1 and C443/P1.

31 Meaney, pp. 28-35. Stanley, pp. 13, 62-63. Wurth, 2006, pp. 36–40, 81-90. NAA: SP1096/1, Box 20, Folder 'Barter', Letter to Minister for Commerce, A.G. Cameron, 2 September 1940.

32 Meaney, p. 20. Wurth, 2006, pp. 47, 59,81, 102–103.

33 Meaney, pp. 1, 89. Wurth, 2006, p. xiii. Stanley, p. 13.

34 NAA: A1067/1, ER46/13/20. NAA: A5466/3, CCJ7C. NAA: A1838/325, 3103/4/1/1 Part 2.

35 Yuichi Murakami, 'Australia's Immigration Legislation, 1893–1901: The Japanese Response,' (eds) Paul Jones and Vera Mackie, *Relations: Australia and Japan,* 2001, pp. 45–69.

Chapter 1 – Pre-federation networks

1 'When opposites attract', Features, *The Australian,* 7 July 2007, author interviewed for this article. Pam Oliver, 'Japanese Immigrants and the Japanese Trading Company Network in Sydney 1880s–1941', Paul Jones and Pam Oliver (eds), *Changing Histories: Australia and Japan,* 2001, pp. 1–24. Yuriko Nagata, *Unwanted Aliens: Japanese Internment in Australia,* 1996. Regina Ganter, *Mixed Relations: Asian-Aboriginal Contacts in North Australia,* 2006 relies on the work of D.C.S. Sissons and Mary Albertus Bain, *Full Fathom Five,* 1982 for the Japanese. Note: Japanese names are normally written surname first. In this book they are written in English style with surname last because this is the way they appeared in Australian records.

2 Available online at au.travel.yahoo.com.guide/australia/western-australia /broome/history.html, www.kimberleyaustralia.com/broome-history.html and www.broomeport.com/about_broome_history.html.

3 Sarah Yu, 'Broome Creole: Aboriginal and Asian Partnerships along the Kimberley Coast', *Queensland Review,* Vol. 6, No. 2, November 1999, p. 59.

4 Available online at www.broomeport.com/about_broome_history.html.

5 Pam Oliver, *Empty North: The Japanese Presence and Australian Reactions, 1860s–1942,* 2006, pp. 129–32. NAA: M10, 2.

6 Available online at www.osatwar.com/ozatwar/tvbomb01.htm, 'Townsville at War – A Soldier Remembers', by Herbert C. Jaffa, p. 30.

7 Available online at home.st.net.au/~pdunn/thejaps.htm, www.anzacday.org. au/history/ww2/bfa/townsville.html and home.st.net.au/~dunn/locations/ macintv.htm.

8 'Ishida and the Sydney Camera Circle', Museum of Sydney, January to May 2004. ABC TV, *Asia Pacific Focus,* 2 August 2004. Nagata, 1996. Noreen Jones,

Number Two Home: A Story of Japanese Pioneers in Australia, 2001. Ganter, 2006, pp. 169–70.

9 Neville Meaney, *Towards a New Vision: Australia and Japan through Time*, 2007. Patrick Lindsay, *The Spirit of Kokoda: Then and Now*, 2002, p. 19.

10 The newly opened material is NAA: SP1098/4 to SP1098/14 and SP1101/1, WOS Controller of Enemy Property Records. See also NAA: A1379/1, EPJ WOS. Please note: because of the very large number of folios used to obtain information in this book, references to particular folios such as letters and memos are cited fully in the text. The file numbers only are cited in endnotes. Analysis of whole series K1145 for WA, Melbourne Japanese series B13/0, and Queensland series J2773/1. Also see Oliver, 2001, for merchants and the network and Oliver, 2004, for sources.

11 Wikipedia. Figures for Australia are difficult to establish with accuracy. Census records are not a reliable measure for the entire period. Japanese people did not always fill out forms after completing their first entry document. The entry documents provide a longitudinal picture of the number of Japanese who stayed for varying lengths of time in Australia. Noreen Jones' study of entries to WA pre 1941 has identified 10,000 people. Queensland is known to have had 3,264 in 1900 and the figure was relatively stable until it decreased before 1941. NSW entry figures amount to over 4,000 based on National Archives entry records but many of these are multiple frequent entries by merchants based in Sydney who travelled regularly to New Zealand, the Pacific and Japan and also include seamen visiting regularly on Japanese merchant ships for short stays on shore. The more stable population in Sydney in the 1930s was approximately 500, estimated on the 319 families listed by the security services, the wages books of Japanese companies and the estimated number of laundrymen. The state had hundreds of other Japanese visitors on short stay at any given time. Victoria's known population never exceeded 250 at any one time, peaking in the 1930s, based on company wages books and security service records. NAA Whole Series C123/1; K1145; B13/0; A1; A8; BP242/1, SP1098, SP1096. NAA: A11804, 1915/236.

12 H.P. Willmott, *Empires in the Balance: Japanese Allied Pacific Strategies to April 1942*, 1982. Quote from Henry Frei, *Japan's Southward Advance and Australia from the Sixteenth Century to World War II*, 1991, p. 3.

13 W.R. Wray, 'The 17th-Century Japanese Diaspora: Questions of Boundary and Policy', web article available online at eh.net/XI11Congress/cd/papers/10Wray383. pdf. Brett L. Walker, 'Foreign Affairs and Frontiers in Early Modern Japan: A Historiographical Essay', *Early Modern Japan*, Fall, 2002, pp. 44–62.

14 Wray web article, pp. 2, 6 and 9. Michael S. Laver, *Japan's Economy by Proxy in the Seventeenth Century, China, the Netherlands and the Bakufu*, 2008, pp. 31–4.

15 Frei, pp. 75–6. Leonard Blussé, *Bitter Bonds: A Colonial Divorce Drama of the Seventeenth Century*, 1997.

16   Christopher Howe, *The Origins of Japanese Trade Supremacy: Development and Technology in Asia from 1540 to the Pacific War*, 1996, pp. 22–32.

17   K. Yoshihara, *Sogo Shosha, The Vanguard of the Japanese Economy*, 1982, p. 22. See also P. Barr, *The Coming of the Barbarians: A Story of Western Settlement in Japan 1853–1870*, 1997. D.C.S. Sissons, 'Early Australian Contacts with Japan', *Hemisphere*, 1972, Vol. 16, No. 4. H.J. Jones, *Live Machines: Hired Foreigners in Meiji Japan*, 1974. H.S. Williams, *Tales of the Foreign Settlements in Japan*, 1958. Tallermann's business activities are listed in J. Sand, *NSW Directory, Sydney & Suburbs, Trades and Professions, 1895–1907*. Keiko Tamura, *Forever Foreign: Expatriate Lives in Historical Kobe*, 2006, pp. 32–4. Harold Williams Papers NLA: MS 6681, Box 44, Series 2, folder 64, 'Notes re Henry MARKS, Alexander MARKS, MARKS and Co.', *Japan Herald*, 11 January 1862.

18   Howe, 1996. Frei, 1991, pp. 39, 45–6, 75–6. Pam Oliver, *Allies Enemies and Trading Partners: Records on Australia and the Japanese*, 2004, p. 23.

19   Mark R. Peattie, *Nan'yō: The Rise and Fall of the Japanese in Micronesia, 1885–1945*, 1988, pp. 20–33.

20   D.C.S. Sissons, 'Japanese Acrobatic Troupes Touring Australasia 1867–1900', *Australasian Drama Studies*, No. 35, October 1999, pp. 73–107.

21   Neville Meaney, *Towards a New Vision: Australia & Japan through 100 Years*, 1999, pp. 43–7.

22   Frei, pp. 48–51. Sissons Papers NLA: MS 3032, 2/1978/11 'Japan and the Australian Wool Industry, 1868–1936'.

23   D.C.S. Sissons, 'Australian-Japanese Relations – The First Phase', pp. 24–6, unpublished, NLA MS3092, Series 1.1, cited hereafter as ' The First Phase'. Frei, p. 55.

24   Sissons on Watanabe 1977, pp. 12–14. Also Frei, p. 40 mentions Manjiro Inagaki in 1893 who reported on Sir Henry Parkes' speech about the danger of the Chinese invading Australia.

25   Yuichi Murakami, 'Civilised Asian: Images of Japan and the Japanese as Viewed by Australians from the Early Nineteenth Century to 1901', PhD thesis, University of Queensland, 1999, p. 78.

26   W.D. Wray, *Mitsubishi and the N.Y.K., 1870–1914: Business Strategy in the Japanese Shipping Industry*, 1984, pp. 3, 4, 57, 285. W.R. Purcell, 'The Development of Japan's Trading Company Network.' *Australian Economic History Review*, Vol. 21, No. 2, 1981. John G. Roberts, *Mitsui: Three Centuries of Japanese Business*, 1989, (1973). Shinichi Yonekawa (ed.), *General Trading Companies: A Comparative and Historical Studies*, 1990, pp. 23–4. Yoshihara, 1982, pp. 16–17. S. Tsunoyama, 'The Early History of Japanese-Australian Trade: An Addendum to Japanese Consular Reports', *Business History*, Vol. 23, 1981, pp. 288–91.

27   Frei, pp. 75–6. Peattie, 'Introduction', R.H. Myers and M.R. Peattie (eds), *The Japanese Colonial Empire 1895–1945*, 1984, p. 9. Howe, 1996, pp. 370–3. Willmott, pp. 19–23.

28 Peter Post, 'Japan and the Integration of the Netherlands East Indies into the World Economy, 1868–1942', *Review of Indonesian and Malaysian Affairs*, Vol. 27, Winter/Summer 1993, pp. 134–65.

29 Murakami, pp. 62–4, 204.

30 Murakami, pp. 83–5. *The Argus*, 17 October 1890. Queensland *Figaro*, 29 November 1884. David Askew, 'The Birth of Kanematsu Shoten: Kanematsu Fusajiro and Early Australia-Japan Relations 1845–1890', *Ritsumeikan Journal of Asia Pacific Studies*, Vol. 11, March 2003, p. 14 with information from Kanematsu Shoten Chosabu, *Goshu*, pp. 559–61, Table 705.

31 Available online at au.travel.yahoo.com.guide/australia/western-australia /broome/history.html, www.kimberleyaustralia.com/broome-history.html and www.broomeport.com/about_broome_history.html.

32 Su Jane Hunt, *Spinifex and Hessian: Women in North-west Australia 1960-1900*, 1986, pp. 126, 128. Frei, pp. 75–6. Henry Reynolds, *North of Capricorn: The Untold Story of Australia's North*, 2003. Ganter, 2006, NAA series K1145 and E752. D.C.S. Sissons, 'Karayuki-san: Japanese Prostitutes in Australia, 1887– 1916 -1', *Historical Studies*, Vol. 17, No. 68, April 1977, p. 328.

33 NAA: BP242/1, Q30581 Part 1.

34 Sissons, 'The First Phase' 1978, p. 19.

35 Meaney, 1999, pp. 56–8.

36 Sissons, 'The First Phase', 1978, p. 10.

37 NAA: A1, 1930/9356.

38 NAA: A1, 1930/9356, report on interview dated 20 October 1910.

39 NAA: MP508/1, 255/40/348.

40 NAA: A367/1, C69262.

41 NAA: MP529/3, TRIBUNAL 4/119.

42 Frei, p. 51. NAA: MP529/3, TRIBUNAL 4/74. NAA: A367/1, C69851. J. Sand, 1902–05, NAA: SP1098/12. NAA: SP1098/11.

43 W.R. Purcell, 'The Nature and Extent of Japanese Commercial and Economic Interests in Australia 1932–41', PhD thesis, University of New South Wales, 1980, pp. 38–41.

44 Documents provided by Kanematsu Australia to the author: 'Mr. Tonanosuke Kitamura – His Life and Success' and 'Origin of Kanematsu Organisation in Australia', nd.

45 NAA: A1/1, 1931/2515. R Yokouchi was listed in J. Sand, *Post Office Directory* in 1893 and T.O. Sata & Co. Japanese Art Painters in the same Quong Tart Chambers in King Street. Sissons, 'The First Phase', 1978, pp. 20, 23.

46 NAA: ST1233/1, N19133. NAA: MP1103/2, NJ17060. Interviews with Nakamura's daughters, October 1997. NAA: A1, 1930/9356.

47 Christine Choo, 'Asian Men on the West Kimberly Coast, 1900–1940', Jan Gothard (ed.), *Asian Orientations: Studies in Western Australian History*, No. 16, 1995, pp. 89–111 maps the early trade routes. Oliver, 2006, pp. 1–4. Analysis of NAA: K1145 and PP14/1. For the estimated numbers of prostitutes in

towns before 1901 see Sissons, 'Karayuki-san -1', 1977, pp. 323, 328, 330. D.C.S. Sissons, 'Karayuki-san: Japanese Prostitutes in Australia, 1887–1916 -11', *Historical Studies*, Vol. 17, No. 69, October 1977, p. 484.

48   NAA: PP14/3, 1928/1008.

49   NAA: PP9/2, 1952/63/6472. NAA: K1145, 1920/3.

50   NAA: PP14/3. Hunt, 1986, pp. 123ff.

51   Hunt, p. 151. Sissons, 'Karayuki-san -1', 1977, pp. 333, 335–6.

52   NAA: A712/1, 1899/K6473.

53   Ganter, 2006, chs. 1–2. Oliver, 2006, ch. 1. Sarah Yu, 'Broome Creole: Aboriginal and Asian Partnerships along the Kimberley Coast', *Queensland Review*, Vol. 6, No. 2, November 1999.

54   Sissons, 1977, p. 325. Hunt's argument, pp. 123–6, that prostitutes arrived before the shopkeepers is not sustainable. NAA: K1145, 1912/154 and 1916/145.

55   Oliver, 2006, pp. 10–12. P.F. Donovan, *A Land Full of Possibilities: A History of South Australia's Northern Territory*, 1981, pp. 200–1. Ganter, 2006, pp. 62–4. Sissons, 1977, p. 12.

56   D.C.S. Sissons, 'Japanese in the Northern Territory 1884-1902', *South Australiana*, Vol. 16, No. 1, 1977, pp. 12–14.

57   Sissons, 1977, p. 18. Information from NAA records are an analysis of all Japanese files in the series NAA: E752, Whole of Series, Certificates Exemption from Dictation Test and E755/1 Whole of Series, Certificates of Exemption-Japanese landed ex fishing vessels.

58   Sissons, 1977, p. 328. Reported in the *Boomerang* on 12 May 1888. NAA: E752/o,WOS. E752/o, 1924/10 and NAA: K1145, 1915/79. NAA: K1145, 1934/2. NAA: PP4/2, 1934/18.

59   Frei, p. 58. Regina Ganter, *The Pearl Shellers of Torres Strait: Resource Use, Development and Decline1860s–1960s*, 1994, pp. 17–19, 23–50.

60   List of Japanese aliens in Queensland, NAA: J25/120, 1951/5447. BP242/1, Q30511, pp. 64–5. Sissons, 'Karayuki-san-1', 1977, pp. 323–31 lists numbers of arrivals.

61   Analysis of NAA: J2773/1 files and NAA: BP242/1, Q30589 Part 1.

62   NAA: A367/1, C69678. NAA: MP1102/3, QJ16195. NAA: MP1102/3, QJ 16098. NAA: A/15, 1926/4456, Collector, Cairns, to Secretary, telegram, 29 November 1916.

Chapter 2 – Through the great white walls, 1901–22

1   Figures appear in a chart compiled by Kanematsu Shōten Chosabu, *Goshu*, Table 705, pp. 559–61 represented in English in David Askew, 'The Birth of Kanematsu Shōten: Kanematsu Fusajirō and Early Australia-Japan Relations, 1845–1890', *Ritsumeikan Journal of Asia Pacific Studies*, Vol. 11, March 2003,

p. 14. See Wikipedia for relative currency values prior to World War One. At this time $4.85 US was equivalent to £1 sterling and ¥2 to $1 US.

2　The term comes from Charles A. Price, *The Great White Walls are Built: Restrictive Immigration to North America and Australasia, 1836–1888*, 1974. See also: A.T. Yarwood, *Asian Migration to Australia: The Background to Exclusion, 1896–1923*, 1964, Chapter 5 includes the Japanese.

3　NAA: A1/15, 1914/11249, Note hand-written by Atlee Hunt on Department of External Affairs Memorandum 3 July 1914. NAA: A1, 1925/18600, Memorandum, Department of External Affairs signed by H. Ryan 8 September 1916. For a discussion of the question of citizenship and Japanese people in Australia see Pam Oliver, 'Citizens without Certificates or Enemy Aliens? Japanese Residents before 1947', J. Beaumont, I. O'Brien and M. Trinca (eds), *Under Suspicion, Citizenship and Internment in Australia during the Second World War*, 2008, pp. 125–41.

4　NAA: B13/0, 1930/7813. NAA: B13/0, 1935/20434. NAA: A1/15, 1925/27797.

5　NAA: A2, 1918/892.

6　D.C.S. Sissons, 'Australian-Japanese Relations – The First Phase', unpublished. NLA: MS3092, Series 1.1. Akita, p. 20, cited hereafter as 'The first phase'. NAA: B13/0, 1923/2809. NAA: B13/0, 1923/3303. NAA: B5020. NAA: A9/1, A1902/35/156.

7　NAA: B13/0, 1925/16532. NAA: A1/15 1925/27797. NAA: A9/1, A1902/35/156. NAA: B741/1, V/187.

8　NAA: A367/1, C69262. NAA: MP529/3, TRIBUNAL 4/119.

9　J.B. Suttor, Intelligence Department, New South Wales, Bulletin No. 2, Report on the Trade of Japan for the Year 1904, p. 10.

10　J.B. Suttor, Immigration and Tourist Bureau, New South Wales, Bulletin No. 36, Report on the Trade of Japan, 1908.

11　J.B. Suttor, Intelligence Department, New South Wales Bulletin No. 19, Reports on the Trade of Japan and Korea 1906, p. 3. Immigration and Tourist Bureau, NSW Bulletin No. 18, Report on the Trade of Japan, 1907, pp. 8, 14. Sissons Papers, NLA: MS3032, 2/1978/11 'Japan and the Australian Wool Industry 1868–1936', p. 10.

12　Sissons: 'Wool industry', p. 8.

13　J.B. Suttor, Immigration and Tourist Bureau, New South Wales, Bulletin No. 47, Report on the Trade of Japan, 1910, p. 11.

14　Sissons, 'The First Phase', pp. 21–2. NAA: A981/4, JAP 55. NAA: SP42/1, entry series for Sydney; NAA: A1/15, 1931/2515.

15　NAA: A367/1, C69851. NAA: MP1103/1, NJ17077. NAA: MP1103/2, NJ 17077.

16　NAA: A1/15, 1907/7834, re. query from consulate and replies by Atlee Hunt began with Ide of the firm Osawa Co. Eastern Merchants on 26 July 1907. Ide was told he had to get a Certificate of Domicile before leaving Sydney.

17 W.R. Purcell, 'The Nature and Extent of Japanese Commercial and Economic Interests in Australia 1932–41', PhD thesis, University of New South Wales, 1980, pp. 197, 206, 238, 242–3. K. Yoshihara, *Sogo Shosha: The Vanguard of the Japanese Economy*, 1982, p. 71.

18 Graham Eccles, 'The Hirodo Story: A Three Generational Family Case Study of Bi-cultural Living', Michael Ackland and Pam Oliver (eds), *Unexpected Encounters: Neglected Histories behind the Australia–Japan Relationship*, 2007, pp. 135–54.

19 NAA: SP1098/16. NAA: SP1098/9, Box 1, Letter 20 January 1917 in letter book for 1917 and Boxes 2, 4, 7, 8, 11, 12, 32. Interviews: conducted by the author with Joan and Naida, daughters of Nakamura, surnames withheld, October 1997.

20 NAA: SP1098/4, Box 13, Ledger 117 for customer lists in 1926. Customer accounts for 1918 in Box 1, Book 30.

21 Mitsui cash books 1916–1918 for example in NAA: SP1098/4, Box 303–304. NAA: SP1098/4, Box 14, Ledger 186, Import account for 1932.

22 Mitsui references to entertainment expenses for example for 1912 are found in NAA: SP1098/4, Box 9, Ledger 8. Such expenses are found throughout the accounts to 1941.

23 Mitsui references to donations are found throughout the accounts to 1941 on a regular basis.

24 Letter to the author from AANSW January 1997.

25 Noreen Jones, *Number 2 Home: A Story of Japanese Pioneers in Australia*, 2001, p. 115.

26 Jones, pp. 111–12, 115, 120–3. NAA: K1145 Whole of Series and NAA: PP14.

27 NAA: A1/15, 1932/770, Suzuki to Home and Territories, Letter, 3 November 1924. His position as Honorary President of the Japanese Society was with the approval of Home and Territories, February 1924.

28 NAA: A1/15, 1932/770, Memo Sub-Collector of Customs, Broome from Secretary Quinlan, 2 February 1924. Umeda had written to them for approval of his position on 17 January because he was on exemption.

29 NAA: A721/1, 1899/K6473.

30 *Ibid.* State Library of Western Australia, Battye Library, MN1216, ACC3700A/1-52 and ACC2628A/1-12, Diaries and Accounts of Jiro Muramatsu. NAA: A1379/1, EPJ1396. NAA: MP742/1, 259/43/572.

31 NAA: J2773/1, 230/11. NAA: J2773/1, 171/13, Hobbs, Wilson & Ryan to Sub- Collector, 21 January 1913. NAA: J2773/1,913/18.

32 NAA: A1/15, 1923/24399.

33 *Ibid.*

34 Australian Dictionary of Biography on line. NAA; SP1098/7, Box 53, Section M and Section R.

35 *Ibid.*, folder B.

36 Pam Oliver, 'A Matter of Perspective: Two Australian-Japanese Families'
Encounters with White Australia, 1888-1946', Ackland and Oliver (eds), 2007,
pp. 126-7. See also NAA: A1/15, 1911/16228; NAA: A367/1, C68609 and
NAA: A367/1, C65778.

37 See for example NAA: SP1098/10, Miscellaneous Records of Mitsubishi
Shoji Kaisha for dealings in minerals in Australia through the head office in
Sydney, correspondence and accounts Box 73 'Minerals' folder and Box 74
'Minerals' folder; Box 42 'Minerals' folder; Box 20 'overseas trade' folder.
NAA, SP1098/4, Miscellaneous Records of Mitsui & Co. Box 13, Ledger 117,
customer lists for 1926; Box 1, Book 30, Customer accounts for 1918; Boxes
303–304, Mitsui & Co. cash books 1916–1918; Box 14, Ledger 186, import
accounts for 1932. Pam Oliver, 'Japanese Relationships in White Australia: The
Sydney Experience to 1941', *History Australia*, Monash University ePress, Vol.
4, No. 1, June 2007, pp. 05–12–16.

38 NOTE: The Department of External Affairs was responsible for immigration
matters from 1903 to 1916. However, name changes and reorganisations over
time before World War Two placed immigration matters from 1916 to 1928
with the Department of Home and Territories and from 1932 to 1938 with the
Department of the Interior.

39 Atlee Hunt papers MS: NLA52 documents 1336 and 1335. Letter from E.M.
Foxall to Altee Hunt, 30 October 1916, and from Hunt to Foxall, 2 November
1916. See also E.W. Foxall, *Colorphobia: An Exposure of the "White Australia"
Fallacy*, 1903, where he demonstrates his enthusiasm for Japanese immigration.

40 Hunt papers NLA: MS 52/1312 -15. Letters to Hunt dated 3 December 1908,
11 December 1908 and 4 February 1910.

41 No documentary evidence is extant to confirm this date of arrival. The story of
the Umino family in this article is a summary of all documents contained in
the following files. Pieces of information extracted from dozens of documents
have been put together to form the narrative. NAA: A1/1, 1935/1444. NAA:
A367/1, C66114.NAA: A367/1, C18000/833. NAA: MP529/9, 4/72; NAA:
MP529/3, 4/48; NAA: A659/1, 41/1/3872; NAA: SP1714/1, N27827.

42 To become a Japanese subject, a wife would need to be registered as such and
entered in the family register in Japan. As Umino intended to stay in Australia
permanently, according to his files in the NAA, he had not registered his wife
or Australian-born children in Japan or with the Consul-General in Australia.
Tamaki correctly says, from the Japanese point of view, they were not Japanese
subjects. Australian law was amended in 1937 to enable wives who had lost
British subject status through marriage to apply for its reinstatement. Violet
Umino applied in 1940. See NAA: SP1714/1, N27827.

43 *Kiichiro Ishida and the Sydney Camera Circle*, 2004.

44 NAA: C123, 9904. Beth Hise and Pam Oliver, 'Kiichiro Ishida', *Insite*, Summer
2003, pp. 4–5.

45 NAA: A1/15, 1924/24078.

46   Ronald Moore, 'The Management of the WA Pearling Industry, 1860 to the 1930s', *Great Circle*, Vol. 16, No. 2, 1994, p. 130.

47   NAA: A659/1, 1943/1/7347, NAA: A7359/101, items 6 & 9.

48   For example, see NAA: SP1098/7, Box 53 for Tashima Co. of Townsville.

49   NAA: A406/62, E1945/1 Part 1 ATTACHMENT. NAA: A1497/1, VOLUME 19 P441 to 443. NAA: A10078/1.

50   NAA: PP302/1/0, WA17964.

51   NAA: A367/1, C78715.

52   NAA: SP1096/5, Box 47 loose papers.

Chapter 3 – Undercurrents: Japan – an uncomfortable ally, 1901–1920s

1   Michael Ackland and Pam Oliver (eds), *Unexpected Encounters: Neglected Histories behind the Australia-Japan Relationship*, 2007. Paul Jones and Vera Mackie (eds), *Relations: Japan and Australia, 1870s–1950s*, 2001. Neville Meaney, *Towards a New Vision: Australia and Japan across Time*, 2007.

2   D.R. Walker, *Anxious Nation: Australia and the Rise of Asia, 1850–1939*, 1999 pp. 3–4. Peter Stanley, *Invading Australia: Japan and the Battle for Australia, 1942*, 2008, Part 1.

3   Walker, p. 18. Stanley, p. 32. Robert Dixon analysed race, gender and nation in Anglo-Australian popular fiction in *Writing the Colonial Adventure: Race, Gender and Nation in Anglo-Australian Popular Fiction, 1875–1914*, 1995.

4   D.C.S. Sissons, 'Attitudes to Japan and Defence, 1890–1923', MA thesis, University of Melbourne, 1956, pp. 66–8.

5   H.P. Willmott, *Empires in the Balance: Japanese Allied Pacific Strategies to April 1942*, 1982. Quote from Henry Frei, *Japan's Southward Advance and Australia from the Sixteenth Century to World War II*, 1991, p. 3.

6   Dixon, 1995. John Docker, *The Nervous Nineties: Australian Cultural Life in the 1890s*, 1991.

7   Neville Meaney, *The Search for Security in the Pacific, 1901–1914*, 1976, pp. 22–3. R.C. Thompson, *Australian Imperialism in the Pacific the Expansionist Era*, 1820–1920, 1980, p. 33. Sissons, thesis, pp. 1–2.

8   Sissons says this argument came from Jack Shepherd in the 1930s, which Walker uses. Sissons, thesis, pp. 4–7.

9   Meaney, 2007, pp. 49, 54. Sissons, thesis, pp. 20b, 20d, 20e, 21. Eric Andrews, *The Australian Centenary History of Defence Volume V: The Department of Defence*, 2001, pp. 18, 21–2, 30.

10   Sissons, thesis, pp. 20f, 20g, 24–5, 31–9, 43.

11   NAA: MP124/6, 603/203/117, 13 February 1924. NAA: B168/0, 1904/32 Part 4, p. 21. NAA: B168/0, 1904/32 Part 7.

12   Christopher Howe, *The Origins of Japanese Trade Supremacy: Development and Technology in Asia from1540 to the Pacific War*, 1996, pp. 370–4. Willmott, p. 17.

13   Sissons, thesis, pp. 20c, 20d, 47–50.

14   Andrews, pp. 21–2, 30.

15   *Lone Hand*, 1 June 1907, p. 206.

16   NAA: MP84/1, 1902/7/47A.

17   Andrews, pp. 32–5.

18   I.F. Clark, *Voices Prophesying War, 1763–1984*, 1966, pp. 85, 158.

19   Dixon, 1995, Chapter 8 is particularly relevant to Japan, also pp. 179–80, 200.
     See also, Clarke, 1966. Stanley, 2008, pp. 31, 52. It was actually blood from
     a horse they sacrificed for the purpose, not that of the soldier. *Lone Hand*, 1
     February 1909. p. 561.

20   *Lone Hand*, 1 March 1911, pp. 409–11, available online at www.awm.gov.
     au/units/unit_10831.asp and www.awm.gov.au/atwar/ww1_flying.asp.

21   *Lone Hand*, 1 February 1909, p. 422.

22   NAA: MP472/1, 16/13/883.

23   *New Idea*, p. 900.

24   Jones and Mackie, 2001.

25   *New Idea*, March 1905, Vol. 3, pp. 129–30.

26   *Ibid.*, p. 829

27   Stanley, 2008. Meaney, 2007. Dixon, 1995. Walker, 1999. *Lone Hand*, pp.
     156–60.

28   NAA: MP1049/1, 1913/0286, 'Confidential – Japanese – Pacific Islands etc',
     13.10.13, and article from the *South China Morning Post*, 6 October 1913, 'The
     Direct Export of Coal'. A.R. Colquhuon, *The Mastery of the Pacific*, 1902, pp.
     348–56.

29   *Lone Hand*, pp. 117–22.

30   NAA: MP1049/1, 1913/0286 as above.

31   NAA: MP472/1, 1/12/6574. Phillipe Palombo, *La Présence Japonaise in
     Nouvelle-Calédonie, (1890– 1960), Les Relations Économiques entre le Japon et la
     Nouvelle-Calédonie à travers L'Immigration et L'Industrie Minière*, ANRT, Lille,
     France, 2001.

32   All from NAA: MP1049/1, 1913/0286.

33   Peattie, pp. 27–33. Naval intelligence reports in the 1910s support Peattie's
     accounts of Japanese activities in the Pacific in NAA: MP1049/1.

34   NAA: MP84/1, 1877/5/5, Letter 17 May 1909 to Minister for Defence, p. 4.

35   NAA: MP84/1, 2021/1/35.

36   Clark, p. 160.

37   NAA: MP84/1, 1888/1/16.

38   NAA: MP84/1, 1888/1/18, 'Armament for coast defences 1/12/1910', p. 2 and
     'Strategical considerations', p. 4.

39   Admiral Kobayashi was hailed in 1928 at the Perth War Memorial for Japan's
     part in the war. See pp. 5–8 of Extracts from Australian Naval Intelligence
     Statements NAA: MP1049/1, 1918/0773.

40   NAA: MP472/1, 1/15/8560, 'Ceremonial for the Official Visit of the Japanese Training Squadron'.

41   NAA: MP1049/1, 1920/090, 'Pacific Island Groups in Japanese Occupation', 'Islands occupied by Japan: and New Caledonia', 1918–1920. NAA: MP1049/1, 1913/0286, 'Memorandum from Governor General to Prime Minister', 10 July 1913.

42   NAA: MP1049/1, 1914/0455.

43   NAA: MP1049/1, 1916/047.

44   NAA: MP1049/1, 1914/0455.

45   NAA: MP1049/1, 1920/090, 'Precis of Events connected with the surrender and occupation of German possessions in the Pacific', prepared by Naval Intelligence', p. 5, 'Islands occupied by Japan: and New Caledonia', 1918–1920.

46   NAA: MP1049/1, 1914/0461.

47   NAA: MP1049/1, 1915/054, 'Commonwealth of Australia Defence of' – 22 March 1915'. See also folder in file: 'Naval Policy – Defence of Australia and the Pacific Policy'.

48   NAA: A3934/1, SC14/22, Memo No. 430 to the Foreign Office, from E.F. Crowe, 30 August 1916. NAA: A3934/1, SC14/9, Letter to A. J. Balfour, Secretary of State for Foreign Affairs London from Ambassador H. Norman, British Embassy, Tokyo, 9 August 1917, p. 1–2.

49   NAA: A1/15,1918/9022. 'C. Extracts from Australian Naval Intelligence Statements and From Diaries etc. H.C. 1 Expansion southwards of Japanese influence' November 1917. NAA: MP 1049/1, 1918/0773.

50   Howe, pp. 376, 381, 397.

51   Howe, pp. 414–20.

52   Howe, pp. 394, 424, 429.

53   NAA: MP472/1, 5/17/7761, letter, J.C.T. Glassop, 13 July 1917, to Navy Office Melbourne.

54   NAA: MP1049/1, 1918/0773, From Secret Abstracts of Intelligence, Straits Settlements, December 1917, item 44, p. 11.

55   NAA: A1/15, 1918/9022, 'Present day Australia', pp. 2–3.

56   NAA: MP84/1, 1902/7/77. NAA: MP1049/1, 1920/0271.

Chapter 4 – Under the power of the *zaibatsu*, 1920s–40

1   *Daily Standard*, 6 August 1923, p. 6. Thanks to Nick Guogh of ANU for bringing this to my attention.

2   NAA: SP822/45, Box 4, Japanese Chamber of Commerce, Sydney, 1941–42, Investigation: Trading with the Enemy Act 1939–40.

3   Howard Wolfers, 'The Big Stores between the Wars', Jill Row (ed.), *Twentieth Century Sydney: Studies in Urban and Social History*, 1980 pp. 18–33.

4   NAA: SP1098/4, Box 13, Ledger 117 for customer lists in 1926. Customer accounts for 1918. NAA: SP1098/4, Box 1, Book 30.

5   NAA: SP1098/12, Box 7. For example, memoranda in 1939 from Nosawa records indicate a number of personal interviews and meetings to organise sales.

6   Mitsui customer lists for example for 1920 in NAA: SP1098/4, Box 19, Ledger 47. Such lists are found in ledgers for all years throughout the series.

7   NAA: SP1098/7, Box 53. NAA: A367/1, C78715, K. Onishe, news items for 1920–1922. W.R. Purcell, 'The Nature and Extent of Japanese Commercial and Economic Interests in Australia, 1932–41', PhD thesis, University of New South Wales, 1980, p. 201. NAA: A981/1, JAP 55. NAA: C443/P1, J170. K. Yoshihara, *Sogo Shosha: The Vanguard of the Japanese Economy*, 1982, pp. 53, 58.

8   NAA: SP1908/7, Box 53. NAA: SP1233/1, 17060.

9   NAA: SP1098/7, Box 53.

10   *Ibid.* NAA: ST1233/1, N19133, letter, 3 November 1937, Commonwealth Investigation Branch, Sydney.

11   NAA: SP1098/12, Boxes 3, 4, 7, analysis of invoices for 1938 and correspondence for 1939.

12   NAA: SP1098/12, Box 5, letter 30 September 1939 correspondence for 1939.

13   NAA: SP1098/12, Boxes 3, 5, correspondence for 1940.

14   D.C.S. Sissons, 'Australian-Japanese Relations – The First Phase'. Unpublished. NLA: MS3092, Series 1.1. pp. 21–2. NAA: A981/1, JAP 55. NAA: SP42/1, entry series for Sydney; NAA: A1/1, 1931/2515.

15   Araki & Co., NAA: SP1098/7, Box 53. NAA: SP1233/1, 17060. Interview: Joan, daughter of Nakamura, January1997.

16   NAA: MP529/3, TRIBUNAL 4/74. NAA: A367/1, C69851. J. Sand, 1902–05. NAA: SP1098/12. NAA: SP1098/11.

17   Purcell, pp. 198, 206. The defence forces noted relationships and rivalries between firms. See Eastern Command 'G' Branch records, Intelligence summaries and diaries, AWM193, 2.

18   Opening of Melbourne branches: Z. Horikoshi, NAA: B13/0, 1923/18611; T. Nakano, NAA: B13/0, 1925/16532; Iida & Co., NAA:B13/0, 1926/6886; Mitsui and Kanematsu in Mitsui Melbourne to T. Urabe, 15 May 1922, 'Victoria as a wool-producing country'. NAA: SP1096/5, Box 47, loose papers. The early accounts for Mitsui are found in NAA: SP1098/4, Boxes 1–30. NAA: SP1096/5, Box 47. NAA: B13/0, 1930/7813. B13/0, 1933/4210. B13/0, 1935/20434. B13/0, 1937/13330. D&W Murray, University of Melbourne Archives, UM74/71.

19   Pam Oliver, 'A Matter of Perspective: Two Australian-Japanese Families' Encounters with White Australia, 1888–1946', Michael Ackland and Pam Oliver (eds), *Unexpected Encounters: Neglected Histories behind the Australia–Japan Relationship,* 2007, pp. 126–7. See also NAA: A1/15, 1911/16228. NAA: A367/1, C68609. NAA: A367/1, C65778.

20 Interviews: Northern Territory Archives Service, NTRS 226, TS 773. Names of interviewees have been withheld in this book for the sake of privacy. See also loose catalogues in Nosawa & Co., NAA: SP1098/4, Box 12.

21 NAA: MP529/3, TRIBUNAL 4/155. *The Northern Standard*, 9 September 1938. *The Northern Territory Times and Gazette*, 10 January 1920, 3 February 1925.

22 NAA: A7359, 9.

23 NAA: A1/15, 1932/770, Pickett to Collector of Customs Fremantle, 1 November 1924.

24 NAA: A1/15, 1932/770, Quinlan to Consul General, 11 December 1924.

25 NAA: A1/15, 1932/700, Memorandum, 14 August 1923; Akiyama to Secretary, re. wife of Tsutsumi, 10 February 1925; Pickett report, 12 November 1924; A.R. Peters note stated that the Minister had said the same for other small firms.

26 NAA: A1/15, 1932/770, McLean to Collector 4 December 1925; Collector to Quinlan, 18 May 1926.

27 NAA: A1/15, 1932/770, Rich to Consul General, 6 June 1930.

28 NAA: A1/15, 1932/700, Information on Tsutsumi.

29 NAA: A1606/1, C18/1.

30 NAA: A443/1, 1940/2/1212.

31 NAA: A433/1, 40/2/2351.

32 Yoshihara, pp. 71, 197, 206. NAA: SP822/45 Box 4, Japanese Chamber of Commerce Sydney, 1941–42, Investigation: Trading with the Enemy Act 1939–40.

33 Purcell, p. 210.

34 NAA: SP1098/4, Box 12, Ledger 247. See for example Mitsui purchases of papers and reviews November 1937 to January 1938.

35 Purcell, pp. 208, 210.

36 NAA: SP1096/1, Box 94. MSK world-wide structure is found in *An Outline of the Mitsubishi Enterprises,* 1937 published by Mitsubishi Goshi Kaisha, Tokyo, Japan, p. 37.

37 NAA: SP1098/10, Box 42, 'Minerals'; Box 20, 'overseas trade'. NAA: SP1096/1, Box 94, *An Outline of the Mitsubishi Enterprises*, p. 37.

38 NAA: SP1098/10, Box 73 Minerals' folder and Box 74 'Minerals', Mitsubishi Sydney to Tokyo Head Office, 14 August 1940, telegrams.

39 NAA: SP1096/1, Box 74, 'Trade with New Zealand and contemplated scheme for marketing', pp. 105–10. NAA: SP1101/1, Box 154, Mitsui's Dunn & Co. credit checks for the 1930s.

40 NAA: SP1096/1, Box 95. NAA: SP1098/10, Box 2 contains wool maps for Australia for 1936. Graham Eccles, 'The Hirodo story: a three generational family case study of bi-cultural living', Michael Ackland and Pam Oliver (eds), 2007, pp. 136–7.

41 NAA: SP1096/5, Box 47 loose papers, Mitsui Melbourne to T. Urabe, 15 May
1922, 'Victoria as a wool-producing country'.
42 NAA: ST1233/1, N39210. NAA: C123, 13529. NAA: SP1098/12, Box 2 for
1940, Box 8, Box 10 for 1938.
43 NAA: A1/15, 1932/770.
44 Compiled from analysis of Mitsui's Journals from 1931 to 1941 in NAA:
SP1096/6, WOS.
45 Interview: Naida, October 1997.
46 D&W Murray, University of Melbourne, UM74/71.

Chapter 5 – Life in suburbia

1 Please note that Japanese names are as they are found in National Archives of
Australia files, which normally list surname last. Nakamura family documents
and photographs kindly provided to the author and used with permission.
Interviews conducted in January 1997 with Naida and Joan, Nakamura's
surviving daughters and Elizabeth his granddaughter. Robert Dixon, *Writing
the Colonial Adventure: Race, Gender and Nation in Anglo-Australian Popular
Fiction, 1875–1914*, 1995, pp. 135–54.
2 Graham Eccles, 'The Hirodo Story: A Three Generational Family Case Study
of Bi-cultural Living', Michael Ackland and Pam Oliver (eds), *Unexpected
Encounters: Neglected Histories behind the Australia-Japan Relationship*, 2007, pp.
136–7.
3 Xavier Archives, Ledger, 1886, pp. 195–6. *The Xaverian*, 1898, p. 52. *The
Xaverian*, 1910, p. 18.
4 See archival records in National Archives of Australia, especially NAA: B13/0
WOS.
5 D.R. Walker, *Anxious Nation: Australia and the Rise of Asia, 1850–1939*, 1999,
pp. 181–93. Ien Ang, 'From White Australia to Fortress Australia: The Anxious
Nation in the New Century', Laksiri Jayasuria, David Walker and Jan Gotthart
(eds), *Legacies of White Australia*, 2003, pp. 51–3.
6 NAA: SP1714/1, N27827.
7 Judith Brett, *Australian Liberals and the Moral Middle Class: From Alfred Deakin
to John Howard*, 2003, pp. 63–4, 84–5.
8 Peter Spearritt, *Sydney's Century: A History*, 2000, p. 34. NAA: SP1098/4,
1935 figures in Box 316 income tax bundle; 1917 figures in Cash Book for
November 1916 to October 1917, Box 303; Salaries for 1940 taken from Box
315 loose papers; Club subscriptions and rent allowance etc. in Box 5, ledger
74. Records of Mitsui contain the salary payments to staff from 1907–41.
Analysis of staff salary lists in ledgers for 1907–41 in NAA: SP1098/4, Boxes
1-30. NAA: ST1233/1, N19133. The Nakamura's employed Australians in
their home. However the nationality of domestic staff in other homes varied.

Managers of companies often brought Japanese maids and governesses to Australia. Others hired Australian maids and certainly the Consulate-General had Australian domestics on its staff. Chauffeurs for Japanese households with Australian born wives tended to be Australian as in the case of the Nakamuras. See NAA: B13/0 WOS and NAA: C123 WOS. However, for other all-Japanese households, laundrymen doubled as chauffeurs. Denzo Umino often chauffeured for the Consulate-General's visiting dignitaries. NAA: A367/1, C66114.

9   NAA: A1/1, 1935/1444.
10 NAA: A367/1, C78715.
11 Mrs Iida, interview by Toshie Swift of MOS, 7 February 2004. Courtesy of Museum of Sydney.
12 New South Wales Marriage Certificate of Kagiyama 1916 and Marriage certificate of his former wife in 1934. Beth Hise and Pam Oliver, 'Kiichiro Ishida', *Insite*, Museum of Sydney, Summer 2003.
13 NAA: C123, 8408. Watarai family. See also travel expenses of Mitsui for 1938–39 for wool purposes. NAA: SP1098/4, Box 15, Ledger 257 and for 1934, NAA: SP1098/4, Box 17, Ledger 217.
14 NAA: SP1098/12, Box 3, loose correspondence letters from Sloane.
15 NAA: A659/1, 41/1/3872. The Act came into force on 1 April 1937. Women were given 12 months to apply.
16 Letter supplied by the family dated 13 March 1942.
17 NAA: SP1714/1 N27827.
18 Mrs Iida, interview by Toshie Swift of MOS 7 February 2004. Courtesy of Museum of Sydney.
19 NAA: A367/1, C71179.
20 Their story is also told by D.C.S. Sissons, 'A Selector and His Family', *Hemisphere*, No. 25, 1980. See also NAA: A1/15, 1925/27797. NAA: A659, 1940/1/5346. NAA: MP729/6, 65/501/147. NAA: MP529/3, TRIBUNAL 4/110.
21 Interview by the author of Naida, Sydney, 27 September 1996.
22 Nakamura hearing against internment NAA: ST1233/1, N19133.
23 NAA: MP529/3, TRIBUNAL 4/117.

Chapter 6 – Undercurrents: The question of espionage to 1937

1   NAA: MP84/1, 1877/5/5, letter 17 May 1909 to Minister for Defence, p. 4.
2   *Ibid.*, pp. 2–3.
3   Hiromi Tanaka, 'The Pacific War and New Guinea', Seminar paper, Remembering the War in New Guinea Project Symposium held at the Australian National University, 19–20 October 2000, Australia–Japan Research

Project at the Australian War Memorial, available online at ajrp.awm.gov.au/ ajrp/remember.nsf/.

4   NAA: MP84/1, 1877/5/5. NAA: MP1049/1, 1911/014. NAA: MP1049/1, 1920/053.

5   NAA: B197, 1877/5/15.

6   *Ibid.*

7   NAA: MP84/1, 1902/7/66.

8   NAA: MP84/1,1877/5/5, Report to Minister for Defence, 17 May 1909, pp. 1–5.

9   Barbara Winter, *The Intrigue Master: Commander Long and Naval Intelligence in Australia, 1913–1945*, 1995, pp. 10–26, chs. 5, 10. NAA: MP1049/1, 1920/0188.

10 NAA: MP1049/1, 1918/0773.

11 *Ibid.*

12 NAA: MP1094/1, 1919/0116. NAA: MP1049/5, 1877/13/88, Report on trip to Japanese Mandated Islands in Nippon Yusen Kaisha S.S. Kasuga Maru (20 August to 12 October 1926).

13 NAA: MP1049/5, 1877/13/213.

14 AWM193, 397 "History of Espionage in NEI" and AWM 54, 883/1/103.

15 NAA: A981/1, JAP 37 (in Dutch translated for the author by Maria van Galen, Franciscan Missionary of Mary, A981/4, JAP 158 Part2. Hiromitsu Iwamoto, *Nanshin: Japanese Settlers in Papua and New Guinea, 1890–1949*, 1999.

16 Tanaka, 'The Pacific War and New Guinea', 2000. NAA: B6121/3, 177. Neville Meaney, *Fears and Phobias: E.L. Piesse and the Problem of Japan, 1909–1939*, 1996.

17 NAA: MP1049/5, 1877/13/148.

18 NAA: A981/1, JAP 55.

19 Meaney, 1996, p. 13. Henry Frei, *Japan's Southward Advance and Australia from the Sixteenth Century to World War II*, 1991, p. 151.

20 NAA: MP124/6, 603/203/347, C.J. Pope, 8 July 1930. NAA: MP1049/5, 2026/8/54.

21 NAA: SP1714/1 N40344, especially p. 2 and Winter, 1995, pp. 92–3, ch. 17.

22 NAA: MP1049/1, 1877/13/140. NAA: MP1049/5, 1877/13/87.

23 NAA: A981/1, JAP 120 Part 1. Note: Surveillance found no militant Japanese party like that alleged by Bob Wurth, 2006, pp. 97–8.

24 NAA: SP1714/1, N40344.

25 AWM124, 3/126. Hiromi Tanaka, 'The Japanese Navy's Operations against Australia in the Second World War, with a Commentary on Japanese Sources', *Journal of the Australian War Memorial*, No. 30, April 1997. NAA: SP1101/ 1.

26 NAA: A367/1, C65778. For the lugger cases see NAA: A1/15, 1938/20318; NAA: A1/15, 20319 and NAA: A1/15, 20322. NAA: MP729/1, 63/401/518.

27 Prue Torney-Parlicki, *Behind the News: A Biography of Peter Russo*, 2005, pp. 53–5.

28 Evidence given by Russo at Inagaki's hearing NAA: MP529/3, TRIBUNAL 4/117.

29 For a fuller understanding of the 1936 Trade Diversion Dispute see: D.C.S. Sissons, 'Manchester v. Japan: The Imperial Background of the Australian Trade Diversion Dispute with Japan, 1936', *Australian Outlook*, Vol. 30, No. 3, 1976. P.B. Murphy, 'Australia and Japan in the Nineteen thirties.' *Journal of the Royal Historical Society*, Vol. 65, No. 4, March 1980. For Sam Hirodo's involvement see Graham Eccles, 'The Hirodo Story: A Three Generational Family Case Study of Bi-cultural Living', Michael Ackland and Pam Oliver (eds), *Unexpected Encounters: Neglected Histories behind the Australia-Japan Relationship*, 2007, pp. 135–54.

30 NAA: C443, J170, Letter from Mr Tomimori to the Managing Director of Kanematsu in Tokio, 30 December 38. This file contains JCC documents in relation to the Trade Diversion Dispute. See also NAA: SP1098/12, Box 10, Item 3.

31 3 May 1924, 'A Japanese Invasion Collaring our Pearling Industry.' By Archie Male; *The Herald*, 3 June 1924; *The Age* 4 June 1924 quoted in NAA: A433/1, 1941/2/2244. NAA: A1/15, 1932/4705. See Pam Oliver, *Empty North: The Japanese Presence and Australian Reactions, 1860s–1942*, 2006 for a full examination of this issue.

32 Oliver, 2006, ch. 5. Norman Bartlett, *The Pearl Seekers*, 1954. The argument in Mary Albertus Bain, *Full Fathom Five*, 1982, pp. 208–9 is almost identical to *The Times*, 19 October 1938, "A pearl case in Australia. Japanese invaders. The issue beyond the courts." which has no supporting evidence or sources given. Regina Ganter, *Mixed Relations: Asian-Aboriginal Contacts in North Australia*, 2006, p. 67 and Regina Ganter, *The Pearl Shellers of Torres Strait: Resource Use, Development and Decline, 1860s–1960s*, 1994, p. 136 and note 16 of p. 270 take Bain's points up without question. There is evidence that Mitsubishi, not Mitsui, was involved in a fishing company at Tampoena by December 1937, NAA: A981/4, JAP 158 Part 3.

33 NAA: BP242/1, Q30589 Part 1.

Chapter 7 – Dangerous years, 1937–42

1 Peter Stanley, *Invading Australia: Japan and the Battle for Australia, 1942*, 2008, p. 52.

2 NAA: C123, 9904.

3 Sandra Wilson, *The Manchurian Crisis and Japanese Society, 1931–1933*, 2002, pp. 96, 185–9. Christopher Howe, *The Origins of Japanese Trade Supremacy: Development and Technology in Asia from 1540 to the Pacific War*, 1996, pp. 366, 397, 398, 411, 424. NAA: C443 P1, J170.

4 Wilson, p. 100.

5   NAA: A981/4, JAP158 Part 1 to Part 5. Over 1,500 documents relating to Japan's expansion into the South Seas after 1935 are found digitised on the NAA website at www.naa.gov.au/record search.

6   NAA: A816/1, 19/304/240.

7   NAA: A981/4, JAP 158 Part 4, Reports of British Consul General Fitzmaurice.

8   NAA: A1196/6, 22/501/9. The interconnectedness of concerns is evident with white pearlers as well. See *The Northern Standard*, 29 March 1940. Gregory & Co. advertisement lists the company as an agent for Nippon Sensui Co. of Tokyo.

9   Shinichi Yonekawa (ed.), *General Trading Companies: A Comparative and Historical Study*, 1990, pp. 170–5, 192. The branches had an important role in catering for the Japanese visitors in their area assisting them with immigration and other processes which were unfamiliar to them the example is Mitsubishi San Francisco's assistance to visiting and immigrant Japanese.

10 NAA: A981/4, JAP 38 Part 2, G. Eliot reported to the British High Commission in London and the Australian Governor General.

11 NAA: A981/4, JAP 158 Part 1 reported on activities in NEI from 1923–33. NAA: A981/4, JAP 158 Part 5, 'Ten years of Japanese penetration in the Dutch East Indies'.

12 NAA: A981/4, JAP 158 Part 5, pp. 13–17.

13 NAA: A981/4, JAP 37.

14 NAA: A981/4, JAP 36.

15 NAA: A981/4, JAP 37.

16 NAA: A981/4, JAP 158 Part 2, *The Herald*, 20 November 1935, 'Japan our next door neighbour. Big lease in New Guinea'.

17 NAA: A1539/1, W39/138. See Mitsui letterhead.

18 NAA: A981/4, JAP 4.

19 NAA: A816/1, 19/304/240.

20 NAA: A981/4, JAP 158 Part 4.

21 Yonekawa, pp. 105–7.

22 Mitsui Gomei Kaisha, House of Mitsui: *A Record of Three Centuries, Past History and Present Enterprise*, 1937, pp. 48–55.

23 NAA: SP1098/4, Boxes 1–30 and 210ff for ledgers for 1907–41.

24 NAA: A816, 19/304/240. NAA: A816/1, 14/301/138.

25 *Ibid*: and NAA: MP1049/5, 2026/8/54.

26 NAA: SP1714/1 N40344, '99. Japanese activities'.

27 W.R. Purcell, 'The Nature and Extent of Japanese Commercial and Economic Interests in Australia 1932-41', PhD thesis, University of NSW, 1980, pp. 285–235.

28 *Queensland Government Mining Journal*, 15 October 1937, p. 348 'Export of Iron Ore' and April 1937.

29 NAA: C443/P1, J24 Part 1. NAA: MP1049/5, 1877/13/148. NAA: A816/1, 19/304/120.

30 *Queensland Government Mining Journal*, 15 September 1937, 'Iron Ore Deposits Ample'.

31 NAA: A2908, Y2 Part 2. No. 771 of 25 June 1938 to PM Canberra, NAA: A2937, 308.

32 NAA: A443/1, 1940/2/180. NAA: C123, 10175. NAA: A373/1, 1759.

33 A.W. Martin, *Robert Menzies, A Life*, Volume 1, 1894–1943, pp. 251–5.

34 NAA: SP1101/1, Box 207, 'pig-iron' folder, correspondence between 15 and 17 November 1938.

35 NAA: SP1098/10, Box 73, folder 'minerals'.

36 NAA: SP1096/1, Box 94, MSK world wide structure is found in "An Outline of the Mitsubishi Enterprises", 1937 published by Mitsubishi Goshi Kaisha, Tokyo, Japan, p. 37. NAA: SP1098/10, Box 95 'copper ore'.

37 NAA: SP1714/1, N60621, Diary entry, 5 February 1941.

38 NAA: MP529/3, TRIBUNAL 4/72.

39 NAA: ST1233/1, N39210, Shimada Report from Police at Parkes 19 May 1941 and Albury 4–15 August 1940.

40 Iwaichi Fujiwara, *F. Kikan: Japanese Army Intelligence Operations in Southeast Asia during World War II*, 1983, p. 8. NAA: SP1714/1, N60621.

41 Fujiwara, pp. 16, 20, 95, 100–8, 128, 138.

42 *Ibid.*, pp. 50–2, 226–8.

43 NAA: SP1098/ 10, Box 1, Correspondence with the Seattle office re Argentina containing detailed maps and charts on the world-wide grain trade. NAA: DP1098/10, Box 94 correspondence mentions maps of Singapore in 1940.It also details Mitsubishi's subscriptions to organisations that supplied circulars and statistical information.

44 NAA: SP1098/4, Box 313, Mitsui account books for 1941. NAA: SP1098/10, Box 54 for Mitsubishi's tender to the army in 1939 and Box 41 for quote of 1940.

45 NAA: SP1098/10, Box 20, folder 'barter', see also 'minerals' folders in Boxes 30, 41, 56, 73, 91.

Conclusion – Saving Australia

1 For a thorough coverage of the internment of Japanese people, see Yuriko Nagata, *Unwanted Aliens: Japanese Internment in Australia*, 1996.

2 NAA: A367/1, C18000/833, pp. 20–1.

3 The argument that combines, especially Mitsui, controlled pearling along Australia's north and that this was a threat originates with M.A. Bain's book, which does not provide any references to its sources on this point. See Oliver, *Empty North* for a full examination of this issue, pp. 145–8. Bain's statement is repeated by every historian since, except Sissons, and most recently by Regina Ganter. It has no basis in fact. The NAA sources on companies provide

a detailed evidence of the structure and interrelationships between Japanese companies throughout the world and their relationship to any Japanese government departments.

4   NAA: MP1587/1, 176 AC Part 2, p. 145. See also Part 1. Both of these files detail what was learned about Japanese espionage after World War Two.

5   For a full account of security files in Australia on the Japanese, see Pam Oliver, *Allies Enemies Trading Partners: Records on Australia and the Japanese*, 2004.

6   NAA: A609, 480/35/2.

7   NAA: A433/1, 40/2/2351, Japanese Merchant entry, 1930–1940.

8   NAA: A606/1, R40/1/35, Memorandum: Peace Settlement with Japan, Secretary, Department of External Affairs, Canberra, 6 August 1947.

9   W.D. Wray, *Mitsubishi and the NYK, 1870–1914: Business Strategy in the Japanese Shipping Industry*, 1984, pp. 3, 76.

10   NAA: MP1185/8, 1945/2/9; NAA: MP1587/1, 176AC Part 2; Stanley, 2008.

11   Australia–Japan Research Project, AWM, Symposium: Remembering the war in New Guinea, 19–21 October 2000. Dr Hiromi Tanaka (National Defence Academy, Yokosuka, Japan), 'The Pacific War and New Guinea', available online at ajrp.awm.gov.au/ajrp/remember.nsf; Henry Frei, 'Why the Japanese were in New Guinea'.

12   AWM124, 2/2, unpublished material on the operation of Japanese submarines in Australian waters in World War 2, p. 10

13   NAA: SP1098/10, Box 6, 1940 'Jute business letters'.

14   NAA: A1838/325,3103/4/1/1 Part 2, pp. 3–4; NAA: A1067/1, ER46/13/20.

15   Wurth, 2006, pp. 36–40.

Bibliography

Government reports

Suttor, J.B., Intelligence Department, NSW, Bulletin No. 2, Report on the Trade of Japan for the Year 1904

Suttor, J.B., Intelligence Department, NSW, Bulletin No. 19, Report on the Trade of Japan and Korea, 1906

Suttor, J.B., Immigration and Tourist Bureau, NSW, Bulletin No. 18, Report on the Trade of Japan, 1907

Suttor, J.B., Immigration and Tourist Bureau, NSW, Bulletin No. 36, Report on the Trade of Japan, 1908

Suttor, J.B., Immigration and Tourist Bureau, NSW, Bulletin No. 47, Report on the Trade of Japan, 1910

Theses

Murakami, Yuichi, 'Civilised Asians: Images of Japan and the Japanese as viewed by Australians from the early Nineteenth Century to 1901', PhD thesis, University of Queensland, 1999

Purcell, W.R., 'The Nature and Extent of Japanese Commercial and Economic Interests in Australia 1932–41', PhD thesis, University of New South Wales, 1980

Sissons, D.C.S., 'Attitudes to Japan and Defence, 1890–1923' MA thesis, University of Melbourne, 1956

Archival sources

Australian War Memorial, Canberra
AWM193, 2
AWM193, 397
AWM54, 883/1/103
AWM124, 3/126
AWM124, 4/339

National Library of Australia
C.L.A. Abbott papers, NLA: MS4744
Atlee Hunt papers, NLA: MS52
D.C.S. Sissons papers, NLA: MS3092, Series 1.1.
Harold Williams papers, NLA: MS 6681

Northern Territory Archives Service
NTRS 226, TS 773

State Library of Western Australia
Battye Library, MN1216, ACC3700A/1-52 and ACC2628A/1-12, Diaries and
 Accounts of Jiro Muramatsu

University of Melbourne Archives
UM74/71, D&W Murray

Xavier College Archives, Kew, Victoria
The Xaverian
Xavier Archives, Ledger, 1886

National Archives of Australia

Canberra
A1 Series, Correspondence files, annual single number series, 1890–1969
A1/15, 1907/7834 Readmission of resident Japanese merchants who make visits to
 New Zealand
A1/15, 1911/16228 Japanese named Nakashiba wishes to take his alleged adopted
 child to Japan
A1/15, 1914/11249 Nishida Yoshitaro
A1/15,1918/9022 Japanese in Australia – Treatment of. (Japanese relations with
 Australia)
A1/15, 1923/24399 E. Tashima Japanese passport
A1/15, 1924/24078 Saburo Muramatsu – Exemption Certificate
A1/15, 1925/18600 Toda, N. – Japanese on passport

A1/15, 1925/27797 Takasuka, J. – Exemption [from dictation test] certificate

A1/15, 1926/4456 Y. Hayami Japanese on passport

A1/15, 1930/9356, Reports regarding certain Japanese who are alleged to be illegally in the Commonwealth

A1/15, 1931/2515 H. Kuwahata exemption certificate nephew re.

A1/15, 1932/770 Tonan Shokai, Broome

A1/15, 1932/4705 Recruiting of Aboriginals for Pearling Industry and other purposes

A1/15, 1935/1444 Denzio [sic] Umino

A1/15, 1938/20318 Japanese Lugger Case – Transcript of Proceedings 22 of 1937 – Dai Nippon Maru

A1/15, 20319 Japanese Lugger Case Transcript of Proceedings in Action No. 13 of 1938 – Seicho Maru

A1/15, 20322 Japanese lugger Case Transcript of Proceedings in Action No.14 of 1937 – Takachiho Maru No. 3 Parts 1 to 6

A2/1, 1918/892 Trade with Japan – Advices re. Firms

A8 Series, Correspondence files, folio System 1895–1905

A9/1, A1902/35/156, Exemption Certificate to Mr Ozawa

A367 Series, Correspondence files, single number series with year prefix, 1916–1927 and 'c' prefix 1927–1953

A367/1, C18000/833 Objection No. 128 – Umino, Violet Maud. Advisory Committee

A367/1, C65778 Russo, Deter. Martyr Graham. Thomas, A.F. Pickering, E.H. Nakashiba, Peter also called Nash Peter

A367/1, C66114 Umino, Denzo

A367/1, C68609 Nakashiba, Samuel

A367/1, C69262, Sato, Ichyo

A367/1, C69678 Oda, Tomize – Internment

A367/1, C69851 Ide Hideichiro

A367/1, C71179 Thomas Nagai [Japanese internee; internment]

A367 /1, C72449 Shimada Ken

A367/1, C78715 Kanematsu Fusajiro and Onisha [sic] Kinjira [sic]. Author note: should be Kinjiro Onishe

A406/62, E1945/1 Part 1 Attachment Jiro Muramats – A native of Japan. Disqualified under Section 39(S) Appeal Before High Court of Australia

A443/1, 1940/2/180 Admission of Japanese to develop Yampi Sound, WA

A443/1, 1940/2/1212

A433/1, 1940/2/2351 Japanese merchants' wives and assistants – Industrial exemption

A433/1, 1941/2/2244 Muramats, J.T. – Pearling applications Cossack, WA and Darwin

A373/1, 1759 Japanese activities – Gulf country, north Queensland

A609, 480/35/2 Sheep breeding in China and Manchukuo

A659/1, 1940/1/5346 Takasuka, I – Naturalisation
A659/1, 1941/1/3872 Umino, Mrs Violet Maude [*sic*] – Retention of British
   nationality
A659/1, 1943/1/7347 Shaw, Taylor and Muramats – Pearling – Complication
   – Cossack
A712/1, 1899/K6473 Muramatsu, Jiro – naturalisation
A816/1, 19/304/120 Yampi Sound. Lease of Iron Ore Deposits by Japanese
A816/1, 19/304/240 Japanese encroachment in Australian waters
A981/4, JAP 37 Japanese activities in New Guinea
A981/4, JAP 55 Japan Espionage – General
A981/4, JAP 120 Part 1 and Part 2 Japanese Minister in Australia General
A981/4, JAP 158 Part 1 to Part 5 Netherlands East Indies Japanese Activities
A981/4, JAP 38 Part 2 Japan, Activities in Pacific General
A1196/6, 22/501/9 Japanese encroachment in Australian waters
A1067/1, ER46/13/20 Allied economic policy towards Japan Dissolution of
   Zaibatsu
A1379/1, EPJ WOS, Correspondence, files single number with EPJ [Enemy
   Property Japan] prefix 1631 items
A1379/1, EPJ1396 Muramatsu, Jiro – Deceased internee
A1497/1, Volume 19 P441 to 443 'Jiro Muramats – Western Australia
   – Application to be enrolled on Commonwealth Roll – Constitution Sec.41
   Commonwealth Electoral Act 1916–1922'
A1539/1,1939/W/138 Export of wool – Mitsui Bussan Kaisha Limited
A1606/1, C18/1 Pearl fishing Broome WA
A1838/325, 3103/4/1/1 Part 2, Zaibatsu. See also Part 1, Part 3 and Part 4
A2908, Y2 Part 2. Yampi Sound
A2937, 308 Yampi Sound
A3934/1, SC14/9 Japanese shipping services
A3934/1, SC14/22 Shipping – Japanese Steamship Lines
A5466/3, CCJ7C Japan – Economic and Financial Provision – Dissolution of the
   Zaibatsu
A7359/101, 6 Identification papers – J. and T. Muramatsu – Pearlers Darwin
A7359/101, 9 T Muramats – Pearlers
A10078/1, Muramats Jiro versus Way HR, Commonwealth Electoral Officer for the
   State of Western Australia
A11804/1, 1915/236 Japanese subjects residing outside of Japan
M10 Personal photographs of the Hon C.L.A. Abbott during his term as
   Administrator of the Northern Territory

Brisbane

BP242/1, Correspondence files relating to national security, single number series
   with Q (Queensland) prefix
BP242/1, Q30511 Japanese – Thursday Island

BP242/1, Q30581 Part 1 Japanese ARO 1.bl
BP242/1, Q30589 Part 1 Japanese activities in Queensland
J2773 Correspondence files, annual single number series
J2773/1, 230/1911 Certificate for exemption from dictation test for Japanese
 – Yeisaburo Tashima and Daisaburo Ishikura
J2773/1, 171/13 Certificate for exemption from dictation test – Kame Tashima,
 Yoshimatsu Tashima
J2773/1, 913/1918 Certificate for exemption from dictation test – Yoshimatsu
 Tashima
J25/120, 1951/5447; List of Japanese aliens in Queensland

Sydney

C123/1, World War II security investigation dossiers, single number series
C123/1, 8408 Watarai, Ryuzo (Japanese)
C123/1, 9904 Kagiyama, Sadako (Japanese) [Box 302]
C123/1, 10175 Okamoto, Hisatoshi [Japanese] [Box 312]
C443/P1, J24 Part 1 Yampi Sound Mining Co.
C443/P1, J170 Japanese Chamber of Commerce, Sydney
SP42/1, Correspondence of the Collector of Customs relating to Immigration
 Restriction and Passports
SP822/45, Box 4 Japanese Chamber of Commerce, Iwai and Company, outwards
 correspondence (enemy property records)
SP1096
SP1096/1, Miscellaneous Records of Mitsubishi Shoji Kaisha Pty Ltd (Melbourne)
SP1096/2, Miscellaneous Records of Mitsui Pty Ltd, Melbourne
SP1096/3, Miscellaneous Records of John Mitchell Pty Co. (Kotoh – Melbourne)
SP1096/4, Miscellaneous Records of Iida & Co. (Melbourne)
SP1096/5, Miscellaneous Records of Mitsui Bussan Kaisha Pty Ltd (Melbourne)
SP1098/4, Miscellaneous Records of Mitsui Bussan Kaisha
SP1098/7, Miscellaneous Records of Araki & Co.
SP1098/8, Miscellaneous Records of Yamashita & Co., pre-1941 records
SP1098/9, Miscellaneous Records of Okura Trading, pre-1941 records
SP1098/10, Miscellaneous Records of Mitsubishi Shoji Kaisha, pre-1941 records
SP1098/11, Miscellaneous Records of Jano & Joko, pre-1941 records
SP1098/12, Miscellaneous Records of Nosawa & Co., pre-1941 records
SP1098/13, Miscellaneous Records of The Japan Cotton Trading Co., pre-1941
 records
SP1098/15, Miscellaneous Records of Kiku Gumi, pre-1941 records
SP1098/16, Miscellaneous Records of Iida & Co., pre-1941 records
SP1099/1 to SP1099/247, Miscellaneous Records of the Yokohama Specie Bank,
 pre-1941 records
SP1101/1, Miscellaneous Records of Mitsui Bussan Kaisha, pre-1941 records
ST1233/1, N19133 Hirokichi Nakamura, Security Services dossier

ST1233/1, N39210 Keiji Shimada
SP1714/1, N27827 Violet Maud Umino
SP1714/1, N40344 Japanese Activities
SP1714/1, N60621 Japanese espionage – Diary of Major Sie Hashida

Melbourne

B13 General and classified correspondence, annual single number series
B13/0, 1923/2809, Usami and Takeo Mori
B13/0, 1923/3303, Kunichi Usami
B13/0, 1923/18611 Kazuhiko Ohtake left Sydney for Japan per SS "Aki Maru"
    21.9.1923
B13/0, 1925/16532 Moshichi Jingu and Fuki Jingu
B13/0, 1926/6886 Iwao Murata ex "Aki Maru" (Sydney) 8.3.1920
B13/0, 1930/7813, Otowo Konishi and Toru Wake
B13/0, 1933/4210. Miss Masakogoto (Japanese student)
B13/0, 1935/20434, Passengers for Melbourne
B13/0, 1937/13330 Naoichi Nagao (Japanese business visitor)
B168/0, 1904/32 Part 4, Report on Russian-Japanese [sic] war by Colonel J.C. Hoad
B168/0, 1904/32 Part 7, Expenses of Colonel J.C. Hoad, attaché with Japanese Army
B197/0, 1877/5/15 Legislation for Protection against Espionage. [Major Asada
    suspected Japanese spy]
B741/1, V/187 Japanese Victoria – names and addresses of
B5020 Series
B6121/3, 179P Japanese Army Preparations for War and Plans for Invasion of Australia
MP84/1, 1877/5/5 Lieut J.G. Fearnley re. Japanese Espionage and a Secret Service
MP84/1, 1888/1/16 Armament, defended ports – Query to UK on effects of shift in
    naval strength
MP84/1, 1888/1/18 Armament for coast defence
MP84/1, 1902/7/66 Review of the results obtained by the Australian Intelligence Corps
MP84/1, 1902/7/47A Reports by Commandants on Work & Training etc. of the
    Australian Intelligence Corps
MP84/1, 1902/7/77 Annual Report – Major-General G.M. Kirkpatrick,
    Inspector-General
MP84/1, 2021/1/35 Creation of Secret Intelligence Service proposed
MP124/6, 603/203/117 Address by Lord Jellicoe to the cadets of the Japanese
    training squadron
MP124/6, 603/203/347 Visit of Japanese Training Squadron
MP472/1, 1/12/6574 Japanese in New Caledonia
MP472/1, 1/15/8560 Visit of Japanese Training Squadron to Australia
MP472/1, 5/17/7761 Exchange of information re training of boys in the RAN
MP472/1, 16/13/883 1912–1913 Visit of Japanese training squadron
MP508/1, 255/40/348 George Taro Furuya
MP529/3, TRIBUNAL 4/48 Transcript of evidence of objection by T. Tanaka

MP529/9, TRIBUNAL 4/72 Transcript of evidence of objection by D. Umino
MP529/3, TRIBUNAL 4/74 Transcript of evidence of objection by H. Ide
MP529/3, TRIBUNAL 4/110Transcript of evidence of objection by S.N. Taksuka [sic]
MP529/3 TRIBUNAL 4/117 Transcript of evidence of objection by M. Inagaki
MP529/3, TRIBUNAL 4/119 Transcript of evidence of objection by Kame Kagami
MP529/3, TRIBUNAL 4/155 Transcript of evidence of objection by J.I. Nakashiba
MP729/1, 63/401/518 Nakashiba [internment of family]
MP729/6, 65/501/147, J57. Sydney Location of Japanese residents
MP742/1, 259/43/572 Darwin, Northern Territory – compulsory land acquisition
      – claim of estate J. Muramats & others
MP1049/1, 1913/0286 Japanese enterprises in South Sea Islands – Admiralty Islands
      alleged control by Japanese
MP1049/1, 1914/0455 Marshall Islands, Caroline Islands, Mariana Islands, Palau,
      Nauru, Bougainville Island, Yap Islands, etc. Arrangements for Occupation of
MP1049/1, 1914/0461 Captured German Islands North of the Equator Australian
      Claims – attitude of Japan
MP1049/1, 1915/054 Australian Naval Defence
MP1049/1, 1916/047 Protection of Trade Routes Proposals with regard to and recall
      of RAN Ships to Australia
MP1049/1, 1918/0773 Military Intelligence Reports Head Quarters Reports
MP1094/1, 1919/0116 Suspicious ships Marine Incidents etc, Pacific and Indian Oceans
MP1049/1,1920/0188 Cdr J.G. Fearnley to Act as Naval Intelligence Officer
MP1049/1, 1920/090 Japanese enterprises in South Sea Islands
MP1049/1, 1920/0271 Appointment of Cdr Fearnley as Commonwealth Coal
      Administration
MP1049/1, 1877/13/140 Suspicious movements of Japanese Merchant vessels off
      Newcastle & other sections of the Australian Coast
MP1049/5, 1877/13/87 Vessel Island Japanese surveying Elcho Island
MP1049/5, 1877/13/88 Report on Japanese mandated Islands
MP1049/5, 1877/13/148 Yampi Sound (WA) Iron Ore Deposits
MP1049/5, 1877/13/213 Japanese Mandated Islands – Intelligence Reports
MP1049/5, 2026/8/54 Visit of Japanese training squadron
MP1103/1, NJ17060 Prisoner of War/Internee: Nakamura
MP1103/1, NJ17077 Prisoner of War/Internee: Ide, Hideichiro aka Henry
MP1103/2, QJ16195 Prisoner of War/Internee: Ugita, Gyogi
MP1103/2, NJ17060 Prisoner of War/Internee: Nakamura
MP1102/3, QJ 16098 Prisoner of War/Internee: Murakami, Utaro
MP1185/8, 1945/2/9 Japanese Plan for the invasion of Australia
MP1587/1, 176 AC Part 1 and Part 2 See B6121/3

Perth

K1145, 1912/154 and 1916/145.Eizo Asari, CEDT to travel to Japan and return
K1145, 1915/79; Shio Hama [Japanese]

K1145, 1934/2 Hama [Japanese]
K1145, 1920/3. Kumazo Asari [Japanese]
PP4/2, 1934/18 Shio Hama [Japanese]
PP9/2, 1952/63/6472 Kumazo Asari [Japanese]
PP14/3, 'Japanese'
PP14/3, 1928/1008 Yamaguchi
PP302/1/0, WA17964 'Jiro [Giro] Muramats'

Darwin
E752. Whole of Series, Certificates Exemption from Dictation Test and
E752/0, 1924/10 Omaki
E755/1 Whole of Series

Interviews

Transcript of interview with Mrs Iida on 07/02/04, conducted by Toshio Swift of the
    Museum of Sydney and used with the permission of Mrs Iida and Ms Swift
Interviews: Naida and Joan, daughters of Hirokichi Nakamura, January 1997, held by
    the author in Sydney and used with the permission of the Nakamura family

Websites and television programs

'Battle for Australia', available online at www.anzacday.org.au/history/ww2bfa.
    'Australia's war 1939–1945', available online at www.ww2australia.gov.au
au.travel.yahoo.com.guide/australia/western-australia /broome/history.html; www.
    kimberleyaustralia.com/broome-history.html
www.broomeport.com/about_broome_history.html
'Townsville at War – A Soldier Remembers', by Herbert C. Jaffa www.osatwar.com/
    ozatwar/tvbombo1.htm
home.st.net.au/~pdunn/thejaps.htm> <www.anzacday.org.au/history/ww2/bfa/
    townsville.html; home.st.net.au/~dunn/locations/macintv.htm
'Ishida and the Sydney Camera Circle', Museum of Sydney, January to May 2004,
    ABC TV, Asia Pacific Focus, 2 August 2004.

Web articles

Frei, Henry, 'Why the Japanese were in New Guinea', seminar paper, and Hiromi
    Tanaka, 'The Pacific War and New Guinea'. Seminar paper, *Remembering
    the war in New Guinea Project Symposium* held at the Australian National
    University, 19–20 October 2000, Australia–Japan Research Project at

the Australian War Memorial, available online at ajrp.awm.gov.au/ajrp/
remember.nsf/
Oliver, Pam, 'In Peace and War: The Japanese Role in the Defence and Security of
Australia to 1943', Public Lecture, 30 October 2007 at 'Speakers' Corner',
National Archives of Australia, Canberra, podcast available online at www.
naa.gov.au
Wray, W.R., 'The 17th-Century Japanese Diaspora: Questions of Boundary and Policy',
web article available at eh.net/X111Congress/cd/papers/10Wray383.pdf

Books and articles

Ackland, Michael and Pam Oliver (eds), *Unexpected Encounters: Neglected Histories behind
the Australia-Japan Relationship*, Clayton, Monash University Press, 2007
Ang, Ien, 'From White Australia to Fortress Australia: The Anxious Nation in the
New Century', in Laksiri Jayasuria, David Walker and Jan Gotthart (eds),
Legacies of White Australia, Perth, University of West Australia Press, 2003
Askew, David, 'The birth of Kanematsu Shoten: Kanematsu Fusajiro and early
Australia-Japan Relations 1845–1890', *Ritsumeikan Journal of Asia Pacific
Studies*, Vol. 11, March 2003
Andrews, Eric, *The Australian Centenary History of Defence Volume V: The Department
of Defence*, South Melbourne, Oxford University Press, 2001
Bain, Mary Albertus, *Full Fathom Five*, Perth, Artlook Books, 1982
Bartlett, Norman, *The Pearl Seekers*, London, Andrew Melrose Ltd, 1954
Barr, P., *The Coming of the Barbarians: A Story of Western Settlement in Japan 1853–
1870*, London, Macmillan, 1967
Blussé, Leonard, *Bitter Bonds: A Colonial Divorce Drama of the Seventeenth Century*,
Princeton, Markus Wiener Publishers, 1997
Brett, Judith, *Australian Liberals and the Moral Middle Class: From Alfred Deakin to
John Howard*, Port Melbourne, Cambridge University Press, 2003
Carruthers, Steven L., *Japanese Submarine Raiders 1942: A Maritime Mystery*,
Narrabeen, Caspar Publications, 2006
Chan, Gabrielle (ed.), *War on our Doorstep – Diaries of Australians in the frontline in
1942*, 2003
Colquhuon, A.R., *The Mastery of the Pacific*, London, 1902
Choo, Christine, 'Asian Men on the West Kimberly Coast, 1900–1940', Jan
Gothard (ed.), *Asian Orientations: Studies in Western Australian History*, No.
16, 1995
Clark, I.F., *Voices Prophesying War, 1763–1984*, London, Oxford University Press, 1966
Daly, Henry, "Americal" 1942–1946, Les Américains en Nouvelle-Calédonie, nd
Dixon, Robert, *Writing the Colonial Adventure: Race, Gender and Nation in Anglo-
Australian Popular Fiction, 1875–1914*, Melbourne, Cambridge University
Press, 1995

Docker, John, *The Nervous Nineties: Australian Cultural Life in the 1890s*, Melbourne, Oxford University Press, 1991

Donovan, P.F., *A Land Full of Possibilities: A History of South Australia's Northern Territory*, St Lucia, University of Queensland Press, 1981

Eccles, Graham, 'The Hirodo Story: A Three Generational Family Case Study of Bi-cultural Living', in Michael Ackland and Pam Oliver (eds), *Unexpected Encounters: Neglected Histories behind the Australia–Japan Relationship*, Clayton, Monash University Press, 2007

Frei, Henry, *Japan's Southward Advance and Australia from the Sixteenth Century to World War II*, Carlton, Melbourne University Press, 1991

Foxall, E.W., *Colorphobia: An Exposure of the "White Australia" Fallacy*, 1903

Fujiwara, Lt General Iwaichi, Akashi Yogi (trans.), *F. Kikan: Japanese Army Intelligence Operations in Southeast Asia during World War II*, Heinemann, Asia, Hong Kong, Asian Studies Series, 1983

Ganter, Regina, *Mixed Relations: Asian-Aboriginal contacts in North Australia*, Crawley, University of Western Australia Press, 2006

Ganter, Regina, *The Pearl Shellers of Torres Strait: Resource use, development and decline1860s–1960s*, Carlton, Melbourne University Press, 1994

Iwamoto, Hiromitsu, 'Nanshin: Japanese Settlers in Papua and New Guinea, 1890–1949', *Journal of Pacific History*, Canberra, Australian National University, 1999

Hise, Beth and Pam Oliver, 'Kiichiro Ishida' Insite, Museum of Sydney, Summer, 2003

Howe, Christopher, *The Origins of Japanese Trade Supremacy: Development and Technology in Asia from1540 to the Pacific War*, Crawford House Publishing, Bathurst, 1996

Horner, David, *Inside the War Cabinet: Directing Australia's War Effort, 1939–1945*, St Leonards, Allen & Unwin, 1996

Hunt, Su Jane, *Spinifex and Hessian: Women in North-west Australia 1960–1900*, Crawley, University of Western Australia Press, 1986

Jones, H.J., *Live Machines: Hired Foreigners in Meiji Japan*, Vancouver, University of British Columbia Press, 1974

Jones, Noreen, *Number Two Home: A Story of Japanese pioneers in Australia*, Fremantle, Fremantle Arts Centre Press, 2001

Jones, Paul and Vera Mackie, *Relations: Japan and Australia, 1870s–1950s*, Parkville, History Department, University of Melbourne, 2001

Kanematsu (Aust.) Pty Ltd, 'Mr. Toranosuke Kitamura – His Life and Success' and 'Origin of Kanematsu Organisation in Australia', nd

Laver, Michael S., *Japan's Economy by Proxy in the seventeenth century, China, the Netherlands and the Bakufu*, New York, Cambria Press, 2008

Lindsay, Patrick, *The Spirit of Kokoda: Then and now*, South Yarra, Hardy Grant books, 2002

Martin, A.W., *Robert Menzies, A Life*, Volume 1, 1894–1943, Australian Lives, Carlton South, Melbourne University Press, 1996 (1993)

McKernan, Michael, *All In! Fighting the War at Home*, St Leonards, Allen & Unwin, 1995

Meaney, Neville, *The Search for Security in the Pacific, 1901–1914*, Sydney, Sydney University Press, 1976

Meaney, Neville, *Fears and Phobias: E.L. Piesse and the Problem of Japan, 1909–1939*, Canberra, National Library of Australia, 1996

Meaney, Neville, *Towards a New Vision: Australia & Japan through 100 Years*, East Roseville, Kangaroo Press, 1999

Meaney, Neville, *Towards a New Vision: Australia and Japan Across Time*, Sydney, University of New South Wales Press, 2007

Mitsuda, Yuri (comp.), Gavin Frew (trans.), *Kiichiro Ishida and the Sydney Camera Circle*, Japan, The Shoto Museum of Art, 2002–04

Mitsui, Gomei Kaisha, *House of Mitsui: A Record of Three Centuries, Past History and Present Enterprise*, Tokyo, 1937

Murakami, Yuichi, 'Australia's Immigration Legislation, 1893–1901: The Japanese Response', in Paul Jones and Vera Mackie (eds), *Relations: Australia and Japan*, Parkville, History Department, University of Melbourne, 2001

Moore, Ronald, 'The Management of the WA Pearling Industry, 1860 to the 1930s', *Great Circle*, Vol. 16, No. 2, 1994

Murphy, P.B., 'Australia and Japan in the Nineteen Thirties', *Journal of the Royal Historical Society*, Vol. 65, No. 4, March 1980

Nagata, Yuriko, *Unwanted Aliens: Japanese Internment in Australia*, St Lucia, University of Queensland Press, 1996

Oliver, Pam, 'Japanese Immigrant Merchants and the Japanese Trading Company Network in Sydney, 1880s to 1941', in Paul Jones and Pam Oliver (eds), *Changing Histories: Australia and Japan*, 2001

Oliver, Pam, 'Interpreting "Japanese Activities" in Australia, 1888–1945', *Journal of the Australian War Memorial*, May 2002

Oliver, Pam, *Allies Enemies Trading Partners: Records on Australia and the Japanese*, Canberra, National Archives of Australia, 2004

Oliver, Pam, *Empty North: The Japanese Presence and Australian Reactions, 1860s–1942*, Darwin, Charles Darwin University Press, 2006

Oliver, Pam, 'Japanese Relationships in White Australia: The Sydney Experience to 1941', *History Australia*, Monash University ePress, Vol. 4, No. 1, June 2007, pp. 05–12–16

Oliver, Pam, 'Citizens without Certificates or Enemy Aliens? Japanese Residents before 1947', in J. Beaumont, I. O'Brien and M. Trinca (eds), *Under Suspicion, Citizenship and Internment in Australia during the Second World War*, National Museum of Australia Canberra, 2008

Phillipe Palombo, *La Présence Japonaise in Nouvelle-Calédonie (1890–1960), Les Relations Économiques entre le Japon et la Nouvelle-Calédonie à travers L'Immigration et L'Industrie Minière*, Lille, France, ANRT, 2001

Peattie, Mark R., *Nan'yo: The Rise and Fall of the Japanese in Micronesia, 1885–1945*, 1988

Peattie, 'Introduction', in R.H. Myers and M.R. Peattie (eds), *The Japanese Colonial Empire 1895–1945*, New Jersey, Princeton University Press, 1984

Post, Peter, 'Japan and the Integration of the Netherlands East Indies into the World Economy, 1868–1942', *Review of Indonesian and Malaysian Affairs*, Vol. 27, Winter/Summer, 1993

Powell, Alan, *The Shadow's Edge: Australia's Northern War*, Charles Darwin University Press, Darwin, 2007

Price, Charles A., *The Great White Walls are Built: Restrictive Immigration to North America and Australasia, 1836–1888*, Canberra, Institute of International Affairs in association with Australian National University Press, 1974

Purcell, W.R., 'The Development of Japan's Trading Company Network', *Australian Economic History Review*, Vol. 21, No. 2, 1981

Reynolds, Henry, *North of Capricorn: The Untold Story of Australia's North*, Crows Nest, Allen & Unwin, 2003

Roberts, John G., *Mitsui: Three Centuries of Japanese Business*, New York, Wetherhill, 1989

Sand, J., NSW Directory, Sydney & Suburbs, Trades and Professions, 1895–1907

Sissons, D.C.S., 'Australian Fears of Japan as a Defence Threat', Senate Standing Committee on Foreign Affairs and Defence – Reference: Japan, 1972

Sissons, D.C.S., 'Early Australian Contacts with Japan', *Hemisphere*, Vol. 16, No. 4, 1972

Sissons, D.C.S., 'Manchester v. Japan: The Imperial Background of the Australian Trade Diversion Dispute with Japan, 1936', *Australian Outlook*, Vol. 30, No. 3, 1976

Sissons, D.C.S., 'A Selector and His Family', *Hemisphere*, Vol. 25, 1980

Sissons, D.C.S., 'Karayuki-san: Japanese Prostitutes in Australia, 1887–1916 -1', *Historical Studies*, Vol. 17, No. 68, April 1977

Sissons, D.C.S., 'Karayuki-san: Japanese Prostitutes in Australia, 1887–1916 -11', *Historical Studies*, Vol. 17, No. 69, October 1977

Sissons, D.C.S., 'Japanese in the Northern Territory 1884–1902', *South Australiana*, Vol. 16, No. 1, 1977

Sissons, D.C.S., 'Japanese Acrobatic Troupes Touring Australasia 1867–1900', *Australasian Drama Studies*, No. 35, October 1999

Spearritt, Peter, *Sydney's Century: A History*, Sydney, University of New South Wales Press, 2000

Stanley, Peter, *Invading Australia: Japan and the Battle for Australia, 1942*, Penguin Group (Australia), 2008

Tamura, Keiko, *Forever Foreign, Expatriate Lives in Historical Kobe*, Canberra, National Library of Australia, 2006

Thompson, R.C., *Australian Imperialism in the Pacific the Expansionist Era, 1820–1920*, Carlton, Melbourne University Press, 1980

Torney-Parlicki, Prue, *Behind the News: A Biography of Peter Russo*, Crawley, University of Western Australia Press, 2005

Tsunoyama, S., 'The Early History of Japanese-Australian Trade An Addendum to Japanese Consular Reports', *Business History*, Vol. 23, 1981

Walker, Brett L., 'Foreign Affairs and Frontiers in Early Modern Japan: A Historiographical Essay', *Early Modern Japan*, Fall 2002.

Walker, D.R., *Anxious Nation: Australia and the Rise of Asia, 1850–1939*, St Lucia, University of Queensland Press, 1999

Wilcox, Craig, 'The Battle of Boucaut Bay', *Wartime*, No. 28, 2004

Williams, H.S., *Tales of the Foreign Settlements in Japan*, Tokyo, Charles E. Tuttle, 1958

Willmott, H.P., *Empires in the Balance: Japanese Allied Pacific Strategies to April 1942*, London, Orbis Publishing, 1982

Wilson, Sandra, *The Manchurian Crisis and Japanese Society, 1931–33*, London, New York, Routledge, 2002

Winter, Barbara, *The Intrigue Master: Commander Long and Naval Intelligence in Australia, 1913–1945*, Brisbane, Boolarong Press, 1995

Wolfers, Howard, 'The Big Stores between the Wars', in Jill Row (ed.), *Twentieth Century Sydney: Studies in Urban and Social History*, Sydney, Hale and Iremonger, 1980

Wray, W.D., *Mitsubishi and the N.Y.K., 1870–1914: Business Strategy in the Japanese Shipping Industry*, 1984

Wurth, Bob, *Saving Australia: Curtin's Secret Peace with Japan*, South Melbourne, Lothian Books, 2006

Wurth, Bob, *1942: Australia's Greatest Peril*, Australia, Pan Macmillan, 2008

Yarwood, A.T., *Asian Migration to Australia: The Background to Exclusion, 1896–1923*, Melbourne University Press, 1964

Yonekawa, Shinichi (ed.), *General Trading Companies: A Comparative and Historical Studies*, Tokyo, United Nations University Press, 1990

Yoshihara, K., *Sogo Shosha: The Vanguard of the Japanese Economy*, Melbourne, New York, Oxford University Press, 1982

Yu, Sarah, 'Broome Creole: Aboriginal and Asian partnerships along the Kimberley coast', *Queensland Review*, Vol. 6, No. 2, November 1999

Index